CONTENTS

Chapter *page*

LIST OF MAPS AND DIAGRAMS ix

PREFACE x

1. FRANCE BEFORE THE FRENCH REVOLUTION . . 1

Introduction—Causes of the Revolution—The Peasantry—The Nobility—The Church—The Bourgeoisie—Government finance—The Government of France—The French Philosophers—Some quotations from the Philosophers—Summary—Questions

2. THE OUTBREAK AND COURSE OF THE REVOLUTION, 1789–1795 9

The situation in 1788–89—The States General, 1789—Capture of the Bastille—The Session of August 4th—The Declaration of the Rights of Man—The Work of the National Assembly—The Church—Summary. The Legislative Assembly—The Outbreak of War, 1792—Insurrection of June 20th, 1792—Establishment of the Paris Commune—The Convention, 1792–95—The War—The Committee of Public Safety—The Reign of Terror—The Worship of Reason—End of the Terror—Date-summary—Questions

3. THE DIRECTORY, CONSULATE AND EMPIRE, 1795–1815 . 21

The new Constitution and the Directory—The war in Italy—The Treaty of Campo Formio, 1797—The Egyptian campaign—State of France on Bonaparte's return—The 'coup d'état' of 18th Brumaire, 1799—The Consulate—Defeat of the Second Coalition—The Peace of Amiens, 1802—Napoleon's reorganization of France—Renewal of the war, 1803—Prussia ends her neutrality—The Treaty of Tilsit, 1807—The Continental System—Effects of the Continental System—The Peninsular War—Austria re-enters the war, 1809—The position in 1810—The Moscow Campaign, 1812—Royalist restoration—The Downfall of Napoleon—Date-summary—Questions

4. THE CONGRESS OF VIENNA, 1814–1815 . . 38

The work of the Congress—Comments on the Congress: (*a*) The Balance of Power; (*b*) Legitimacy; (*c*) Nationality—Summary—Questions

Chapter *page*

5. The Congress System, 1818–1822 43

The Congress of Aix-la-Chapelle, 1818—The Congress of Troppau, 1820—The Congress of Laibach, 1821—The Congress of Verona, 1822—Date-summary—Questions

6. France, 1815–1870 48

Louis XVIII and Richelieu—The Ultra-royalists—Villèle's policy—The Orleanist Monarchy, 1830–48—Foreign policy—Internal affairs of France—Opposition to Louis Philippe—Policy of suppression—Reform banquets—The Second Republic—The political tactics of Louis Napoleon—The Government of Napoleon III—Foreign policy: The Crimean War; Italian policy; the Mexican adventure—The position at home—The Franco-Prussian War—Defeat of France—Summary—Dates—Questions

7. The Hapsburg Empire to 1867 . . . 64

Hungary as centre of discontent—The year 1848 in Hungary—Events in Vienna—Some reasons for the failure of the Austrian revolutions—The Dual Monarchy—Summary—Dates—Questions

8. The Unification of Italy, 1815–1870 . . 69

Italy after 1815—Attempted revolutions—Giuseppe Mazzini and the Society of Young Italy—The risings of 1848—War against Austria—Reasons for Italian failure, 1848–49—The position after 1848—Foreign policy of Cavour—Giuseppe Garibaldi—Summary—Dates—Questions

9. Germany, 1815–1870 79

Germany after the Congress of Vienna—The Zollverein—The Liberal movement in Prussia, 1848—The Frankfort Parliament, 1848–49—The Prussian League—Summary to 1850—German unification under Prussia—Foreign policy: War against Denmark—Defeat of Austria: Seven Weeks' War, 1866—General results of the war—Prussia and France 1866–70—The Spanish Succession, 1869—Summary—Dates—Questions

10. The German Empire under Bismarck, 1870–1890 . 89

The Imperial Constitution—Bismarck's internal problems—Economic policies and industrial development—Bismarck and tariffs—German foreign policy under Bismarck—The DreiKaiserbund—The Congress of Berlin, 1878—The

MODERN EUROPEAN HISTORY

1789–1977

BY

HERBERT L. PEACOCK

THIRD EDITION

Maps by Boris Weltman

HEINEMANN EDUCATIONAL BOOKS
LONDON

By the same author

A History of Modern Britain 1815–1977

A History of Modern Europe 1789–1976

British History 1714 to the Present Day

Europe and Beyond 1870–1976

Heinemann Educational Books Ltd

LONDON EDINBURGH MELBOURNE AUCKLAND TORONTO
SINGAPORE HONG KONG KUALA LUMPUR
NAIROBI IBADAN JOHANNESBURG
LUSAKA NEW DELHI KINGSTON

ISBN 0 435 31711 3

First published 1966
Reprinted 1969
Second Edition 1973
Reprinted 1975
Third Edition 1978

Published by Heinemann Educational Books Ltd
48 Charles Street, London W1X 8AH
Printed in Great Britain at
The Pitman Press, Bath

Chapter *page*

DreiKaiserbund Treaty, 1881—The Triple Alliance, 1882—The Secret Reinsurance Treaty, 1887—Summary—Dates—(domestic policy)—Dates (foreign policy)—Questions

11. THE EASTERN QUESTION, 1815–1878 . . . 97

Introduction—The Greek War of Independence—The Great Powers—Mehemet Ali and the Middle East—The Sultan and Mehemet Ali—The Straits Convention, 1841—The Crimean War—The Treaty of Paris, 1856—The Eastern Question from 1856 to the Congress of Berlin, 1878—Results of the Berlin Treaty—Summary—Dates—Questions

12. FRANCE, 1870–1914 107

The position in 1870–71—The Paris Commune—Establishment of the Republic—Principal events of the years 1880–1914—General Boulanger—The Panama Scandal—The Dreyfus case—The Separation Law—Summary—Dates—Questions

13. RUSSIA TO 1914 113

Introduction—Alexander I—Reactionary period of Alexander I—Nicholas I—Alexander II—Discontent in the reign of Alexander II—Alexander III—Nicholas II—Movements of opposition in the early twentieth century—The Russo-Japanese War—Effects of the defeat in Russia—Summary—Dates—Questions

14. THE ORIGINS OF THE GREAT WAR, 1914–1918 . . 122

The colonization of Africa—Imperialism in the Far East—General comments—The Dual Alliance of France and Russia, 1893—Britain's 'splendid isolation' removed—The first Moroccan Crisis and the Triple Entente—The second Moroccan crisis, 1911—Crises in the Balkans—Effects of the First and Second Balkan Wars—General points—Summary of causes of Great War—Dates—Questions

15. THE GREAT WAR, 1914–1918 131

The German plan—The Eastern Front, 1914: Tannenberg—Turkey and Bulgaria join Germany—The naval war in 1914—The year 1915: Ypres and Gallipoli—The year 1916: the siege of Verdun, battles of Somme and Jutland—The war in 1917: the Russian Revolution—The United States enters the War—The year 1918: the last German offensive—Some reasons for German defeat—Date-summary—Questions

Chapter *page*

16. The Peace Treaties, 1919–1920 140

Principal personalities—Germany—Eastern Europe—General criticism—Wilson's Fourteen Points—The League of Nations—Modern Turkey and the Treaty of Sèvres, 1920—Summary—Questions

17. Russia, 1914–1939 146

Revolution of February, 1917—The return of Lenin, April, 1917—Reasons for Bolshevik success—Bolshevik rule, 1918–27—Internal development of Russia—Stalin v. Trotsky—The Five-year plans—Political developments under Stalin—Summary—Dates—Questions

18. Germany and Italy, 1919–1935 154

The Weimar Republic—General state of Germany—Policy of Stresemann, 1923–29—The great industrial depression and the rise of Adolf Hitler—Economic crisis—The Reichstag fire—Some considerations on the rise of Hitlerism—Italy after 1919: the rise of Mussolini—The Corporate State—Summary—Dates—Questions

19. International Politics, 1919–1939 . . . 163

France and Germany—The reparations problem—The League of Nations—Economic and humanitarian work of the League—The problem of aggression—The weakness of the League of Nations after 1930—The Spanish Civil War, 1936–39—Austria—Czechoslovakia—Poland—Summary—Dates—Questions

20. The Second World War, 1939–1945 . . 170

Poland and Finland—Attack on Denmark and Norway—The collapse of France—The Battle of Britain—Lend-Lease Act—British victory in Cyrenaica—Rommel's first African campaign—Hitler attacks Russia—Pearl Harbour, 1941—1942, Stalingrad and El Alamein—Allied invasion of Italy—D-Day, June 6th, 1944—German counter-offensive—Death of Hitler and Mussolini—The atomic bomb—Reasons for Germany's defeat—Date-summary—Questions

21. The Great War-time Conferences . . . 181

The Atlantic Charter, 1941—The Yalta Conference—The San Francisco Conference—The Potsdam Conference—Summary—Dates—Questions

Chapter *page*

22. THE POST-WAR WORLD, 1945–1953—EASTERN EUROPE 184

The general position at the end of World War II—Eastern Europe—Communist control in Poland, Rumania, Bulgaria, Hungary, Czechoslovakia and Yugoslavia—Effects of the Soviet-Yugoslav quarrel—Austria resists Communism—The Position in Greece, 1944–49—Summary—Questions

23. THE POST-WAR WORLD, 1945–1953—WESTERN EUROPE 190

France—Italy—Germany—Refugee problem in Germany—Economic union of British and American Zones—The Berlin blockade—The Truman Doctrine and the Marshall Plan—The Western alliances—Other movements for European Union—The atomic bomb—Summary—Dates—Questions

24. THE POST-WAR WORLD, 1945–1953—THE MIDDLE AND FAR EAST 200

Syria, Lebanon and Palestine—Egypt—North Africa: Tunisia; Morocco; Algeria—Turkey—Persia—French policy in Indochina—Communism under Mao Tse-tung in China—The Korean war, 1950–53—Effects of Korean war on world affairs—Summary—Dates—Questions

25. THE YEARS 1953–1977 IN EUROPE . . . 212

The post-Stalin period—Eastern Europe, 1955–56—Poland from 1955—The Rising in Hungary—The Common Market—EFTA—Euratom—German re-unification fails—Summit Conference, 1960—The Cuban crisis, 1962—The Test-ban Treaty—Czechoslovakia, from 1967—The Berlin Wall—International developments from 1974—The Helsinki International Agreement—Summary—Dates—Questions

26. THE MIDDLE AND FAR EAST, 1953–1977 . . 230

Tunisia—Morocco—Algeria—Britain and Egypt—The Suez crisis—The Baghdad Pact—Arab–Israeli Conflict—The Yom Kippur War, 1973—Indochina—The Manila Pact—Vietnam 1954–75—Summary—Dates—Questions

27. FRANCE, 1940–1977 242

The War period, 1939–1945: The 'phoney war'; Compiègne armistice; the Vichy government—Committee of National Liberation—The Fourth Republic—Decline of

Chapter *page*

the Fourth Republic—Instability—The Algerian problem—The Fifth Republic—The new constitution—De Gaulle's foreign policy—Domestic policy—Discontent—Colonial policy—The French Community—France, 1970–1977—Summary—Dates—Questions

28. THE UNITED NATIONS 259

Organization—The Security Council—Economic and Social Council—The Trusteeship Council—The International Court of Justice—The Secretariat—Important problems before the United Nations 1945–63—Other moves by the United Nations—Disarmament—General Work—The Trusteeship system—Admission of Communist China 1972—Summary—Dates—Questions

GLOSSARY OF POLITICAL TERMS 270

ANSWERING EXAMINATION QUESTIONS. 273

BIBLIOGRAPHY 277

INDEX 277

LIST OF MAPS AND DIAGRAMS

	page
France in 1789: Causes leading to the Revolution	5
Europe in 1810	26
The rise and fall of Napoleon	35
Europe in 1815	41
The Concert of Europe	47
Problems of Louis Philippe	54
The Unification of Italy	75
Bismarck's policies, 1871–1890	93
Bulgaria, 1878, after San Stefano; Bulgaria, 1878, after the Congress of Berlin	103
Origins of the Great War, 1914–1918	127
The Western Front, 1914–1918	134
Europe, 1914–1918; Europe, 1919–1923	139
Reasons for the rise of Hitler	157
The Sudetenland and the Polish Corridor	167
Germany after 1945	177
Spheres of influence in Europe after 1945	196
The Far East after 1945	209
The Middle East from 1953	235
The French Government from 1946	246
The New Countries of Northern Africa	254

PREFACE

This book aims at presenting an outline of European History from 1789 to the present day for examination candidates.

I have given considerable attention (seven chapters) to the period since 1945, which involves important detail on the history of eastern Europe, the Middle East, North Africa and the Far East. In the twentieth century especially, world history cannot be artificially divorced from the history of Europe, and this is beginning to be recognized in the examination field.

Each chapter is designed to cover the main events and to give essential information which is either new or a revision in compressed form of work already done. While it cannot be absolutely comprehensive, it is hoped that it will be found useful both for current learning and for pre-examination revision.

Names and events when first mentioned are shown in bold type. Summaries, dates and questions are given at the end of each chapter. Maps, diagrams, a glossary of terms and a short bibliography are also included.

H. L. PEACOCK

PREFACE TO THE THIRD EDITION

In this new edition the chapters on Europe, the Middle and Far East, and France have all been updated to the end of 1977.

May 1978 H. L. PEACOCK

CHAPTER ONE

FRANCE BEFORE THE FRENCH REVOLUTION

Introduction

THE **French Revolution** of **1789** was one of the most important events in human history. It is therefore a very natural point at which to begin the study of more recent European history.

It was important because it overthrew an old-established monarchy and introduced new methods and principles of government which have affected all political thinking since. The new ideas of *liberty*, *equality* and *fraternity* affecting all men regardless of class were very attractive to those who had no privileges, or very restricted ones, under the old systems of government. The Revolution, therefore, affected the actions and thoughts of men in other countries as well as in France. The rulers and aristocracy of those countries were naturally the main enemies of the Revolution, but the Revolution found supporters among the peasants, the town workers and the middle class in many countries. The Revolution was, therefore, a 'world-shaking' event.

Causes of the Revolution

The Peasantry

In 1789 the peasantry in France numbered about 23,000,000 in a total French population of 25,000,000. There were still about 1,000,000 outright *serfs*. A larger proportion were *métayer* tenants sharing the profits and losses of cultivation with their lords, while others owned small patches of land which provided only the barest subsistence.

The main burdens on the peasantry were in the form of *direct* and *indirect taxation*. Direct taxation was payable to government collectors. The most burdensone taxes were the *taille* imposed on income and property, the *poll-tax* imposed upon the head of each household, and the *vingtième* imposed on all property. From these taxes the clergy and nobility gained considerable exemption. The indirect taxes (forms of purchase tax) were numerous, but the most burdensome was probably the *gabelle* or salt tax, by which every individual over eight years old was compelled to purchase at least seven pounds of salt each year, and was taxed on the amount purchased. A horde of officials and soldiers was employed to collect this tax, and great harshness was used. Penalties for evasion were ferocious; for many years before the Revolution, thousands were imprisoned for trying to avoid the tax and about five hundred victims were hanged annually or sent to the galleys. The right to collect indirect taxes was given to *tax farmers*, a widely detested class. Another burden on the peasantry was the *corvée* or forced labour for public works, which interrupted their work on their own plots. The peasants still had to make *feudal* payments to their lords. The Church also exacted *tithe*.

Approximately two-thirds of the peasants' earnings went in taxation.

The Nobility

The nobility monopolized the highest positions in the Church and State and only nobles could become army officers. Living as absentee landlords at Versailles or in the towns and cities, the nobility left their estates in the hands of bailiffs and lost their old feudal contacts with their tenants. They were also exempt from most taxation, especially the 'taille' and the 'corvée'. The *Lesser Nobility*, comprising about 90,000 families, had fewer privileges and less political power than the *Greater Nobility*, whom they envied. Their sons all inherited noble titles but had not the means to live up to them, and quite a number threw in their lot with the Revolution.

The Church

Discontent with the Church was increasing before 1789. It owned one-fifth of the land, claimed exemption from taxation, and imposed tithe on the peasantry. Its wealth aroused the increasing envy and distrust of both peasant and merchant. Within the Church extremes of wealth existed. The 60,000 parish priests received stipends of between £30 and £70 a year, while the 134 archbishops and bishops received an average of about £2,500 per annum, and many lived in luxury.

The Bourgeoisie

The grievances of the middle class of merchants and professional men are regarded by many writers as the real cause of the Revolution. Without their leadership the Revolution would have failed. They lived mainly in the towns and enjoyed considerable exemption from taxation. However, the exemptions of the nobility were greater, it was difficult to buy landed estates, and the officer ranks of the army were monopolized by the nobility, as were the highest political appointments. Despite the wealth and education of the middle class, the country was still governed by the King's local officials, the *Intendants* and by the Versailles nobility. They were also seriously discontented with the financial mismanagement of the reign of **Louis XVI**. The French participation in the **American War of Independence (1775–1783)** had greatly increased the *National Debt* and before 1789 the government was bankrupt. The empire in India and Canada had also been lost to the British. The merchant class (as well as the Church and nobility) had subscribed large loans to the government, but their repayment had become impossible by 1789.

Government Finance

Louis XVI, who reigned from 1774 to 1793, had made some early efforts to improve the finances of the state and appointed **Turgot** Controller General of Finances. Turgot abolished thousands of *sinecures*—paid appointments for which little or no work was done—and replaced the *corvée* by a tax on all landowners. However, he was ousted from power by the nobility and the Queen, **Marie Antoinette.** The same fate befell the Swiss banker, **Necker.** The enlightened reforms of both Turgot and Necker were frustrated by the Queen and the Court Nobility, to the further exasperation of all those who were discontented with the régime. When Necker was recalled in August, 1788, it was too late to avoid national bankruptcy.

The Government of France

The government of France was a despotism, with all power vested in the King. He ruled with the *Royal Council* and, in the provinces, with the Intendants. The King's despotic power was expressed most forcibly in his use of the *lettre de cachet* by which he could imprison any individual 'during the King's pleasure'.

But this despotism was becoming more and more inefficient. There was delay and chaos in the government of the country. There were two different systems of taxation, one for the thirteen central provinces, the other for the remainder. The Roman Law dominated the south, the Common Law the north. There was freedom of trade for the central provinces and customs duty for the remainder. These hindrances to administration and trade irritated above all the *bourgeoisie*, and those French economists, known as the **Physiocrats,** denounced this wasteful system. The **Parlement of Paris** claimed the right to criticize the King's decrees and to obstruct them, but by holding a special meeting of the Parlement known as a *lit de justice* the King could bring it into line. Thus there was no possibility of any popular control in the last resort. This compared most unfavourably with the English system, which many French writers admired, despite its defects.

France had supported the American colonies in their revolt, and thus had helped to produce something like a democracy across the Atlantic. This contrast struck the returning French volunteers very forcibly, and their commander, **Lafayette,** was to play a prominent part in the Revolution.

The French Philosophers

French philosophers of the eighteenth century encouraged the pursuit of *Reason* as against *Authority* based on despotism. **Voltaire (1694–1778)**, the great satirist of the age, was essentially destructive. He attacked the Church in his work **'Oedipe' (1718)**, and demanded complete religious toleration. In his **'Letters on the English' (1734)** he

FRANCE IN 1789

CAUSES LEADING TO THE REVOLUTION

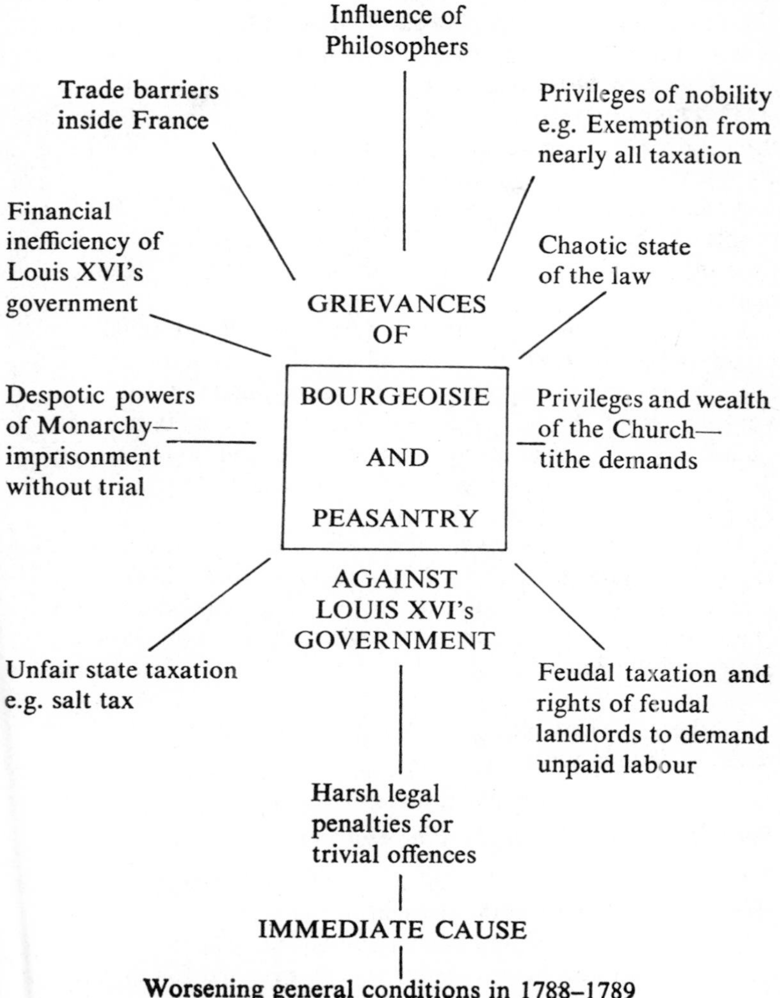

IMMEDIATE CAUSE

Worsening general conditions in 1788–1789

praised the English social and political system as against the French. He did not believe in democracy, but wanted the monarchy to act in the interests of all the people. **Montesquieu** (**1689–1755**) attacked the absolute monarchy in his '**Persian Letters**' (**1721**) and in his '**Spirit of the Laws**' (**1748**) he advocated a monarchy whose powers would be limited by various representative bodies. **Jean-Jacques Rousseau** (**1712–1778**) went further in his criticisms than any other. He preached the goodness of man before man was corrupted by human society. He was the outright democrat who preached the need for the end of monarchy in favour of rule by the whole people—the 'sovereign people'. In his great work, the '**Social Contract**' (**1762**) he expressed these ideas and expressed his faith in the natural goodness of man.

The **Encyclopedists** were contributors to the '**Encyclopédie**' which first appeared in **1751** under the editorship of **Diderot**. It was frequently censored or suppressed, but exerted great influence, even at Versailles itself. Both Turgot and Rousseau were contributors. It challenged every idea based on despotism, and sought to set up Reason as the judge on every issue. It attacked every social evil in France which we have already noted.

Another group of thinkers very influential with the bourgeoisie were the Physiocrats, founded by **Quesnay** (**1694–1774**). They regarded land as the sole source of wealth and demanded the abolition of all existing taxes in favour of a single tax paid by all classes. They demanded freedom of trade and the end of economic interference by the state.

All these thinkers were challenging the old order and did much to shake its foundations.

Some Quotations from the Philosophers

Rousseau's attacks on social inequality and oppression were his greatest contribution to the thought of the age:

'Man was born free, but everywhere he is in chains.'

'Are not all advantages in our society reserved for the rich and powerful? . . . But how different is the spectacle for the poor man! The more compassion society owes him the less he receives. All doors are closed to him, even when he has the right to have them opened.

. . . If a "corvée" is called for, or a military levy made, he is the first to be taken. He bears not only his own burdens but those his neighbour has managed to shift on his back. At the least accident that befalls him all leave him to his fate. If his cart overturns he is unlikely to escape insults from the duke's servants, who hurry by . . .' ('Social Contract').

Kings, argued Rousseau, must be enemies of the people: 'Their own interest demands above all that the people be weak, wretched and unable to resist.'

The Philosophers did not regard themselves as revolutionaries, although their ideas were adopted by outright revolutionaries. They wished society to be changed from above, not from below.

Said Voltaire: 'It is not a question of making a revolution as in the time of Calvin and Luther, but only of bringing one about in the minds of those who govern.'

Another great thinker, **D'Alembert,** said something which was almost similar: 'Freedom is of no benefit to the people, which is like a small child that falls and hurts itself when left to walk alone, and then gets up and strikes its governess.' Again: 'The number of *canaille* is always more or less the same, and the mob is always ignorant and stupid.'

In the same way Montesquieu wanted change, but not a revolution. Yet his words were revolutionary in their effect:

In his 'Persian Letters' the visitor to France from Persia saw that the King 'makes his subjects think as he pleases . . . he gives preference to those who dress him or who hand him a napkin rather than to those who conquer a city or win a battle.' (A clear reference to the Court of Versailles.)

Summary

The causes of the French Revolution are to be found in the deeply unjust and disturbed state of French society. The following considerations should be taken into account, although they are not necessarily in order of importance:

1. The burdens on the peasantry, arising from taxation and the feudal exactions of the lords, made them ripe for revolutionary leadership.

2. The grievances of the educated bourgeoisie who, above all, were influenced by the writings of the philosophers.

3. The despotism of the monarchy.

4. The inefficiency of the monarchy.

5. The obstruction of reforms by the Court Nobles and the Queen of Louis XVI, Marie Antoinette.

6. The influence of the American Revolution and of the English social and political system.

QUESTIONS

1. Why was there discontent among the bourgeoisie before the Revolution?

2. What were the principal burdens on the peasantry before the Revolution?

3. Explain the importance of the following French writers: (a) *Voltaire;* (b) *Rousseau;* (c) *Montesquieu;* (d) *Diderot;* (e) *Quesnay.*

4. What was the position of the nobility before the Revolution?

5. What was the position of the Church, and why was it criticized?

CHAPTER TWO

THE OUTBREAK AND COURSE OF THE REVOLUTION, 1789–1795

The Situation in 1788–1789

IN 1788 a very bad harvest in France led to food shortages, riots and widespread imprisonment. Necker's revelation of the country's bankruptcy in his '*Compte rendu*' caused general dismay. Demands arose for the summoning of the **States General** which had not met since **1614.** Louis was compelled to summon the States General for May, **1789,** and ordered lists of grievances, or *cahiers,* to be prepared by districts.

The States General, May, 1789

Delegates were elected by the procedures of 1614 to the three separate estates. These three estates were the Nobility, the Clergy and the 'Commons' or Third Estate. The delegates' powers were limited to discussing the 'cahiers' prepared by the local assemblies. In general, the 'cahiers' complained of the taxation burdens already referred to (p. 2) and some contained demands for the creation of a limited monarchy in France and the end of noble and clerical privileges.

The States General met at Versailles and consisted of 308 Clergy, 285 Nobles and 621 members of the Third Estate. Louis had accepted Necker's advice that the Third Estate should have the preponderant representation. But Louis insisted that the old system of *voting by estates* should be maintained. This meant that the First and Second Estates could out-vote the Third by two to one.

Louis refused the demand of the Third Estate that voting should be by heads, so on June 12th, 1789, they declared themselves the **National Assembly** and invited the other Estates to join them. This was a critical decision and the first outright conflict with the monarchy.

Louis' reply was to order a *Royal Session* of all the estates at which he would give his orders, and the meeting-place of the National Assembly was closed. The Assembly moved to an adjoining tennis-court building and, under the leadership of **Count Mirabeau,** took the **Tennis Court Oath** not to dissolve 'until the constitution of the kingdom shall be established'. After further resistance by the Third Estate at the Royal Session, Louis gave way, and on June 27th ordered the Nobility and Clergy to join the Third Estate in one assembly.

The court nobles now prepared to use force against the Assembly, and troops were concentrated in Paris under **Marshal de Broglie.** This led to great agitation in Paris, where many of the **Gardes Françaises** sympathized with the National Assembly. A special committee was now set up by the Paris electors and their representatives at the **Hotel de Ville,** and plans were prepared for a **National Guard.** The court party now forced Louis to dismiss Necker, and this aroused further popular agitation.

Capture of the Bastille, July 14th, 1789

Under the leadership of the young journalist, **Camille Desmoulins,** demonstrators seized arms from the **Invalides** and the Hotel de Ville and moved against the **Bastille.** They were joined by some of de Broglie's troops and by deserters from the 'Gardes Françaises'. The Bastille was captured but only seven common criminals were found in the dungeons. *The Bastille was a symbol of despotic oppression,* however, and its capture had immense effect. In the countryside local councils were elected, manor houses attacked, records destroyed and the payment of feudal dues ended. The committee at the Hotel de Ville declared July 14th a national holiday and adopted the tricolor. Louis himself attended the council at the Hotel de Ville and put the new tricolor emblem in his hat. The National Assembly now called itself the **Constituent Assembly,** thus indicating its intention of working out a new form of government for France.

The Session of August 4th, 1789

In thirty decrees, the National (or Constituent) Assembly swept away feudal dues and declared the old systems of taxation illegal. This marked the end of the old financial order in France.

By this time many of the nobility and the King's brothers had fled the country, with the hope of gaining foreign help for the suppression of the Revolution. These people were called the *emigrés*.

The Declaration of the Rights of Man, August 27th, 1789

The **Declaration** by the National Assembly asserted *the legal equality of all men*; *their right to rule*; *their right to freedom in writing and printing*; and their *right to make laws*. Taxation ought only to be imposed through elected representatives and there should be no arbitrary imprisonment.

At this point the monarchy itself was not under attack, and Louis was given the right to veto laws for two consecutive sessions—*the suspensive veto*. But Louis now refused to sign the Declaration of the Rights of Man or accept the decrees of August 4th. Rumours of a military plot against the Assembly were also spread in Paris, and the **Jacobins** organized the **March of the Women** to Versailles, October, 1789, with the avowed purposes of demanding bread and the punishment of officers at Versailles, who had insulted the tricolor. Lafayette followed with a detachment of the National Guard to protect the Royal Palace. However, the mob broke in and Marie Antoinette barely escaped with her life. The King now accepted the Declaration and the decrees of August 4th, and went to Paris where he was lodged in the **Tuileries.** The Assembly also moved to Paris, which thus became the real centre of the Revolution. *The public was now admitted to the Assembly gallery*, and from here the mob under Jacobin inspiration was able to bring its weight to bear on the Assembly.

The Work of the National Assembly, June, 1789–September, 1791

The largest party in the Assembly was the **Feuillants** or Left Centre, numbering about seven hundred. These representatives wished for a limited monarchy and the ending of the old social evils. On the extreme Left were the Republicans who included **Maximilien Robespierre.**

We have already noted the importance of the session of August 4th and the Declaration of the Rights of Man. The Assembly also swept away the old system of local government headed by the Intendants. France was divided into 83 Departments, which were divided into districts or *arrondissements.* The 'arrondissements' were subdivided into *cantons* and these in turn were divided into *communes. The active citizens* (i.e. those over twenty-five years paying taxes and enrolled on the register of the National Guard) elected the members of the various councils. The active citizens also elected the judges in the new law courts set up throughout the country. This electoral system was the attempt to apply the 'sovereignty of the people' to law as well as local government.

The Assembly proceeded to work out a new constitution for France. The King remained head of the State, but he could only delay laws for four years (the suspensive veto). His veto did not, however, apply to financial measures. He no longer controlled the judges, nor could he declare war or peace without the Assembly's consent. He retained his position as head of the armed forces. Even after the attempted flight from France of the royal family and their detention at Varennes, September, 1791, Louis still maintained his place in the constitution, when he was brought back to Paris, although his general popularity had disappeared. The new Assembly of 745 members was to be elected by the active citizens who numbered about 43,000 only. This constitution was essentially the work of the Feuillants.

The National Assembly also abolished torture and the 'lettres de cachet'.

The Church

The National Assembly declared toleration for all religions, abolished the tithe, took over Church property, but guaranteed a minimum salary to the parish priests. Monasteries and nunneries were closed and their inmates given pensions. By the **Civil Constitution of the Clergy, July, 1790,** archbishoprics were abolished and both bishops and parish priests were to be elected by the active citizens. Definite salaries were given to each grade of the clergy. The Pope's power to intervene in the affairs of the French Church was denied. Count Mirabeau, a hater of the old Church, now persuaded the Assembly to demand from the clergy an **Oath of Allegiance** to the Civil Constitution. Fifty thousand parish priests, called the 'non-jurors', who refused, were deprived of their livings. The 'non-juring' priests became enemies of the Revolution. The government now issued *Assignats* as currency on the security of the confiscated Church lands, but successive governments issued them so freely that their value had decreased one hundred times by 1796.

Summary

The Assembly had swept away feudal taxation and privilege, maintained the monarchy with limited powers, swept away the old system of law, set up a new system of local government, and deprived the Church of its privileged position. It had created a new force, the National Guard, to protect the gains of the Revolution. Under the Assembly, the Revolution reached its moderate phase, but Louis' attempted flight played into the hands of the Jacobin Republicans.

The Legislative Assembly, Oct. 1791–Sept. 1792

On a proposal by Robespierre, the National Assembly had barred its members from election to the **Legislative Assembly.** The elections returned 136 Jacobins and supporters, 264 Feuillants, and a Centre group of 350 who, however, were weakened by having no co-ordinated policy. The Jacobins soon split into Jacobins and more moderate **Girondins.** The Jacobins, members of the Jacobin Club, under the leadership of Robespierre and **Marat,** were strongly Republican. The Paris **Cordelier Club,** under **Danton,** was also extremely Republican. In the Legislative Assembly the Jacobins quickly secured the '*appel nominal*' by which each deputy declared his vote aloud. This gave the mob, who were admitted to the public gallery, opportunities of pressure on the deputies.

The Outbreak of War, 1792

In August, 1791, the influence of the 'émigrés' was seen in the **Declaration of Pillnitz** by the **Emperor of Austria** and the **King of**

Prussia. The Declaration said that the cause of Louis XVI was the cause of monarchies everywhere. A royalist insurrection also broke out in western France—**La Vendée.** The Legislative Assembly now ordered the return of the 'émigrés' by June 1st, 1792. If they did not return they would come under sentence of death. As the Jacobins expected, Louis vetoed this law. He also vetoed further laws against the non-juring priests.

The Girondins now wished to bring about war with Austria, hoping that an invasion of France would further discredit the King. The Feuillants also supported a war policy for the opposite reason—that French success would strengthen the King's position. Lafayette, Commander of the Army of the Centre, supported the Feuillants. **Dumouriez,** a Girondin, became Minister of War. The Jacobins opposed the war, fearing a strengthening of the King's position. When **Leopold II,** Emperor of Austria, refused a French demand that he should disown the 'émigrés', France declared war on Austria on April 20th, 1792. At first the French invasion of Belgium was driven back, and Louis replaced his Girondist government by the Feuillants.

Insurrection of June 20th, 1792

The King's vetoes, the appointment of the Feuillant ministry, the rising price of food, the defeats in Belgium, all gave the Jacobins, under Robespierre, Marat and Desmoulins, increasing influence. On June 20th, 1792, a crowd of demonstrators broke into the Tuileries and forced Louis to don the red cap of the Revolution. Despite the apparent danger to his life, he refused to withdraw the vetoes.

Lafayette now attempted to suppress the Jacobins and left his army command to appear in the Assembly. The Jacobins, however, accused him of desertion and were able to turn the Assembly against him. He returned to his army command, but soon afterwards gave himself up to the Austrians.

Establishment of the Paris Commune, 1792

The Jacobins now aimed to increase their power in Paris, and Danton took the leading part in these preparations. At this moment the **Duke of Brunswick,** commander of the Prussian forces, threatened

Paris with attack and punishment if any further attempts were made on the person of Louis XVI. The **Brunswick Manifesto** helped the Jacobins to rouse a patriotic fervour. They had already gained control of the military sections of Paris. On August 10th, 1792, the supporters of Danton seized control of the Hotel de Ville and set up the **Commune.** The King took refuge in the Legislative Assembly. The mob attacked the Tuileries and the Swiss Guards were massacred. The Commune now secured the suspension of the King and the Assembly ordered the election of a **Convention** by *manhood suffrage*, the Jacobins thus securing the ending of the distinction between 'active' and 'passive' citizens. The Commune now became the real ruling force in Paris. It was joined also by Robespierre and Marat, the latter being editor of the revolutionary newspaper '*L'Ami du Peuple*'. Robespierre directed his attacks against the Girondins, a strict censorship of all correspondence was introduced, and the royal family was removed to the Temple prison. Extreme action was next taken against all suspects, and on September 2nd the demands of Marat began to be carried out. Between September 2nd and 11th 1,200 prisoners were hastily tried, convicted and guillotined. The political excuse for the **September Massacres** was the danger of possible traitors in the rear of the French armies. At this time Danton was Minister of Justice.

The Convention, 1792–1795

The elections gave the Girondins a majority, and they aimed at a stable moderate government and the suppression of the Commune. But against them were the Jacobins, and **the Mountain**, so-called from their occupation of the highest seats on the left of the Convention hall. All the twenty-four deputies from Paris were Jacobins, and included Danton, Robespierre and Marat. The main conflicts on policy were now to be between Girondins and Jacobins. It was to be a struggle to the death.

The War

On September 20th, **1792,** the Prussians were defeated at **Valmy** and the French occupied the Austrian Netherlands. On **September**

22nd the **French Republic** was declared. Britain now entered the war against France fearing for her commercial interests in the Netherlands where her ally Holland controlled the Scheldt by a treaty. France had denounced the treaty and now used Antwerp as a naval and trading base and sent warships into the Scheldt. The Convention's **Edict of Fraternity** of November, **1792,** appealing to all peoples against their governments and **the execution of Louis** in January, **1793,** despite the efforts of the Girondins to save him, had alarmed the British government. **William Pitt, the Younger,** who was then Prime Minister, protested and his protests were answered by a French declaration of war on **February 1st, 1793.** Pitt then succeeded in forming the **First Coalition** of Britain, Spain, Holland and the German and Italian states against France. This resulted in French defeats in the Netherlands and the beginnings of a retreat. To meet this sudden turn for the worse the Convention set up three important committees—the **Committee of Public Safety, the Committee of General Security** and the **Revolutionary Tribunal.**

The Committee of Public Safety

The Committee was given control of the army and foreign affairs, and had power to order suspects to appear before the Revolutionary Tribunal; as a result the guillotine became increasingly busy. The Committee of General Security was given charge of police arrangements in Paris.

The Girondins now made a determined effort to defeat the Jacobins, and Marat was made to appear before the Revolutionary Tribunal, which acquitted him of responsibility for the September Massacres. This was followed by the armed forces of the Commune expelling the Girondins from the Convention, and they then attempted to rouse their followers in the provinces to revolt. A royalist insurrection also broke out in La Vendée and the French armies suffered further defeats.

The Reign of Terror

The Committee of Public Safety now made gigantic efforts to retrieve the military situation. Under **Carnot's** direction 700,000 troops were raised and ruthless discipline was imposed by the Committee's Representatives with the armies. A *levée en masse* was decreed by the Convention by which the whole population of France was brought into the war effort. At the same time Terror became a legal weapon after the Committee had secured the passage of the *Law of Suspects* by which not only political suspects could be summarily tried and executed, but also speculators in grain who were not observing Robespierre's **Law of the Maximum** which had fixed a maximum price for corn. The Terror extended all over France, and in Girondist Lyons over 1,500 people were executed. Fifty thousand revolutionary committees were established throughout France to bring suspects to trial. The Girondist leaders were executed, as also was Queen Marie Antoinette. On the military front Carnot's efforts secured the recovery of the French armies and the defeat of the Austrians, Prussians and the British.

The Worship of Reason

The Committee of Public Safety and the Commune were now the two directing forces of the Revolution. In the Commune the extreme terrorist and atheist, **Hébert**, gained power. A non-Christian calendar was introduced by the Convention and events were to date from **Year One of Liberty**—September 22nd, **1792.** Notre Dame became a **Temple of Reason,** as well as many other churches in France.

Robespierre was opposed to Hébert. Following Rousseau, he considered belief in a Supreme Being to be necessary. At the same time he wished to destroy the Commune in favour of the Committee of Public Safety which he controlled. Danton also opposed Hébert's policy of continuing the Terror. A combination of Robespierre and Danton secured the execution of Hébert and his principal followers in March, 1794.

Danton's open opposition to the Terror, now the armies had recovered, and his opposition to carrying the Revolution into foreign countries, led Robespierre to attack him violently in the Committee. Robespierre secured his arrest and execution on April 5th, 1794.

The End of the Terror

Robespierre now insisted on the recognition by the Convention of the **Supreme Being,** but at the same time he increased the Terror and denounced all his enemies in a powerful speech in the Convention. This, however, led to a hardening of opposition against him; he was casting his net too wide, for in the period of his domination (about seven weeks) more victims than ever went to the guillotine. On July 27th, 1794, he was greeted in the Convention by cries of 'Down with the tyrant' and he joined the Commune at the Hotel de Ville. Before he could move, the troops of the Convention attacked the Hotel de Ville, arrested him, and he was guillotined on July 28th. The majority of the Commune were soon afterwards executed. This marked the end of the Terror and of Jacobin control. The Jacobins made several attempts to revolt against the Convention, but the Jacobin Club was closed and the Convention forces maintained their control.

Summary

The Revolution passed through the following important phases:

Phase One. 1789–1791

1789	
May	**Meeting of the States General.**
June	**Third Estate declares itself the National Assembly.**
July 14th	**Capture of the Bastille.**
August	**Abolition of feudal dues and taxation and privileges of Church and Nobility.**
	Declaration of the Rights of Man.
October	**March of the Women to Versailles.**
	Royal family brought to the Tuileries.
1790	
July	**Civil Constitution of the Clergy.**
	Oath of Allegiance.
	Non-juring priests.
1791	
June	**The flight to Varennes.**
August	**Declaration of Pillnitz.**
	'Émigré' activity increases.
	Louis vetoes laws against 'émigrés.'

Phase Two. October, 1791–September 20th, 1792

	The Legislative Assembly:
	136 Jacobins returned in elections.
	Increased Jacobin influence on affairs.
	The Jacobin Club.
	The Gallery.
	The 'appel nominal'.
1792	
April	Girondist ministry declares war against Austria.
June	Demonstrators invade the Tuileries.
	Louis refuses to abandon his vetoes.
August	Establishment of the Paris Commune.
	The Brunswick Manifesto.
	Royal family lodged in the Temple prison.
September 2nd–11th	The September Massacres.
September 22nd	Declaration of the Republic.

Phase Three

	The Convention, September, 1792–October, 1795.
1792	
September 20th	Prussians defeated at Valmy.
November	Edict of Fraternity.
1793	
January	Execution of Louis XVI
February 1st	France declares war on Britain.
	First Coalition formed against France.
	Establishment of:
	Committee of Public Safety.
	Committee of General Security.
	Revolutionary Tribunal.
	Royalist revolt in La Vendée.
	French armies defeated on eastern frontier.
	Carnot organizes the 'levée en masse'.
	Law of Suspects.
	The Reign of Terror.

November	**Worship of Reason.**
1794	**Execution of Hébert.**
April	**Danton executed.**
July	**Robespierre executed.**
	End of the Terror.
	Jacobin Club closed by Convention.

QUESTIONS

1. What was the importance of the National Assembly?

2. Why did France become a Republic and not a constitutional monarchy?

3. By what means did the Jacobins gain increasing control of the Revolution?

4. Why did the Reign of Terror occur and what were its results?

5. Write notes on three of the following: (a) *Declaration of the Rights of Man;* (b) *the Declaration of Pillnitz;* (c) *the Edict of Fraternity;* (d) *the Worship of Reason.*

6. How would you account for the fall of Robespierre?

CHAPTER THREE

THE DIRECTORY, CONSULATE AND EMPIRE, 1795–1815

The New Constitution: The Directory, 1795–1799

THE new constitution devised by the Convention consisted of the **Council of Ancients** (250 members over forty-five years of age) and the **Council of Five Hundred** (comprised of men of thirty-five years of age or over). The executive was to consist of five **Directors,** one retiring each year and his successor being appointed by the legislature. To reduce the possibility of royalist or Jacobin representation, two-thirds of the Council of Ancients and of the Five Hundred were to be chosen from the Convention.

Opposition at once broke out to this arrangement, and an attempt to organize an insurrection against the Convention was defeated by **Napoleon Bonaparte**'s '*Whiff of grapeshot*' which put an end to the insurrection of 13th Vendémiaire (October 5th, **1795**).

Another conspiracy was organized by **François Babeuf** and his communistic **Society of Equals.** The murder of the Directors was planned, but this rising was betrayed and suppressed.

The War in Italy

By 1795 the victories of the French army, which **Carnot's** organizing genius had brought about, had begun to break up the First Coalition. There was disunity among the allies. Both Austria and Prussia were more concerned with their gains in Poland than with fighting the Revolution. They both feared that **Catherine II** of Russia would gain in Poland. This fear weakened their efforts in the west. The new tactics developed by the French armies also proved effective against older military ideas. By 1795 Prussia, Spain and Holland were out of the war. Austria, Britain, the German states, and Piedmont still remained in arms against France.

Carnot (now one of the Directors) planned two great military thrusts into southern Germany and into northern Italy respectively—both aimed at the defeat of Austria. The command of the first army was given to Generals **Jourdan** and **Moreau**, that of Italy to Napoleon Bonaparte (**1769–1821**), whose ideas had impressed Carnot.

Bonaparte's Italian campaign, quite unexpectedly, stole the thunder. He took over a demoralized army on the Piedmontese frontier, thoroughly reorganized it, promised them 'honour, wealth and glory' and, despite a two-to-one superiority of his opponents, defeated the Piedmontese, then the Austrians successively at **Lodi** (**May, 1796**), at **Rivoli** (**January, 1797**) and marched towards Vienna. At **Leoben** the Austrian Emperor sued for peace.

The campaign had shown Bonaparte's genius in speed of manœuvre and his uncanny capacity to observe and strike at the enemy force's weakest point. His revolutionary claim to be the 'liberator' of the Italians from the foreign yoke also gained him useful support. His armies lived on the country, and were thus unhampered by unnecessary transport. The conquered states were made to meet his military expenses—for example, the **Duke of Modena** was forced to pay 10,000,000 francs. Numerous works of art were seized and sent to France.

The Treaty of Campo Formio, October, 1797

Austria abandoned Belgium, and France gained the left bank of the Rhine. Austria also had to leave Lombardy and recognized the new **Cisalpine Republic** created by Bonaparte in northern Italy. Bonaparte unscrupulously handed over Venice to Austria and seized the Venetian navy for France. The treaty really brought the First Coalition to an end, for only Britain was left in opposition to France. Bonaparte had achieved political and military glory and it was a decisive stage in his gradual rise to power.

The Egyptian Campaign

The Directory's schemes for the invasion of Britain had been defeated by the naval victory of **Jervis** and **Nelson** over the Spanish fleet at **Cape St. Vincent, 1797,** and the defeat of the Dutch fleet by **Duncan** at **Camperdown, 1797.** This had prevented the joint use of the French, Spanish and Dutch fleets to cover the invasion. An attempted French invasion of Ireland had also failed. A decision was made to strike at Britain's trade and empire through an Egyptian expedition. Bonaparte, whose popularity the Directory feared at home, accepted the command and in May, **1798,** set out from Toulon with an army of 40,000 and a hundred scholars. He captured **Malta,** landed in Egypt, seized **Alexandria,** defeated the **Mamelukes** outside Cairo at the **Battle of the Pyramids, July, 1798.**

At this point Nelson destroyed the French fleet at the **Battle of the Nile, August, 1798,** and Bonaparte struck out towards Turkey through Syria. The British fleet supplied Acre with reinforcements and Bonaparte was forced to retreat to Egypt.

During this appalling campaign in which the French soldiers died in thousands from thirst and disease, Bonaparte continued to send to the Directory glowing and exaggerated accounts of the glories of the campaign.

In **1799** the **Second Coalition** of Britain, Austria and Russia was formed against France. Russia feared French eastern ambitions, while the Austrians had been encouraged to join the coalition by Britain's successful resistance and her offer of financial aid. The difficulties of the Directory at home were well known, as also was the real failure of Bonaparte's expedition.

In these circumstances, Bonaparte left the army of Egypt under **Kléber's** command and returned to France.

State of France on Bonaparte's Return

The Directors had never been completely united on policy. In 1795 three were in favour of continuing the war policy, two were against it. The minority were also inclined to look towards some form of royal restoration. The Directory tended to become more and more dictatorial and in September, **1797** (the *coup d'état* of 18th Fructidor) they disbanded the Legislature by military force because it opposed them. At this time Carnot fled to Switzerland. General economic conditions became bad. The *assignats* were now almost worthless and prices were very high. There was a great increase of brigandage in France. The Directors themselves were open to corruption and took enormous bribes. The defeat of the First Coalition gave them some credit, and the peasants were in general prosperous at this time. But Britain gained important naval victories, and on land the French armies deteriorated. The Second Coalition gained considerable victories against the French in 1799, driving them from Italy, Switzerland and the German states. In Switzerland the victories of the Russians under **Suvoroff** were especially humiliating. It was at this point that Bonaparte returned from Egypt and decided to intervene directly in the politics of France.

The Coup d'État of 18th Brumaire (*November 9th, 1799*)

The **Abbé Sieyès,** one of the Directors, aimed at achieving a constitution for France which would end the virtual dictatorship of the Directory. By securing the dismissal of his opponents he gained a majority support in the Directory, but he required military support to put an end to the Directory system. Bonaparte decided to throw in his lot with Sieyès, who was popular in France. The Council of Ancients supported Bonaparte and Bonaparte was given command of the forces of Paris. His brother **Lucien Bonaparte** was also in the key position of President of the Council of Five Hundred, where, however, Napoleon met opposition. He was ejected from the Council of Five Hundred when he appeared before them, but his brother Lucien, promising that Bonaparte would protect the liberty of Frenchmen, persuaded the soldiers to invade the Council of Five Hundred and expel the members. A small, carefully chosen commission secured the end of the Directory and the appointment of two of the former Directors (Sieyès and **Ducos**) to govern with Bonaparte while a new constitution was devised.

The Consulate

Bonaparte dominated the constitution-making committee which eventually appointed him **First Consul**. He held the main power in the state, whilst the Second and Third Consuls were only advisers. The First Consul appointed all the main state officials, both military and civil. He could decide on war or peace. He proposed laws, which were then drafted by a **Council of State.** The elected **Legislative Body** could then either reject or accept laws without discussion. The First Consul also appointed the **Préfets** of the departments and the **Maires** of the 'communes'.

One of Bonaparte's first acts was to dismiss Sieyès and Ducos and secure his supporters, **Cambacérès** and **Le Brun,** as Second and Third Consuls.

Thus the end of the Directory saw the beginnings of Bonaparte's despotic power in France. The glamour of the Egyptian expedition and the calamities of France in 1799 had opened the way for him. He was widely popular in the country.

Defeat of the Second Coalition

Bonaparte now retrieved the military situation by defeating the Second Coalition. The latter had already shown signs of strain in 1799 because of disputes between Austria and Russia over the aims and strategy of the Coalition.

Bonaparte crossed the **Great St. Bernard Pass** with 40,000 men and defeated the Austrians at **Marengo, June 14th, 1800.** Moreau also defeated the Austrians at **Hohenlinden, December 3rd, 1800.** By the *Treaty of Lunéville, 1801*, France regained the territories she had won by the Treaty of Campo Formio.

Bonaparte had formed the **League of Armed Neutrality** at the end of **1800**. It consisted of those nations most aggrieved by the exercise of the British Navy's right of search of neutral vessels. The League consisted of Russia (where the unstable **Czar Paul** had now become an admirer of Bonaparte), Sweden, Denmark and Prussia. Denmark and Sweden closed the Kattegat to British vessels, but in **April, 1801,** Nelson destroyed the Danish fleet at **Copenhagen (Battle of the Baltic).** The League collapsed soon after the murder of the Czar Paul.

The Peace of Amiens, 1802

The position of stalemate between Britain and France led to the **Peace of Amiens.** Pitt was replaced by **Addington** as Prime Minister. Britain restored the captured French colonies, but retained **Ceylon**

NORWAY
SWEDEN
UNITED KINGDOM
DENMARK
BALTIC SEA
Copenhagen
Tilsit
Friedland
Eylau
NORTH SEA
RUSSIAN EMPIRE
PRUSSIA
WESTPHALIA
GRAND DUCHY OF WARSAW
London
CONFEDERATION OF THE RHINE
Jena
R. Rhine
Boulogne
Austerlitz
AUSTRIAN EMPIRE
Wagram
Vienna
Paris
Brest
BADEN
Ulm
BAVARIA
SWITZERLAND
FRENCH EMPIRE
BLACK SEA
Rochefort
R. Danube
DALMATIA
KINGDOM OF ITALY
ADRIATIC SEA
KINGDOM OF NAPLES
TURKISH DOMINIONS
Corunna
CORSICA
SARDINIA
Fuentes d'Onoro
PORTUGAL
Torres Vedras
Madrid
Lisbon
SPAIN
BALEARIC ISLES
MEDITERRANEAN SEA
SICILY
C. St. Vincent
C. Trafalgar
Sts. of Gibraltar

and **Trinidad.** Britain promised to evacuate Malta and Egypt. France's boundaries of 1802 were recognized. France also promised to evacuate **Naples** and the **Papal States.**

Napoleon's Reorganization of France

Attempts were made by both Jacobins and Royalists to assassinate Napoleon, but his power in France increased. He became *First Consul for life in 1802* and **Emperor in 1804.** A plebiscite overwhelmingly confirmed his rise to power.

The years 1800–1810 saw great social changes in France, mainly owing to the direct influence of Napoleon. He promoted soldiers on merit—the *career open to talent*—and this produced remarkable military efficiency. He also allowed an increasing number of 'émigrés' to return.

By the **Concordat of 1802** with the Church, he hoped to end a hostility that many clergy had felt against the state after the Revolution. The Catholic religion was recognized as that of 'the great majority of the French people'. Bishops were appointed by Napoleon, but the Pope invested them. Bishops appointed the clergy with government approval and were to be paid by the state. The Pope now recognized the sale of Church lands which the Revolution had brought about.

The **Code Napoleon** brought about clarification of the law and made it uniform for all people. The strengthening of the family was based on increasing the father's authority—he could even have his own children imprisoned. The position of the wife became inferior and she could not acquire or sell property without her husband's consent. A *system of assize courts* was set up. Accused persons were tried in public, but the preliminary hearing of witnesses was in secret. *Divorce* was now permitted.

In education the *lycées* were established, and many technical schools founded, as also was the **University of France** (the Imperial University at that time). All these changes were aimed at producing an *élite* leadership through the 'lycées' and at improving general, scientific and industrial education.

A special *Society for the Encouragement of National Industries* was set up, composed of manufacturers and scientists. Industry was also aided by the establishment of the **Bank of France,** which was given a monopoly of note issue. A gold standard helped to stabilize prices. Roads, canals and seaports were extended and improved. The *beet-sugar industry* was established and the cotton, woollen and silk industries flourished. The peasantry above all prospered.

Napoleon inaugurated the **Legion of Honour**. 'Men', said Napoleon, 'are led by toys.'

Renewal of the War, 1803

Napoleon continued to send spies to Egypt; Britain refused to evacuate Malta and would not recognize French occupation of the Austrian Netherlands. Napoleon complained of attacks on him in the 'émigré' press in London and the British of attacks on them in the official French 'Moniteur'. Britain declared war on France in May, 1803.

Napoleon seized Hanover and declared the whole of the European coastline closed to British trade. He assembled troops and boats at Boulogne for an invasion of Britain. His attempt to gain control of the Channel with the combined French and Spanish fleets was frustrated by Nelson's blockade of **Admiral Villeneuve's** fleet at Toulon and **Collingwood's** blockade of the Brest fleet. Napoleon, to meet the danger from Austria, who had now joined the Third Coalition, broke up his invasion army at Boulogne and marched across Europe. Nelson's victory at **Trafalgar, October 21st, 1805,** finally settled any possibility of a French invasion of England.

Pitt had replaced Addington and proceeded to form the **Third Coalition** of Britain, Austria and Russia. Russia had joined the coalition because the **Czar Alexander I** disliked Napoleon's occupation of Hanover, and the Czar's relative the **Duc d'Enghien** had been tried, unjustly condemned and executed on a charge of plotting to murder Napoleon. Austria was determined to regain her Italian territories. Prussia remained neutral, as she had been since 1795.

Napoleon's reply was to launch a major campaign against Austria and Russia without delay. He marched 500 miles across Europe in 21 days and defeated the Austrians at **Ulm, October, 1805.** He occupied Vienna and then defeated the combined Austrian and Russian armies at **Austerlitz, December, 1805.** By the **Treaty of Press-**

burg, 1805, Venetia was taken from Austria and incorporated in Napoleon's Kingdom of Italy. Austria also lost other territory to the German states created by Napoleon.

Prussia Ends her Neutrality

Prussia, although isolated, now entered the war against Napoleon. Her trade losses through Napoleon's control of Hanover had been enormous. But she over-estimated her power. Her army was composed of serfs officered by incompetent men. The result was the overwhelming defeat of the Prussians at **Jena, October, 1806.** In **June, 1807,** Napoleon defeated the Russians at **Friedland.**

By the great victories of Ulm, Austerlitz, Jena and Friedland, Napoleon's control of Europe was greater than ever and the Third Coalition had collapsed. Pitt, its creator, had died in 1806 after the news of Austerlitz.

The Treaty of Tilsit, July, 1807

Napoleon and the Czar Alexander I met on a raft on the River Niemen. Napoleon gave Alexander freedom to conquer Finland and extend his territory in the Balkans against Turkey. Alexander recognized Napoleon's control of Europe. Prussia lost all territory west of the Elbe and this became part of the new Kingdom of **Westphalia** under **Jerome Bonaparte.** The Czar and Napoleon secretly agreed that if Britain rejected Alexander's peace-making efforts, then he would support Napoleon's **Continental System.**

The Continental System

Napoleon's aim was to bring Britain down by economic ruin, as an alternative to invasion. He compelled Prussia to accept the system after Jena, gained Alexander's support in 1807 and Austria's in 1809. He issued a series of decrees as follows:

1. **Berlin Decrees, 1806.** All ports in French-controlled and allied states were closed to British trade.
2. **The Warsaw Decrees, 1807.** All British goods in north German ports were to be seized.

3. **The Milan Decrees, 1807.** Neutral ships changing course from a French to British port were liable to seizure.

4. **The Fontainebleau Decrees, 1810.** All English goods in French territory to be seized and burnt.

Britain replied by various **Orders in Council** forbidding neutrals to trade with ports which excluded British goods. Neutrals sailing to French-controlled ports were told to go to a British port, where their goods would be put in bond and re-exported on favourable terms.

Effects of the Continental System

Widespread smuggling of British goods into the Continent began. British exports were in such demand that not even Jerome Bonaparte, King of Westphalia, could be relied upon to implement his brother's decrees. The same applied to the French-appointed **King of Sweden, Bernadotte.** Napoleon himself was forced to give special permits for British goods to enter France. Neutral traders were almost extinguished, and Britain gained the world carrying trade. In Europe the merchant class became seriously discontented, especially in Holland, Prussia, Russia and Sweden. The system led, in part, to the downfall of Napoleon. The latter's **imprisonment of the Pope** in **1809** was partly due to the Pope's refusal to apply the system to the Papal States. It also led on to the **Peninsular War** when Portugal refused to ban British trade, and it was in the Peninsula that the first serious cracks in Napoleon's rule of Europe appeared. Alexander eventually deserted the system, and Napoleon's fatal **Moscow Campaign** was the result.

The Peninsular War, 1808–1814

In **1808** the Portuguese rejected the Continental System, and a a Franco-Spanish army invaded Portugal. In Spain itself there was conflict between **Charles IV** and his son who became **Ferdinand VII.** At a conference at Bayonne, Napoleon forced the King and Queen to abdicate, imprisoned Ferdinand, and made his own brother, **Joseph Bonaparte, King of Spain.** This led to a national rising in Spain and the first defeat of Napoleon's forces for many years. **Marshal Dupont** capitulated to a Spanish force at **Baylen, July, 1808,** and Joseph

Bonaparte fled from Madrid. The Spaniards now began the organization of *guerrilla warfare.*

The Portuguese appeal for help led to the arrival of **Arthur Wellesley** (later **Duke of Wellington**) with an English army. The French, isolated in Portugal, capitulated and, by the **Convention of Cintra, August, 1808,** evacuated Portugal.

Napoleon now took command himself, invaded Spain with 200,000 men and entered Madrid. **Sir John Moore** organized a delaying attack from the north, but was forced to retreat to **Corunna, 1809,** where he was killed before he could re-embark. But the diversion enabled Wellesley to establish round Lisbon the defensive lines of **Torres Vedras,** in front of which the country was laid waste for thirty miles.

The critical point in the war was the attack by Napoleon's great **General Masséna** on Portugal in **1810** with 70,000 men. He reached the lines of Torres Vedras in October, 1810, but they proved too strong for him. He retreated, losing 20,000 men, many of whom died of starvation because of the Spanish 'scorched earth' policy and guerrilla attacks. Wellington pursued Masséna and defeated him at **Fuentes d'Onoro in May, 1811.** All French forces were thus cleared from Portugal.

The defeat at Fuentes d'Onoro encouraged the other nations of Europe, especially the Prussians and Russians, to strengthen their resistance to Napoleon and prepare for further action. The new national resistance to Napoleon began in Spain.

Wellington was able to carry the war into Spain in the following years, with fluctuating success, but eventually defeated the French army under **Marshal Soult** at **Toulouse** in **1814.**

The Peninsular War proved fatal to Napoleon. 200,000 men were permanently tied down there. Wellington's holding of Lisbon enabled British reinforcements to arrive easily by sea. Despite an uncertain start, the Portuguese and Spanish fighters greatly improved as the war went on. The French found the country too poor to adopt their old tactics of living on it. The British soldiers in Spain proved excellent and superior to the French. The French found that the geography of the country, with north–south rivers and mountain ranges, made their customary rapid movement of men and supplies very difficult.

Austria re-enters the War, 1809

Austria decided to strike again while the French were distracted in Spain. **Francis I** now appealed to a national spirit. His armies were reorganized and a new national militia created. But at this time neither Prussia nor Russia assisted her, although her armies under the **Archduke Charles** gave a better account of themselves than hitherto, and Napoleon was beaten at the **Battle of Aspern, 1809.** The Austrians were unable to follow up this success and were decisively defeated by Napoleon at **Wagram, 1809.** By the **Peace of Vienna, October, 1809,** Austria lost a large part of Poland to Russia, provinces on the Adriatic to France, and had to accept the Continental System. Hoping to guard against future Austrian opposition and having divorced **Josephine,** Napoleon now married the Emperor's daughter, the **Archduchess Marie Louise.**

The Position in 1810

At this highest peak of Napoleon's power new forces were at work against him. The force of *nationalism* was beginning to operate in Spain, Austria and in Prussia. The Continental System was causing economic hardship throughout Europe, as were French taxation and indemnities. In Prussia, the leading ministers of **Frederick William III, Stein** and **Hardenberg,** did much to create a new national spirit. The **University of Berlin** was established and became a centre of patriotism, *serfdom was abolished*, the middle class were given a voice in the new town councils, and the land was redistributed to the advantage of the peasantry. Under **Gneisenau's** guidance a trained militia was created, giving an armed reserve of 120,000 men by 1811.

In Russia, Alexander found the Continental System a burden on his merchant class trading with Great Britain. He was no nearer gaining Napoleon's consent to the taking over of Constantinople by the Russians, and he feared the effect on Russian Poland of Napoleon's creation of the Grand Duchy of Warsaw. He resented the seizure of **Oldenburg** by Napoleon in **1810** to enforce the Continental System, especially as its ruler was Alexander's brother-in-law.

The Moscow Campaign, 1812

When Alexander broke completely from the Continental System in **1811,** Napoleon decided on the invasion of Russia. He marched across Europe but when he entered the deserted city of Smolensk on August 18th he had already lost 100,000 men—more from sickness and desertion than fighting, which the Russians avoided by organized retreat and a 'scorched earth' policy. At the **Battle of Borodino** on September 7th, **1812,** he lost another 80,000 men, and the Russians continued their retreat. On September 14th, Napoleon found Moscow empty and in flames, and Alexander showed no signs of being willing to negotiate. On October 18th Napoleon's retreat began. The greatest military calamity yet known to history resulted, and not more than 20,000 out of the invading force of 600,000 returned to Europe. As the *Grande Armée* had been made up of contingents from other European states besides France, the calamity was widely felt. It was the beginning of the end for Napoleon. An almost immediate result was the **Treaty of Kalisch, 1813,** between Prussia and Russia for a united attack on Napoleon. The **War of Liberation** had begun.

Napoleon's organizing genius was now seen at its most astonishing. He raised another army of 300,000 men and won the battles of **Lutzen** and **Bautzen, 1813.** An armistice brought about by Austria, however, enabled the alliance of Austria, Prussia, Russia and Great Britain to be cemented. In August, **1813,** Napoleon defeated the Austrians at **Dresden,** but at the **Battle of the Nations at Leipzig, October, 1813,** he was defeated and had to retreat across the Rhine. The French-created **Confederation of the Rhine** now turned against him and allied forces entered France. By this time Wellington's armies were in southern France. After the entry of the Prussians and Russians into Paris, Napoleon capitulated and was exiled to **Elba.**

Royalist Restoration

Louis XVIII, brother of **Louis XVI,** was restored as **King of France** in **1814.** He accepted a parliamentary system of government for France, but his Royalist supporters proved very unpopular when they secured the abolition of the tricolor flag. They also forced the dismissal of Napoleon's officers, and demanded back the lands gained by the peasantry at the Revolution.

Thus, when Napoleon escaped from Elba and returned to France in **March, 1815,** there was sufficient discontent to sway the people once again towards him, and Louis XVIII fled.

The statesmen meeting at Vienna to settle the future of Europe disbanded and prepared for the final battle with Napoleon. **Waterloo,** fought near Brussels, **June 18th, 1815,** was the result.

Napoleon's efforts to defeat the British by attacking the point of junction of the British and Prussian armies nearly succeeded. Wellington's troops, however, held firm until **Blücher's** Prussians reached the main battle area. Napoleon's final effort to turn the tide by throwing in the **Imperial Guard** against the British was a failure. He was defeated and went to his final exile on **St. Helena.**

The Downfall of Napoleon

The following points should be considered in discussing the reasons for Napoleon's downfall. They are not necessarily in order of importance.

1. *Britain's naval power* and its effects, especially in preventing the invasion of Britain and combating the Continental System.

2. *Britain's financial power* which enabled her to subsidize her allies in the three coalitions, and also at the time of the War of Liberation.

3. *Britain's industrial and agricultural resources* enabled her to avoid outright starvation, although there was much distress. Napoleon himself realized that he could not secure complete victory while Britain remained against him.

4. *The Continental System and its effects* in arousing opposition to the French from the merchant and working class of Europe. The impossibility of completely enforcing it.

5. *The rise of nationalism* and the importance of Portugal and Spain in this respect. Napoleon's defeats in Spain encouraged his main opponents immensely. The drain of 200,000 French troops to Spain crippled his schemes. The very ideas of the Revolution—Liberty, Equality, Fraternity—had been spread by the French armies, and this in itself led to the new spirit of nationalism, which eventually turned against Napoleon.

THE RISE AND FALL OF NAPOLEON

Difficulties of and conflicts within the Directory	1796	The Italian Campaign
	1797	Campo Formio
	1798	Egyptian Campaign
	1799	First Consul
	1800	Marengo
Internal reforms	1804	**Emperor**
Code Napoléon	1805	**Austerlitz**
Control of Europe complete Continental System in operation	1806	Jena
	1807	Treaty of Tilsit Friedland
	1809	Wagram
	1810	Masséna defeated in Portugal
	1811	Alexander deserts Continental System
	1812	**Moscow Campaign**
	1813	French retreat in Spain Battle of the Nations (Leipzig)
	1814	Elba
	1815	Waterloo
		St Helena
	1821	Death

6. *The power of Russia,* her size, climate and strong national spirit and Alexander's desertion of Napoleon, leading to the calamity of the Moscow campaign.

7. *The imprisonment of the Pope* in 1809 lost Napoleon much support.

8. *Napoleon's military judgement* seemed to *decline* after 1810, although this is a controversial matter. The Moscow campaign was ill-judged. He under-estimated Spanish national resistance and boasted at one time that he would master Spain with only 30,000 troops. The battle of Waterloo requires study in itself, but it appears that he waited too long to throw in the Imperial Guard. There is little doubt that the battle was long in the balance. He tended to under-estimate Wellington as a soldier, and expressed his contempt for him even on the field of Waterloo.

Dates

1795–96	**Defeat of the First Coalition.**
	Bonaparte's Italian Campaign.
1797	**Treaty of Campo Formio.**
	British naval victories at Cape St. Vincent and Camperdown.
1798	**Bonaparte's Egyptian expedition.**
	Battle of the Pyramids.
	Nelson's victory at the Battle of the Nile.
1799	**Second Coalition formed against France.**
	Bonaparte returns to France and becomes First Consul.
1800	**French victories of Marengo and Hohenlinden.**
	League of Armed Neutrality.
1801	**Treaty of Lunéville.**
	Nelson's victory at Copenhagen.
1802	**Peace of Amiens.**
	The Concordat.
	Napoleon commences the social and legal reorganization of France.
1803	**Renewal of the war.**
	Seizure of Hanover by Napoleon.
1804	**Napoleon becomes Emperor.**

1805	**Formation of the Third Coalition.**
	Trafalgar.
	French victories at Ulm and Austerlitz.
	Treaty of Pressburg.
1806	**Prussians defeated at Jena.**
	The Continental System began.
1807	**Russians defeated at Friedland.**
	Treaty of Tilsit between Napoleon and Alexander I.
1808	**British army under Wellesley in Portugal.**
	Peninsular War began.
	Convention of Cintra.
1809	**Sir J. Moore at Corunna.**
	Austrians defeated at Wagram.
	Peace of Vienna.
1810	**Spirit of nationalism developing against Napoleon—Spain, Portugal, Austria, Prussia.**
1811	**Alexander turning away from Continental System.**
1812	**Moscow Campaign.**
	Battle of Borodino, September 7th.
1813	**Treaty of Kalisch between Prussia and Russia.**
	The War of Liberation began.
	Napoleon's victories at Lutzen, Bautzen and Dresden.
	Napoleon defeated at Leipzig (Battle of the Nations).
1814	**Napoleon exiled to Elba.**
	Louis XVIII restored but he aroused much opposition in France.
1815	**Napoleon escaped from Elba, March.**
	Battle of Waterloo, June 18th.

QUESTIONS

1. *What were the achievements and failures of the Directory, 1795–1799?*
2. *Why was Bonaparte able to become First Consul in 1799?*
3. *What part did British naval power play in the years 1795–1815?*
4. *What reforms did Napoleon introduce in France?*
5. *Why did the French ultimately fail in the Peninsular War?*
6. *What were the main reasons for the defeat of Napoleon?*

CHAPTER FOUR

THE CONGRESS OF VIENNA, 1814–1815

THE President of the Congress was **Metternich,** and the Congress was attended by representatives from every European state, including Alexander I of Russia, Frederick William III of Prussia, Francis I of Austria and, for Britain, **Lord Castlereagh,** the Foreign Secretary. **Talleyrand** was the chief French representative. The Great Powers really decided the main issues, but Talleyrand succeeded in gaining a place for France in the Committee of Eight which undertook the Congress preliminaries.

The Work of the Congress

The first aim was *the prevention of future aggression by France.* Belgium (Austrian Netherlands) and Holland were united to make a barrier on France's north-eastern boundary. In northern Italy, the King of Piedmont was restored and his kingdom strengthened by the addition of Genoa. On the eastern frontier of France, Prussia took over the rule of the Rhine provinces.

Certain territories were assigned to the Great Powers and Alexander demanded the whole of Napoleon's Grand Duchy of Warsaw and those parts of Poland given to Prussia in the partitions at the end of the previous century. Prussia would only agree provided she received the whole of the Saxon kingdom. Talleyrand exploited these differences to the advantage of France and brought her into alliance with Britain and Austria against Russia and Prussia. He revived the *Balance of Power principle* which was to the advantage of France. Napoleon's escape from Elba interrupted the Congress but, after Waterloo, compromise proved easier. Russia was given the territory she demanded and Prussia gained Danzig and Posen, the greater part of Saxony, Western Pomerania—from Sweden—and the Rhine provinces.

Austria received Lombardy and Venetia in place of the former Netherlands. These areas were richer and nearer to her own domain. She also received Illyria, Dalmatia and the seaport of Cattaro on the Adriatic. From Bavaria she obtained the Tyrol and Salzburg. Thirty-nine states were formed into the **German Confederation** of which Austria was to be the president.

Britain gained Cape Colony, Ceylon, the West Indian islands of Tobago, Santa Lucia and Trinidad. She also gained Mauritius, the North Sea naval base of Heligoland, Malta, and the Ionian islands protectorate. These acquisitions greatly strengthened Britain as an imperial and naval power.

Sweden gained Norway from Denmark partly to compensate her for the earlier loss of Finland to Russia and as a reward for Bernadotte's part in the War of Liberation. Denmark had remained loyal to Napoleon.

Comments on the Congress

(*a*) The Balance of Power

Talleyrand exploited the principle of the Balance of Power in the interests of France (see p. 38). Castlereagh and Metternich pursued united policies towards Russia, whose anti-Turkish ambitions they distrusted. In general, all four Great Powers gained from the Congress without any one being dominant, or any combination being dominant.

(*b*) Legitimacy

This was the principle that hereditary rulers (or their heirs) who had been deposed by the Revolution and Napoleon should be restored where possible.

Talleyrand's influence was seen here, but it suited the aims of most of the Great Powers. **Ferdinand IV** was restored to the Kingdom of Naples and **Ferdinand VII** to Spain; they were both violent reactionaries. The restored rulers of Parma, Modena and Tuscany were connected with the **Hapsburgs,** and Naples had an alliance with Austria. These restorations suited the aims of Metternich in Italy, and destroyed Napoleon's Kingdom of Italy.

(*c*) Nationality

The principle of nationality, which had been given stimulus in Spain, Portugal, Poland, Italy, and Germany during the Napoleonic period, was in the main ignored. Belgium and Holland were an unnatural union; Alexander gained the Polish-inhabited Grand Duchy of Warsaw, and Finland; Italy was again fragmented in Austrian interests, as was Germany; the union of Sweden and Norway proved impermanent. The settlements were in the interests of states rather than people.

The Quadruple Alliance

The **Quadruple Alliance** of Britain, Prussia, Austria and Russia was formed by the **Treaties of Chaumont** of **1814–1815.** These countries had maintained their union against Napoleon and agreed to meet in congresses to discuss and settle the affairs of Europe. Castlereagh was a keen advocate of the congress system, but he despised and distrusted Alexander's scheme of the **Holy Alliance** by which the powers were to pledge themselves to be guided by the principles of Christianity. The Alliance, signed by Austria, Prussia and Russia, had little effect.

Summary of the Results of the Congress

The Treaty of Vienna was one of the most important attempts to settle the affairs of Europe and to guarantee the continuance of peace among the Great Powers. A long period of peace did, in fact, follow and was not really broken until 1854. There was, however, opposition to the idea of nationality and this part of the settlement was fraught with the most danger, and caused immediate internal disturbance especially in Italy. The later struggles for Italian and German unification were movements against the Metternich system devised at Vienna. The earliest breach in that part of the settlement was the **Belgian Revolution** of **1830.** (Prussia, however, having gained a German population was later to be in a strong position to lead German national unification.) The Congress also showed the forces of Legitimacy and Balance of Power strongly at work.

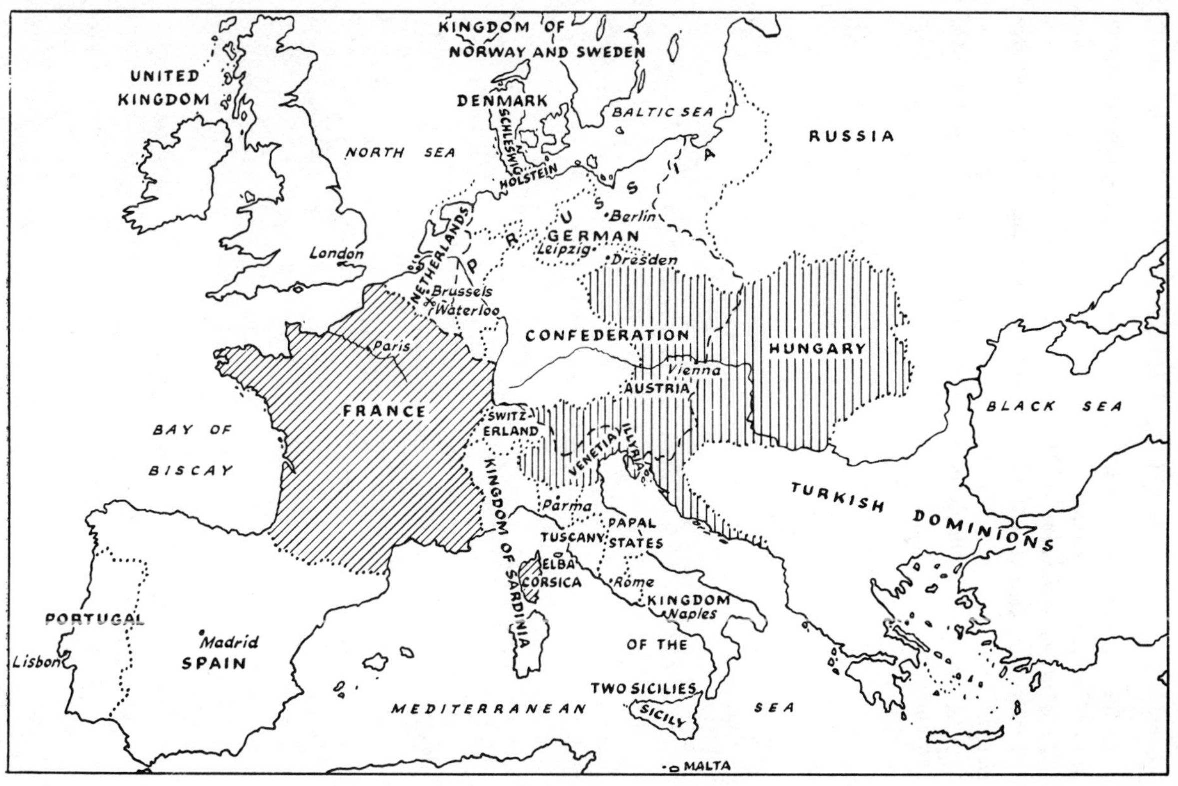
UNITED KINGDOM
KINGDOM OF NORWAY AND SWEDEN
DENMARK
SCHLESWIG
HOLSTEIN
BALTIC SEA
NORTH SEA
RUSSIA
London
NETHERLANDS
Brussels
Waterloo
Paris
FRANCE
BAY OF BISCAY
PORTUGAL
Lisbon
Madrid
SPAIN
P R U S S I A
Berlin
GERMAN
Leipzig
Dresden
CONFEDERATION
Vienna
AUSTRIA
HUNGARY
BLACK SEA
SWITZ-ERLAND
VENETIA
ILLYRIA
KINGDOM OF SARDINIA
Parma
TUSCANY
PAPAL STATES
ELBA
CORSICA
Rome
KINGDOM
Naples
OF THE
TWO SICILIES
SICILY
MALTA
MEDITERRANEAN SEA
TURKISH DOMINIONS

QUESTIONS

1. What differences of interest were there among the Great Powers at the Congress of Vienna?

2. What were the aims of Metternich?

3. To what extent was the principle of nationality ignored or resisted?

4. Attempt a summary of the good and bad aspects of the 1815 settlement.

CHAPTER FIVE

THE CONGRESS SYSTEM, 1818–1822

The Congress of Aix-la-Chapelle, 1818

THIS was attended by Francis I and Metternich, Frederick William III, Alexander I, Castlereagh, and **Richelieu** for France. The latter gained the withdrawal of occupation forces in France and France began to settle down under its limited monarchy. The Quadruple Alliance was secretly renewed to check any revolution in France, but the French signed a special Declaration with the powers of the Quadruple Alliance affirming respect for treaties and abstention from interfering in the internal affairs of other states without being asked to do so. The Declaration met both Castlereagh's and Metternich's fear of Russian intervention in Europe. On the same grounds Castlereagh opposed a Prussian suggestion that forces under Wellington should be permanently stationed in Belgium to police Europe against revolution. Castlereagh also secured the rejection of a Russian offer of naval help in the Mediterranean against the Barbary pirates. Sharp differences between members of the Alliances were already evident. The Quadruple Alliance became the **Quintuple Alliance** by the accession to it of France in 1818.

The Congress of Troppau, October, 1820

The years 1818–1821 saw revolutionary movements and disturbances in Spain, Naples, Italy and Germany. After the murder of **Kotzebue,** Alexander's spy, in 1819, the latter ceased to play with liberal ideas and fell strongly under Metternich's influence. Metternich now wished to use the Quintuple Alliance as a counter-revolutionary organization. Britain and France both opposed this, especially when Alexander suggested a joint naval foray across the Atlantic to bring the rebellious colonies of Spain and Portugal back to the mother countries. This was also against Britain's trading interests. Castlereagh, however, accepted Austria's right, under a treaty of 1815, to restore the monarchy's power in Naples, where a revolution had occurred.

Britain and France did not, therefore, sign the **Troppau Protocol of 1820** by which Austria, Russia and Prussia bound themselves to intervene in any state which had undergone revolution and thus threatened other states.

The Congress of Laibach, 1821

This was the adjourned Congress of Troppau. **Ferdinand** of Naples met Metternich, and an Austrian army restored Ferdinand to Naples. A liberal revolution in Piedmont was also suppressed by 80,000 Austrian troops. The Troppau Protocol was revived, despite British protests. However, the outbreak of the **Greek War of Independence, 1821,** once again brought Britain and Austria together against Russia, who wished to intervene in the dispute. Alexander was 'persuaded' to accept the attempted mediation of Austria and Britain in the conflict.

The Congress of Verona, October, 1822

Before the Congress, Castlereagh had committed suicide and was succeeded by **George Canning (1770–1827)** as British Foreign Secretary. Wellington went as the British representative. Alexander wished to send 150,000 Russian troops to Spain to suppress the liberal revolution there against Ferdinand VII. Britain, France and Austria opposed him. France, however, where the Ultra-royalists were now in power, wished to use her own army in Spain, and to this the **Protocol powers** (Austria, Prussia and Russia) agreed. Wellington thereupon withdrew from the Congress. In 1823 a French army entered Spain and restored the despotic powers of Ferdinand VII. Canning, however, threatened British naval action if the Protocol powers or France made any move against the former Atlantic colonies of Spain and Portugal, and Britain made treaties with Brazil,

Mexico and Colombia. The **Monroe Doctrine** of **1823** also assisted Canning's aims.

The Greek War of Independence saw the end of the Congress System. Canning's aim was to prevent unilateral intervention by Russia, and in **1827** the **Treaty of London** with Russia and France resulted in joint intervention and the destruction of the Turkish fleet at **Navarino.** Metternich was isolated and was greatly offended, but Canning had prevented the new Czar, Nicholas I, from taking unilateral action.

Thus the Congress System failed to work with the general harmony Castlereagh had hoped for; serious oppositions of policy occurred and the system was abandoned. The net result, however, of the Congress of Vienna settlement, of the Congress System, and of the general exhaustion produced by twenty years of war, was that no major international war occurred till the Crimean War in 1854. It must also be remembered that the idea of the settlement of disputes by the concerted efforts of the Great Powers—the **Concert of Europe**—remained a strong influence right up to 1914.

Dates

1818 **Congress of Aix-la-Chapelle.**
Liberal revolutionary movements.
Russian proposals rejected.
Army of occupation withdrawn from France.
1819 **Murder of Kotzebue.**
1820 **The Congress of Troppau.**
The Troppau Protocol.
1821 **Congress of Laibach.**
Ferdinand restored in Naples by Austrians.
Greek War of Independence.
1822 **Congress of Verona.**
George Canning, British Foreign Secretary, resists Russian proposals for intervention in Spain and South American republics.
Canning opposes French intervention in Spain.
1823 **Monroe Doctrine strengthens Canning's Atlantic policy.**
French army enters Spain.
1827 **Treaty of London.**
Death of Canning.

QUESTIONS

1. Explain the relations between Russia and the other Great Powers in the years 1818–1827.

2. What were the principles of British foreign policy as shown at the congresses?

3. Why did the Congress System cease after 1822?

4. Did the Congress System achieve anything constructive?

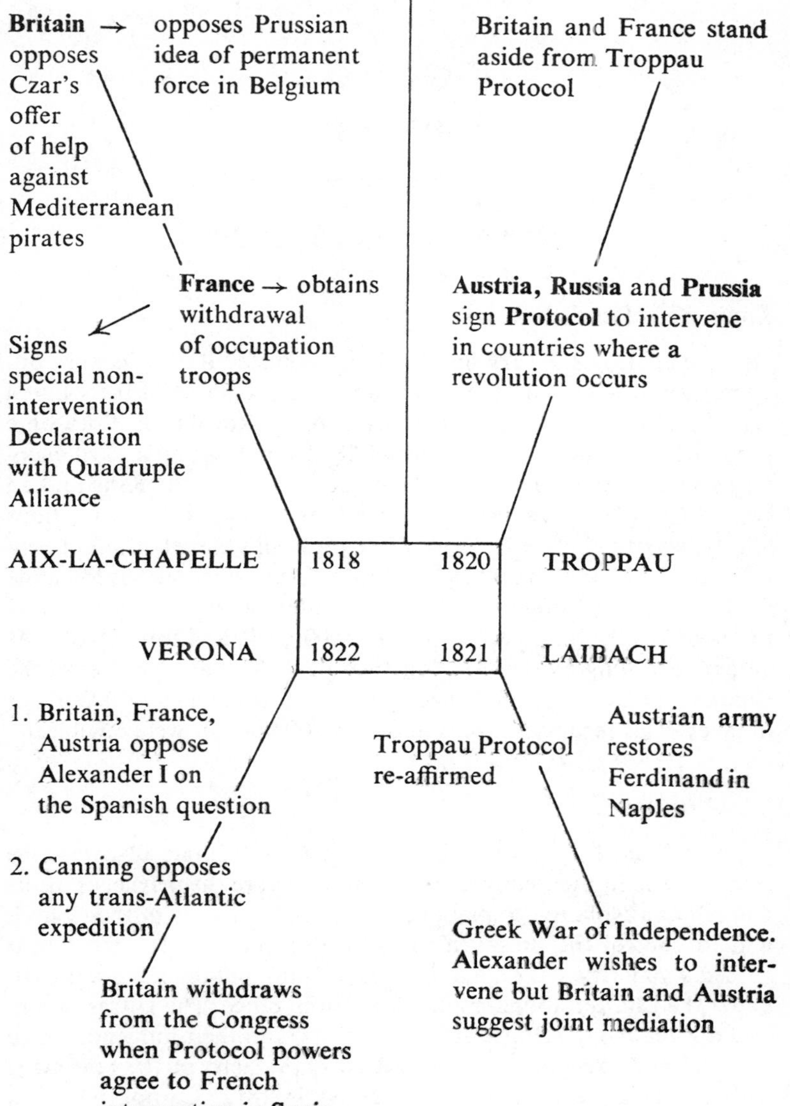

THE CONCERT OF EUROPE
Britain → opposes Czar's offer of help against Mediterranean pirates
opposes Prussian idea of permanent force in Belgium
Britain and France stand aside from Troppau Protocol
France → obtains withdrawal of occupation troops
Signs special non-intervention Declaration with Quadruple Alliance
Austria, Russia and Prussia sign Protocol to intervene in countries where a revolution occurs
AIX-LA-CHAPELLE
1818
1820
TROPPAU
VERONA
1822
1821
LAIBACH
1. Britain, France, Austria oppose Alexander I on the Spanish question
2. Canning opposes any trans-Atlantic expedition
Britain withdraws from the Congress when Protocol powers agree to French intervention in Spain
Troppau Protocol re-affirmed
Austrian army restores Ferdinand in Naples
Greek War of Independence. Alexander wishes to intervene but Britain and Austria suggest joint mediation

CHAPTER SIX

FRANCE, 1815–1870

Louis XVIII and Richelieu

BOTH Louis XVIII and his chief minister **Richelieu** were opposed to any attempts to restore the privileges of the Church and Nobility which had been lost by the Revolution. Both were prepared to maintain the **Charter of 1814** which set up a parliamentary system with a **Chamber of Peers** nominated by the King and an elected **Chamber of Deputies.** The Charter also guaranteed religious liberty, equality before the law, a free press and the retention of property by all those who had gained through the confiscations from the Church and the Nobility in 1789. The voters were, however, limited to about 100,000 in a population of 29,000,000, and were eligible as voters according to the taxation they paid. To be a member of the Chamber of Deputies a man had to be over forty and pay 1,000 francs in taxes. This meant that only about 12,000 persons were eligible.

The Ultra-royalists

The **Ultras,** led by the King's brother, the **Comte d'Artois** (the leader of the former 'émigrés') wanted to restore the privileges of the Church and Nobility, to place education in the hands of the Church and to control the press. In the first elections of 1815 the Ultras gained a majority in the Chamber of Deputies, but the King was able, under the Charter, to maintain Richelieu in office. The Ultras organized a *white terror* against their opponents, and their influence led to the trial and execution of **Marshal Ney,** the hero of the rearguard action during the retreat from Moscow in 1812. Carnot, who had returned to France, was forced into exile. There were a number of assassinations of former supporters of the Revolution and Napoleon.

Louis XVIII and Richelieu saw the dangers of this policy, especially when, due to fears of the confiscation of their land, the peasants of Grenoble revolted in 1816. Louis dissolved the ultra-royalist Chamber, and the elections returned a majority of his supporters. There had been a reaction against the *white terror*. In **1818** Richelieu was able to secure the withdrawal of occupation troops and a reduction of the indemnity imposed on France because France now appeared to be stable.

But from **1819–1824** the Ultra-royalists regained influence. This was in part because Louis himself became alarmed when in 1819 the electors returned twenty-one extreme Republicans, among them the **Abbé Grégoire,** one of the leaders of the anti-Church and anti-monarchical elements of 1789. Louis managed to unseat Grégoire—much to the delight of the Ultras. Then in 1820 **Louvel** assassinated the **Duc de Berri,** second son of the Comte d'Artois. The Duc de Berri was in direct succession to the throne on the Bourbon side. Richelieu himself now imposed a press censorship, abolished the secret ballot in elections and gave a double vote to the great landowners. However, the Ultras succeeded in replacing Richelieu by **Villèle,** who was more to their liking. He remained Chief Minister till 1827.

Villèle's Policy

He was prepared to strengthen the position of the Ultras, and the important Catholic **Society of the Congregation** secured increasing influence for the Catholic Church through Villèle's support. The Ultras also regained control of the Chamber of Deputies, and Villèle introduced an amendment to the Charter by which elections were to be held every seven years in place of the Charter's old arrangement by which fifty deputies retired each year and elections were held to fill their places. This gave the Ultras a long run of power.

Louis died in 1824 and was succeeded by the Comte d'Artois who took the title of **Charles X.** The ultra-royalist policy was now pressed forward. Villèle gave compensation to the 'émigrés', but the Bourgeoisie disliked the reduction of their interest on the National Debt to pay for it. The revival of old laws which had protected the property of the Church and imposed harsh penalties was increasingly resented by the middle and lower classes. They feared a complete return to the old alliance of Church and State which had existed before 1789.

The fears of the middle and working class as well as the peasantry led to increasing opposition to Charles X. In 1827 the old revolutionary Lafayette was significantly elected to the Chamber of Deputies. He had already attempted a rising against Louis XVIII in 1821 and had been organizing secret revolutionary groups. The National Guard also became unreliable, for they regarded themselves as the protectors of the Charter of 1814. Charles X now disbanded the National Guard and imposed further censorship. The Chamber of Peers, originally appointed under the 1814 Charter, had continuously opposed the policies of Charles and Villèle. The latter resigned in 1827, and was followed by **Martignac** till 1829, then **Polignac,** an even more extreme Ultra. In the elections of 1829 Charles lost fifty of his supporters, whereupon, refusing to accept the voters' verdict, he issued the **Ordinances of St. Cloud** by which he set aside the elections, restricted the franchise and placed newspapers under government control.

This led to immediate revolt in Paris and a government was set up in the **Hotel de Ville** under Lafayette. Barricades were thrown up by the middle and working class of Paris. The royalist troops made little resistance and Paris was under revolutionary control once again. Charles X fled to England on August 1, **1830.**

The movement for a constitutional and limited monarchy had won a victory against attempts to restore the doctrine of the **Divine Right of Kings.**

The Chamber of Deputies, rejecting Republicanism, elected **Louis Philippe** to succeed Charles X.

The Orleanist Monarchy, 1830–1848

Louis Philippe was the son of Philippe 'Egalité', **Duke of Orleans,** who had voted for the execution of his cousin Louis XVI. Louis Philippe was styled *King of the French* to indicate his popular support. His general style was middle class and reflected the fact that he relied upon the support of the new rising class of merchants and manufacturers of the French Industrial Revolution.

The new **Charter of 1830** abolished the power of the King to issue decrees, and the parliament could now introduce laws itself and not merely, as hitherto, debate those put before it by the King. The voters were increased to 200,000 with a middle-class property qualification. The population of France was now about 30,000,000.

Foreign Policy

Louis wished for peace and industrial progress, but he was under pressure from various directions to take strong action abroad. **Bonapartists, Legitimists** (Bourbon supporters), **Liberals** and **Republicans** all wanted a strong foreign policy.

In 1830 the Belgians revolted against their union with the Dutch which had been arranged under the Vienna settlement. Their Dutch king favoured his own people, and there were other grievances over trade, taxation, parliamentary representation and Church control of education. Louis was expected to intervene on behalf of the Belgians, but he feared the alignment of the other Great Powers against him. When the Belgians offered the throne to the **Duc de Nemours,** the second son of Louis Philippe, the British Foreign Secretary **Palmerston** forced him to withdraw and **Leopold of Saxe-Coburg,** uncle of the future **Queen Victoria,** was elected. Both Britain and France assisted the Belgians against a Dutch offensive in **1831,** and in **1839,** Russia, Austria, Prussia, France and Britain all guaranteed the independence and neutrality of Belgium by the **Treaty of London, 1839.**

Thus although Louis had played some direct part in helping the Belgians, he was really controlled by the other Great Powers.

In 1830 the Poles revolted against Russia and the Italians against Austrian control. Louis was urged to take supporting action, but he preferred peace and the absence of opposition from the Great Powers. The Chamber of Deputies was guided by self-interest and influenced by official bribery to support Louis.

In **1833, Mehemet Ali,** ruler of Egypt, had seized Syria from his overlord the **Sultan of Turkey,** but in **1839** the Turks launched an attack against him. **Adolphe Thiers,** Louis' Prime Minister, wished to support Mehemet Ali and build up French influence in the Middle East. Britain again opposed this, and Palmerston arranged a settlement to which France eventually agreed after Thiers had been dismissed. Mehemet lost both Syria and Crete, and Thiers and the French Liberals were thus frustrated.

In **1846** the **Spanish marriages** question broke the official friendship between Britain and France. The circumstances of the marriage of the **Duc de Montpensier** into the Spanish royal family made possible a future union of France and Spain, which was regarded by Britain as a threat to her Mediterranean interests and the Balance of Power in Europe. Almost as a reply to Louis' breach of the agreement with Britain over Spain, Palmerston's diplomacy led to the defeat of the Catholic 'cantons' by the Protestants in the **Swiss Civil War.** Louis had supported the Catholic cause, and his defeat was displeasing to the Church in France.

Thus the cautious policy of Louis, while it pleased a considerable section of the commercial middle class by keeping France at peace, was violently attacked by Bonapartists, Legitimists, Liberals and Republicans.

Internal Affairs of France, 1830–1848

Louis' cautious middle-class policy was typified by the attitudes of **Guizot,** Prime Minister **1840–1848.** Working- and lower-middle-class demands for the vote were met with determined opposition. He bribed the Chamber of Deputies, but this meant that the Chamber became increasingly out of touch with the needs and demands of wider sections of the people.

Opposition to Louis Philippe

Although on the throne for eighteen years, Louis' position was never entirely secure. There were several conspiracies to assassinate him, and in 1830–1835 there were six serious revolts. He could, however, rely on the Chamber of Deputies and the middle-class National Guard. The Socialists, under the leadership of **Louis Blanc,** led a determined resistance on behalf, especially, of the workers of the industrial towns, where living conditions and wages were bad. Louis Blanc propounded the theory of the State's duty to provide work, and his **L'Organisation du Travail** had great influence. The socialist conspirator **Blanqui** also attempted a rising against Louis in **1832.**

The Republicans demanded the end of the monarchy and the extension of the franchise. The Bonapartists under **Louis Napoleon Bonaparte,** nephew of the great Napoleon, aimed at a Bonapartist restoration. Attempts were made in 1836 at Strasbourg and 1840 at Boulogne, but both failed. The Liberals demanded closer control of the government by a more democratic Chamber of Deputies, and the Legitimists aimed at the restoration of the Bourbon line.

To appease the French memories of Napoleon, Louis Philippe permitted the return of Napoleon's body from St. Helena in 1841.

Policy of Suppression

Louis' reply to agitation was suppression. The **Law of Associations** made illegal the activities of most of his opponents already mentioned. The press was heavily censored. The armed forces were used on several occasions to suppress working-class revolts (e.g. at **Lyons** in **1834**).

Reform Banquets

In **1843** the Socialists and Republicans united in their demands for parliamentary reform, but **Guizot** resisted all demands for a debate on the franchise in the Chamber of Deputies. **Reform Banquets** were now organized and some members of the Chamber of Deputies participated. It was Louis' banning of the great Reform Banquet in Paris on February 22, **1848,** which sparked off the revolution against him and led to his flight to England on February 24th. Both the working and middle class of Paris had overthrown him with the active support of the National Guard.

The following points should be considered in accounting for the fall of the Orleanist monarchy:

1. The instability of Louis Philippe's position from the start.
2. The general acceptance by the Chamber of Deputies of the King's and Guizot's policies forced criticism into conspiratorial channels outside the Chamber of Deputies.
3. The policy of suppression and the failure to reform very bad working-class conditions in the industrial towns caused unrest.

4. Refusal to extend the franchise led to the decisive union of Socialists and Republicans.
5. A foreign policy whose apparent timidity caused a looking-back to Bonapartism.
6. The Church was displeased to lose many of the gains of the previous reign.

Parties of both Right and Left had every cause to seek the overthrow of Louis Philippe, yet in many ways he had shown skill, craft and statesmanship in maintaining his precarious position for eighteen years.

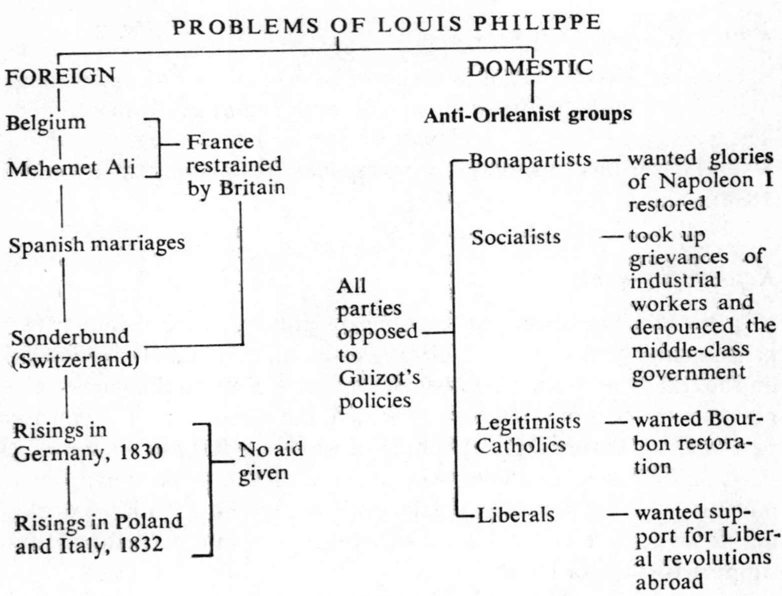

The Second Republic, 1848–1852

The republican poet **Lamartine** now became head of the Provisional Government of which Louis Blanc was also a member, but the majority were opposed to anything like a 'Red' republic, and Lamartine ordered the suppression by the **Garde Mobile** of a great socialist demonstration on **April 16, 1848.**

In May, elections for a Constituent Assembly were undertaken on the basis of *manhood suffrage*, every man over twenty-one having the vote. Four Socialists were returned for Paris, but the new Assembly was *overwhelmingly middle class and anti-Socialist* and even 130 Legitimists were returned.

The *National Workshops* to provide work for the unemployed were now demanded by the Socialists. The government allowed a partial, half-hearted experiment which brought in thousands of unemployed from outside the city, produced little useful work, and was resisted by the wealthy taxpayers from the start. When the schemes were abandoned a rising took place in June in the eastern districts of Paris under socialist leadership and fighting lasted for four days. **General Cavaignac** suppressed the rising with 10,000 casualties among the insurgents.

Under the new constitution, now approved, a single Chamber of Deputies (750) was to be elected by *universal male suffrage*, as was also the President, who was to hold office for four years only. The President was head of the armed forces and appointed his own ministers.

In December, 1848, Louis Napoleon Bonaparte gained an overwhelming majority for the Presidency. The reasons were many—the 'Napoleonic legend' which he had cultivated; the attraction of his schemes for the relief of poverty which he had evolved during his imprisonment after 1840; the belief of the French peasantry that he would guarantee their property as his uncle had done; his promises to strengthen the position of the Catholic Church; and the feeling of the propertied classes that he would produce order in the state and protect them from Communism and Socialism. He was also assisted by the fact that the Socialists were discredited after the events of February–June, 1848, and that the Royalists failed to produce a candidate.

The Political Tactics of Louis Napoleon, 1848–1852

Louis Napoleon now strengthened his position by giving posts in his government to Orleanists, Legitimists and Catholics, with a Bonapartist as Chief of Police. He gained further support from the Church by sending **General Oudinot** to Rome to suppress the Roman

Republic of **Mazzini** and **Garibaldi**. He left a permanent French garrison there to protect the Pope. Republican and Socialist societies were widely suppressed by the police and their publications banned. This enabled him to control the Chamber of Deputies. But he skilfully maintained the support of the mass of the people and resisted an attempt of the Chamber of Deputies to disfranchise 3,000,000 unskilled workers. He thus appeared to be the protector of the Republic. In 1851 he was opposed by the Chamber when he demanded the extension of the Presidency to ten years. He felt confident of support for this from the people, and he began the imprisonment and exile of many of his political opponents. They numbered about 20,000 in all, including many members of the Chamber of Deputies. On **December 2nd, 1851,** a plebiscite (partly 'fixed') gave him an overwhelming vote for the ten-year Presidency. The next twelve months saw him touring the country, reviving the old Napoleonic military parades and the eagle standards and generally courting popularity. He became the **Emperor Napoleon III on December 2, 1852.**

He had gained power by skilful political manœuvres, by using to his own advantage the control of the armed forces and the police, by appealing to the people against the Chamber, by promising order and progress, and by the outright suppression of his more determined opponents.

The Government of Napoleon III, 1852–1870: The Second Empire

Napoleon declared that *order must come before liberty,* and a rigid central control of the country was imposed. He created an army loyal to himself and imposed an oath of allegiance in both military and civil spheres. In elections only candidates were acceptable who were approved by the government. The 'Préfets' of the Departments were chosen by the Emperor and controlled all important posts in local government. Newspapers were censored and could be fined or suppressed. The University of Paris was closely watched, and an army of spies carried out a continuous surveillance.

During his early years as Emperor, Napoleon III attempted to redeem some of his social promises. He reduced, for instance, profiteering in food and introduced work schemes to assist the unemployed. Slum clearance was undertaken vigorously, and Paris itself was transformed under the supervision of Baron Haussmann. An important motive for the sweeping away of narrow streets and the creation of wide boulevards was to make impossible the barricades of left-wing revolution.

The economic development of the country was rapid. New canals, roads and harbours were constructed. Special investment banks were set up for the benefit of the new Bourgeoisie. Farming was also improved by land-drainage schemes and improved credit facilities. Railways were rapidly extended.

Up to 1860 Napoleon III was in a strong position for three reasons: (1) the suppression of his opponents; (2) the economic development of the country; (3) a reasonably successful foreign policy.

Foreign Policy

1. **The Crimean War.** In **1853**, war broke out between Russia and Turkey over the claims of the Czar Nicholas I to be the protector of the Balkan Christians against Turkey and the protector of the Holy Places in Jerusalem for the Greek Orthodox Church. France claimed to protect the Holy Places, too, and Russia countered by occupying the Principalities (Wallachia and Moldavia). British policy aimed above all at maintaining the integrity of the Turkish Empire. Both Britain and France entered the war in support of Turkey in 1854.

Napoleon III's motives for entering the struggle were: (1) military glory to be gained by a quick victory over the old enemy of 1812; (2) the desire to take up the cause of the Catholic Church in the Holy Land; (3) the wish to revive French influence in the Middle East which had been frustrated by Louis Philippe's cautious policy; (4) the desire to make France once again the main European Power and the centre of diplomatic affairs; (5) the wish to alter the Vienna settlement of 1815.

After great casualties and muddle the war was won by the Allies and Napoleon presided at the **Paris Peace Conference** of 1856. His main aims had been achieved.

2. **Italian Policy.** In his young days Napoleon III had supported the Italian *Carbonari* struggling against Austria, and he was under

considerable public pressure to assist the Italians. On the other hand, the Catholic Church in France was reluctant to support any moves against the principal ally and support of the Pope—namely, Austria. The Sardinians, however, had assisted France and Britain in the Crimean War, and at Paris in 1856 **Count Cavour** had pressed Napoleon for assistance against Austria. While still hesitating, the urgency of the Italian question was brought home to Napoleon III by the attempt of the anarchist **Orsini** to assassinate him in **1858**. On July 20th, **1858**, he made the **Compact of Plombières** with Cavour. He promised to assist Piedmont to expel the Austrians from northern Italy, and in return was to receive Nice and Savoy. The Pope, however, was to retain power in the Papal States and an independent kingdom of Central Italy was to be formed.

After a variety of manœuvres and provocations, the Austrians attacked Piedmont, whereupon Napoleon III poured his troops into northern Italy and won the costly battles of **Magenta (1859)** and **Solferino (1859)** against the Austrians.

At this point he made the **Truce of Villafranca** with the Austrians, **1859**. This was a devastating blow to his allies the Piedmontese. Various motives have been attributed to Napoleon III's decision, such as the heavy French casualties; the rising demand from all the Italian states for union with the Kingdom of Piedmont-Sardinia, which would leave the Pope's position in Rome weakened and exposed; Napoleon's fear of creating a strong Italian state which would challenge the position of France in the Mediterranean; and finally Napoleon's dislike of the Republicans in the Italian movement. He could not control and limit the Italian movement as he had hoped. The Prussians had also begun to increase the number of their troops on the Rhine.

Napoleon gained **Savoy** and **Nice,** and Sardinia gained **Lombardy** but not Venetia, which she had been promised in 1858.

Napoleon was denounced in France by the Liberals for having failed to carry through the struggle, and by Catholic opinion for having gone too far, especially when popular revolts in the smaller Italian states led to their union with Sardinia. The Romagna, part of the Papal States, joined Sardinia.

3. The Mexican Adventure. In 1861 the Mexican government repudiated its foreign debts. Britain, France and Spain sent a joint expedition to Mexico and forced her to resume payments. The English and Spanish withdrew, but Napoleon maintained his troops in Mexico. He was dazzled by the prospect of setting up a new Latin Empire under French control, and he persuaded the **Archduke Maximilian**, of Austria, to accept the role of **Emperor of Mexico.** The project was a disastrous failure; huge sums of French money were wasted and Napoleon was forced to withdraw when the U.S.A. (where the Civil War had just ended) threatened to invoke the Monroe Doctrine. Maximilian was executed by the Mexicans, and great damage was done to Napoleon's prestige.

The Position at Home

The Emperor was now experiencing opposition in France, and the **Free Trade Treaty** of **1860** with Britain caused offence to many French commercial interests. He was compelled by circumstances to make concessions to the liberty he had promised. In 1859 he granted an amnesty to political prisoners and exiles and permitted the Senate and Legislature to criticize the government's measures. Under Adolphe Thiers the **Third Party** developed, demanding more democratic rights for parliament. In 1868 the control of newspapers was abandoned and political meetings permitted. More freedom was thus given to Napoleon III's critics and in the elections of 1869 over 3,000,000 votes were gained by his critics out of a total of 8,000,000. This compelled him to allow the Legislature to introduce laws and vote on financial matters and to appoint a Prime Minister, **Ollivier,** to take over much of the control of the cabinet hitherto in the hands of the Emperor. The so-called *Liberal Empire* was thus created.

The Franco-Prussian War, 1870

By **1869** the strength of Prussia under **Bismarck** had become obvious, and among Napoleon's advisers there were a number, including the **Empress Eugènie** herself, who regarded a successful war against Prussia as the only way of safeguarding France's future in Europe.

By 1866 the diplomatic initiative had passed to Prussia. Napoleon had incorrectly expected the **Austro-Prussian War** of **1866** to be long drawn out, exhausting to both sides, and thus ensuring France's superiority over both countries. It lasted seven weeks, ending in an overwhelming Prussian victory. Bismarck, who had met Napoleon in Biarritz in 1865, now used Napoleon's early demands for Luxembourg, parts of the left bank of the Rhine, and Belgium, to bring the South German states under Prussian influence. These disclosures also helped to isolate Napoleon from the other European powers.

The immediate cause of war with France was the Spanish succession question involving the candidature of a **Hohenzollern** for the Spanish throne. The affair of the **Ems telegram** (see p. 86) was used by Bismarck to provoke the war party in France, and he succeeded.

Defeat of France

Napoleon III had been misled by his advisers as to the state of preparedness of the French army, which was disorganized. The heroism of the French soldier could not compensate for muddle and mismanagement. The French war party interfered with strategy and Napoleon, already ill, could not resist. It was such interference which prevented Napoleon from organizing a defensive retreat of his main armies on Paris and led to the calamity of **Sédan (1870)** and the **Siege of Paris (Sept. 1870–Jan. 1871)**. The heroic efforts of **Léon Gambetta** to organize prolonged resistance in Paris and the provinces proved in vain.

By the **Treaty of Frankfort, 1871,** France was to pay Germany an indemnity of 5,000,000,000 francs, the surety for which was a German army of occupation. **Alsace-Lorraine,** with its valuable minerals and agriculture, went to Germany.

Summary of Napoleon's Downfall

Napoleon III had attempted to revive the glories of the earlier age of his uncle, Napoleon I, but the internal and external position of France was far different in Napoleon III's day. His foreign policy was only partially effective because he was too hesitant. It also caused many human casualties and was very costly. There was much corruption and bribery among his ministers. His later liberal policies were forced upon him by difficulties rather than granted by his own free will. The attempted defeat of Prussia was a desperate gamble to retrieve an already weakened position, though many of his advisers did not see it in its true light.

Summary

The restored French monarchy of 1815 had had to face opposition from the Ultra-royalists and Republicans. Charles X's efforts to create an ultra-royalist French society brought about the united opposition of the French middle and working classes in 1830. Louis Philippe, however, relied exclusively on the middle class, refused to extend democracy and followed only a partly effective foreign policy. He experienced the continuous opposition of various conspiratorial movements. His overthrow in 1848 led to attempts by the Socialists to force the pace of events, and against them the propertied classes sought the support of Louis Napoleon Bonaparte. As Emperor he attempted to carry out his social promises, and for some years his position was strong. But he embarked on an adventurous foreign policy without the strength to carry it through. He was out-manœuvred by Bismarck and with the disaster of the Franco-Prussian War of 1870, the Second Empire collapsed.

Dates

1814	**The Charter.**
1815–16	**The White Terror.**
	Peasant revolt in Grenoble.
1818	**Occupation troops withdrawn.**
1819	**The Abbé Grégoire unseated.**
1820	**Louvel assassinates Duc de Berri.**
1824	**Accession of Charles X.**
1830	**Ordinances of St. Cloud.**
	Fall of Charles X.
	Accession of Louis Philippe.
	Charter of 1830.
	Belgian revolt.
	Polish revolt.
1833	**Mehemet Ali seizes Syria.**
1834	**Law of Associations.**

1836	**Failure of Louis Napoleon Bonaparte's first attempted 'coup'.**
1839	**Thiers supports Mehemet Ali against Turkey.**
	Complications with Britain and dismissal of Thiers.
	Publication of Louis Blanc's 'L'Organisation du Travail'.
1840	**Louis Napoleon Bonaparte's attempted 'coup' at Boulogne.**
1841	**The Emperor Napoleon's body brought from St. Helena.**
1843	**Alliance of Socialists and Republicans to demand extension of the franchise.**
1846	**The Spanish marriages.**
1848	**Paris Reform Banquet (Feb. 22nd).**
	Dismissal of Guizot.
	Fall of Louis Philippe.
	National Workshops.
	Four days of civil war, June 23–26.
	Louis Napoleon Bonaparte elected President.
1849	**General Oudinot goes to the help of Rome.**
1851	**Louis Napoleon Bonaparte made President for ten years (Dec. 2).**
1852	**Louis Napoleon Bonaparte becomes Emperor Napoleon III (Dec. 2).**
1853–56	**Crimean War.**
1856	**Peace of Paris.**
1858	**Orsini's attempted assassination of the Emperor.**
	Compact of Plombières.
1859	**Battles of Magenta and Solferino.**
	Truce of Villafranca.
	More political freedom accorded at home.
1861–67	**Failure of the Mexican adventure.**
1867	**Execution of Maximilian.**
1866	**Austro-Prussian War.**
	Napoleon fails to gain concessions from Bismarck.
1868	**Control of press abandoned.**
	Political meetings permitted.
1869	**Growth of opposition to Napoleon III.**
	Legislature permitted to introduce laws and vote on financial

	questions.
	The Spanish Succession question.
1870	**Franco-Prussian War.**
	Fall of Napoleon III.
1871	**Treaty of Frankfort.**

QUESTIONS

1. What part was played by the Ultra-royalists during the years 1815–1830?

2. What were the causes of the revolution of 1830?

3. How do you explain the fall of Louis Philippe in 1848?

4. By what means was Louis Napoleon Bonaparte able to rise to power in the years 1848–1852?

5. Did the Emperor Napoleon III bring any benefits to France?

6. What were the main reasons for the fall of the Second Empire in 1870?

CHAPTER SEVEN

THE HAPSBURG EMPIRE TO 1867

THE history of Austria during the years 1815–1849 is dominated by **Prince Metternich (1773–1859).** An aristocrat with a deep knowledge of European society, he defended the old social and political systems and was opposed to the doctrines of nationalism and equality preached by the French Revolutionists.

Nationalism in Austria would have broken the country to pieces—as it did after 1918—and would have led to the domination of the German Confederation by Prussia. The Empire was composed of Czechs, Slovaks, Germans, Magyars, Serbs, Croats, Slovenes, Poles, and Italians.

The Emperor Francis I and Metternich worked hand in hand to prevent the spread of liberalism and ideas of national independence. The universities and schools were closely watched, and a censorship of books and periodicals imposed.

It was an *autocratic empire* with every individual responsible to the Emperor. But its increasing inefficiency caused criticism from sections of the middle class of industrialists and traders. Government revenue rarely balanced expenditure, and high tariffs on imports designed to raise revenue, handicapped both industry and trade.

The Austrian nobility held the key posts in the country, were exempt from compulsory military service and governed their estates by feudal courts. Their privileged position annoyed the Bourgeoisie. State appointments were also confined to Roman Catholics and this was a cause of grievance to religious minorities.

Hungary as a Centre of Discontent

In Hungary the ruling people were the **Magyars.** They had **been** successful in retaining their own **Diet** with which the Emperor discussed affairs of state. They had also succeeded in gaining the acceptance of Magyar as the official language in place of the old imperial Latin. Magyar nationalism, however, attempted to impose its language and law on minorities in Hungary such as the **Croats.** This led to resistance by the Croatians to Magyar domination and a demand for their own Assembly and the official use in Croatia of their own language. Thus, for these various reasons, nationalism developed in Hungary both among the Magyars and the Croats.

A leading part in opposition to official imperial policy in Hungary was taken by **Louis Kossuth,** a journalist. But his demands went beyond mere Magyar nationalism and, although a Magyar himself, he denounced the social privileges they enjoyed in relation to both middle class and peasantry. He demanded an elected parliament and the equality of all before the law. He was elected a member for Budapest in the Hungarian Diet of **1847**.

The Year 1848 in Hungary

The **revolution of 1848** in France had immediate effects in Hungary. In the Diet, Kossuth put forward the demands of his supporters in the important speech of March 3, 1848. The Hungarian liberals were encouraged by the outbreak of revolution in Vienna itself.

The Hungarian Diet now adopted the **March Laws** put forward by a supporter of Kossuth, **Francis Déak.** These created a Hungarian government responsible to the Hungarian parliament alone and not to Vienna. It gave parliament control of taxation, the army and foreign affairs. *Serfdom* and the *privileges of the Magyar nobility were also abolished.* The middle class and a section of the peasantry were given the vote in elections and a **National Guard** was established. At this point the Emperor was still recognized as the head of state.

But Kossuth's refusal to give similar liberties to the Croat minority led to the establishment of a separate Croatian assembly at Agram. The Croatian leader **Count Jellacic** now joined the Emperor in the hope that he would grant Croatian independence, and in July, 1848, Croatian and imperial Austrian forces moved against Budapest. A fatal division had thus appeared in the national movement in Hungary.

Kossuth now declared Hungary a separate Republic. The Emperor's reply was to call in the willing aid of Czar Nicholas I who was alarmed both by the social reforms in Hungary and by the prospect of a Republic on his frontier. Austrian victories in Italy also released forces against Hungary. Under **General Haynau,** the Austrian imperial forces, with the aid of 200,000 Russian troops, crushed Hungarian resistance, and Kossuth fled. The name 'Hyena' given to Haynau by his opponents was a comment on the ruthless revenge taken against the Hungarian patriots. The Croats and Slovenes failed to gain the rights they had hoped for.

Events in Vienna

On March 12, **1848,** the **Emperor Ferdinand,** who had succeeded Francis in 1835, was compelled to receive a *Students' Petition* which demanded the sweeping away of the censorship and the holding of elections for a popular parliament. Some demonstrators were killed by the imperial troops, but the general movement of intellectuals, the middle and working classes was so strong that Metternich fled from Vienna on March 15th. On April 14th the Emperor decreed a constitutional monarchy and the holding of elections for a parliament to which the government would be responsible. The people had also established a **Revolutionary Committee** to rule Vienna and a **National Guard.** In May, 1848, the Emperor left Vienna for Innsbruck where he would be less under popular control. In December, 1848, the Emperor Ferdinand, who was weak-minded and incapable, abdicated in favour of his nephew, **Francis Joseph** (1848–1916).

At this time the risings on similar lines by the Czechs in Prague and by the Poles in Galicia were beginning to fail.

The new parliament meeting in Vienna failed to achieve strength and union against the Emperor and among its various factions. One of the most serious divisions was between the Slavs and Germans. Eventually the Slav representatives left Vienna altogether and the revolutionary movement in the city was overwhelmed by the army that **General Windischgratz** brought against it. The Emperor's powers were in the main restored under the new despotic Chancellor **Prince Schwarzenberg.** Serfdom, however, was not restored.

Some Reasons for the Failure of the Austrian Revolutions

The following points can be considered:

1. Conflicts *within* the national movements prevented a complete union of all anti-imperial forces. The Emperor was able, for instance, to exploit to his own advantage the divisions between Croats and Magyars and between the Germans and Slavs.

2. The imperial Army remained intact, and its victories in Italy and also against the revolution in Prague enabled it to bring its full might against Vienna.

3. The intervention of the Czar Nicholas I in Hungary was decisive.

4. The lack of success of the liberal revolutions in Germany and Italy also weakened the Hungarian and Viennese movements by their effect on morale.

The Dual Monarchy

In 1859, because of Austrian defeats by Napoleon III in northern Italy and resultant discontent, the Emperor agreed to restore the Magyar Diet in Hungary. He also allowed Magyar to be the official language again. After the defeat of Austria by Prussia at **Sadowa** in 1866, the Dual Monarchy was established by a compromise—the *Ausgleich*. Hungary was given equality with Austria in the Empire. For matters of common interest special committees composed equally of Hungarians and Austrians were established, but for all purely internal affairs Hungary was self-governing. Despite a number of changes, Magyar domination in Hungary itself continued.

Summary

For more than thirty years Metternich succeeded in suppressing liberalism and nationalism in Austria-Hungary. Liberal and national discontent had, however, developed beneath the surface, and the French Revolution of 1848 brought it into the open. The early successes of the revolutionaries were destroyed by divisions amongst themselves and by the strength of the imperial forces. The intervention of Nicholas I had a decisive effect in ending the revolutionary movement in Hungary and, by its effects, elsewhere. Neither France nor Britain were able or willing to give direct aid to Continental liberalism and nationalism. Hungarian nationalism was recognized by the *Ausgleich* of 1867, but not in the form Kossuth had demanded.

Dates

1848 Revolutions in Vienna, Prague and Budapest.
1849 Suppression of the Hungarian revolution.
1859 Austrians defeated by Napoleon III in northern Italy.
1867 The Dual Monarchy established.

QUESTIONS

1. Why was there discontent in the Hapsburg Empire in 1848?

2. What was Kossuth's policy and why did the Hungarian revolution of 1848 fail?

3. What were the general causes of failure of the revolutions in the Hapsburg Empire, 1848–1849?

4. What was the 'Ausgleich' and how did it come about?

CHAPTER EIGHT

THE UNIFICATION OF ITALY, 1815–1870

Italy after 1815

NAPOLEON'S control of Italy had *encouraged the idea of unity*. He had imposed French rule, but at the same time had improved communications, administration and law. The Bourbons had been removed from Naples and other petty rulers had also been overthrown. The French had been welcomed by a considerable number of Italians, especially of the middle class, whose interests were promoted in government and trade. Eventually, however, French control became onerous, particularly because of heavy taxation, and there was a demand that all foreign control should be removed.

The Vienna settlement went contrary to all ideas of Italian union and liberalism. Austria received Lombardy and Venetia, and their inhabitants were subjected to heavy taxation and to a severe police control. **Victor Emmanuel I** became **King of Sardinia** and he undid much of the progressive work of the French. **Ferdinand I, King of the Two Sicilies,** ruled with despotic cruelty. In the Papal States the Inquisition was used against liberalism, and the government would not allow either railways or telegraph systems to be developed. In Modena, Parma and Tuscany there was more political freedom, but their rulers were Austrian or under Austrian domination.

Explanatory Note. At the time of which we are speaking, the Kingdom of Sardinia comprised both the island of Sardinia and Piedmont in northern Italy. Since they had gained control of Sardinia in 1718, the rulers of Piedmont had adopted the title of 'King of Sardinia'. Piedmont was thus a part of the whole kingdom. There was, strictly speaking, no such territory as the Kingdom of Piedmont, though the term is sometimes used. To avoid confusion, the term 'Kingdom of Sardinia' is used in this chapter and Piedmont is referred to as a territory only. The capital of the Kingdom of Sardinia was Turin in Piedmont. It must also be emphasized that Piedmont was the wealthiest and most important part of the kingdom.

Attempted Revolutions

Liberal risings occurred in both **Naples (1820)** and in **Piedmont (1821)**, but through Austrian intervention (requested by their rulers) both movements were suppressed. In **1830**, at the time of the revolution against Charles X in France, armed revolts occurred in **Parma, Modena** and the **Papal States.** Aid was hoped for from Louis Philippe, but was not forthcoming. Austrian power was too great and the efforts of the Italian secret society—the **Carbonari**—failed. No co-ordinated movement had yet arisen.

Giuseppe Mazzini and the Society of Young Italy

Giuseppe Mazzini (1805–1872), a member of the Carbonari, was exiled to France in 1830 for his opposition to the Sardinian monarchy. From there he organized in 1831 a new movement, **Young Italy,** whose appeal was to all classes, including the town workers and the peasants—a wider appeal than the Carbonari had. In **1831** Mazzini's appeal to the new King of Sardinia, **Charles Albert,** to lead a movement for national unity and liberation, brought no response. Louis Philippe expelled Mazzini from France. From Switzerland in 1833 he attempted an invasion of Savoy with a band of followers in order to raise a general rebellion in Piedmont. This failed. In the same year the Swiss expelled him and he then went to live in England. His outlook was now Republican.

Other ideas for Italian unification were put forward, especially the **Federalist** idea propounded by the writer **Gioberti,** who wished to see a *federation under the Pope*. This idea was strengthened in **1846** when the new **Pope Pius IX,** despite Austrian protests voiced by Metternich, set up a municipal council for Rome, released political prisoners and introduced other liberal reforms.

The Risings of 1848

During 1848 Europe was in a revolutionary turmoil. In **January, 1848,** the people of Sicily expelled the garrison of **Ferdinand II,** who was forced to grant a liberal constitution for the Kingdom of the Two Sicilies (Naples and Sicily). In **March, 1848,** popular pressure caused Charles Albert to accept a liberal constitution in Piedmont-Sardinia, and Pius IX did the same for the Papal States. Metternich was also forced to flee from Austria, and the people of Milan expelled the 20,000 troops under **Radetsky,** who retired with his troops to the **Quadrilateral fortresses.** In Venice, a Republic was proclaimed under **Daniele Manin.**

War against Austria

After some hesitation Charles Albert declared war against Austria and marched into Lombardy. Troops arrived from Naples to assist him, but Pius IX refused all aid. Charles was defeated at **Custozza** and Radetsky reoccupied Milan. An armistice was signed, but in March, 1849, Charles Albert resumed the offensive only to be defeated at **Novara.** He abdicated in favour of his son **Victor Emmanuel II.**

In southern Italy Ferdinand II regained control and bombarded Sicily into submission. In the Papal States Mazzini and **Giuseppe Garibaldi (1807–1882)** gained control and established the **Roman Republic.** The Pope fled to **Gaeta** in the Neapolitan kingdom. He then appealed to the new French President, Louis Napoleon Bonaparte, who despatched General Oudinot with a French force to Rome. The Republicans were defeated and a French garrison installed to protect the Pope. In the north Venice was bombarded into submission.

The Italian Failure, 1848–1849

This attempt to unite Italy failed for the following reasons: (1) Early hesitation of Charles Albert gave Radetsky valuable time; (2) lack of support from the Papacy; (3) intervention of Louis Bonaparte at Rome; (4) lack of co-ordination, partly due to Charles Albert's dislike of the Republicans, who were strong in Venice, Lombardy and

Rome—and their dislike of him; (5) failure of revolution in Austria liberated Austrian forces for action in Italy; (6) Radetsky's skilful use of the Quadrilateral fortresses.

The Position after 1848

Most of the Italian rulers regained their previous powers, but Victor Emmanuel II was determined to retain the liberal constitution in the Kingdom of Sardinia and to bide his time for a future move against Austria. A more determined character than his father, he had learnt the lesson that Sardinia must take the lead in the future; she must gain foreign support and she must be economically much stronger.

The aristocratic liberal, **Count Camillo Cavour (1810–1861),** an agriculturist, a free-trader, an admirer of the British parliamentary system and the editor of **'Il Risorgimento',** was destined to play the main role in securing these three principal aims. He was elected to parliament in 1848. He strongly supported the policy of Victor Emmanuel II which was aimed at reducing the power of the Church in the Kingdom of Sardinia. In 1850 he was appointed Minister of Commerce and Agriculture, and in 1851 Minister of the Navy and Finance. In **1852** he became **Prime Minister.**

Cavour's internal policy greatly strengthened the Kingdom of Sardinia, promoting the interests of the middle class. New banks were created to aid investment in railways, shipping and agriculture. Producers' co-operative societies were encouraged and a free-trade policy was promoted, especially with industrialized Britain. Cavour greatly strengthened the army and facilitated the promotion of middle-class officers. His anti-Church policies were carried a further step forward in **1853** when he imposed taxation on Church estates and confiscated for general use the lands of a number of religious orders. This aroused Papal opposition, but the laws were passed by the parliament at Turin. Increased government revenue was the result.

Foreign Policy of Cavour

Cavour sent Sardinian troops to the Crimean War, where they played a distinguished and efficient part. At the Paris Peace Conference he voiced *the grievances of Sardinia* against Austria and sought the support of Napoleon III. The latter was inclined to support Sardinia for three main reasons. Firstly, a defeat of Austria would further strengthen the position of France in Europe. Secondly, Napoleon III himself had professed, as a former Carbonaro, an interest in national struggles for liberty, and here was an opportunity to carry this into practical effect. Thirdly, a successful campaign in northern Italy, the scene of his famous uncle's triumphs against the same enemy, would strengthen his claim to be the true inheritor of the Napoleonic legend.

But against Napoleon III in France was a great proportion of the Catholic Church, which regarded itself, France and Austria as the protectors of the Pope in Rome.

The Orsini attempt to assassinate Napoleon III in 1858, far from losing Cavour the support of the Emperor, had the opposite effect. In June, **1858,** Cavour and Napoleon III concluded the secret Compact of Plombières. Napoleon was to assist Sardinia in driving the Austrians from the whole of northern Italy and was to receive Nice and Savoy in return. The Pope was to retain the Papal States and Ferdinand II was to remain in Naples. This agreement was designed to assist Sardinia, but at the same time to appease Catholic opposition whilst also satisfying liberal demands in France that something should be done for Italy.

Cavour manœuvred the Austrians into the position of apparent aggressors (see p. 58). Napoleon III's forces moved into northern Italy, and defeated the Austrians at Magenta and Solferino. Soon afterwards he concluded the truce of Villafranca, 1859, with the Austrians. In the notes on France (p. 58) the probable reasons for this astonishing move have been considered. This dramatic change of front caused the temporary resignation of Cavour and seemed to justify the distrust of Napoleon III openly avowed by the extreme Left in Piedmont, who were represented especially by the supporters of Garibaldi and Mazzini. However, in Modena, Parma, Tuscany and the Romagna, popular revolts compelled their rulers to agree to plebiscites which gave an overwhelming verdict for union with Sardinia. Nice and Savoy, however, were handed over to France, much to the disgust of the Garibaldians.

Giuseppe Garibaldi

Garibaldi was a native of Nice and an early supporter of Mazzini's Young Italy movement. He took part in Mazzini's abortive invasion of Savoy in 1833 (see p. 70). He then fled to South America where he developed the famous *guerrilla* tactics in support of Uruguay against Brazil and Argentina. In 1848 he set up the Roman Republic with Mazzini, but after its defeat through French intervention, he fled once again to America, returning later to cultivate his farm at Caprera. In 1859, he fought very successfully in the Alps against the Austrians. The Villafranca episode and the loss of Nice and Savoy strengthened his conviction that the Italians must fight their own battles. He detested both Cavour and Napoleon III. In **1860** a popular rebellion broke out in Sicily against Francis II, known as 'King Bomba'. Garibaldi gathered his famous **1,000 redshirts** (of mixed nationalities) at Genoa, sailed to Sicily and landed at Marsala under cover of British warships. He captured Palermo. Palmerston refused to accept Napoleon III's suggestion that Garibaldi should be prevented from crossing to the mainland. Garibaldi crossed the Straits of Messina and moved against Naples, which he captured with the aid of a popular rising.

The position of Cavour and Victor Emmanuel II was now difficult. While openly disavowing Garibaldi in order not to come in direct conflict with the Austrians and the French, they did not prevent his sailing from Genoa. Cavour now moved Piedmontese troops illegally into the Papal States in order to forestall Garibaldi's threatened attack on Rome. The Papal States declared by plebiscite for union with the Kingdom of Sardinia. Thus the anti-Papal and republican aims of Garibaldi and Mazzini (who had joined Garibaldi in Naples) were frustrated, but at the same time Cavour had gained control of the Papal States. Victor Emmanuel II entered Naples towards the end of 1860, where he was welcomed by Garibaldi. The latter was persuaded, much against his real inclination, to disband his volunteers. He once again retired to Caprera.

Cavour's policy had succeeded in: (*a*) gaining the union of the Papal States and Lombardy with Sardinia: (*b*) safeguarding the position of the Pope in Rome itself: (*c*) preventing the spread of support for the Republican supporters of Garibaldi and Mazzini: (*d*)

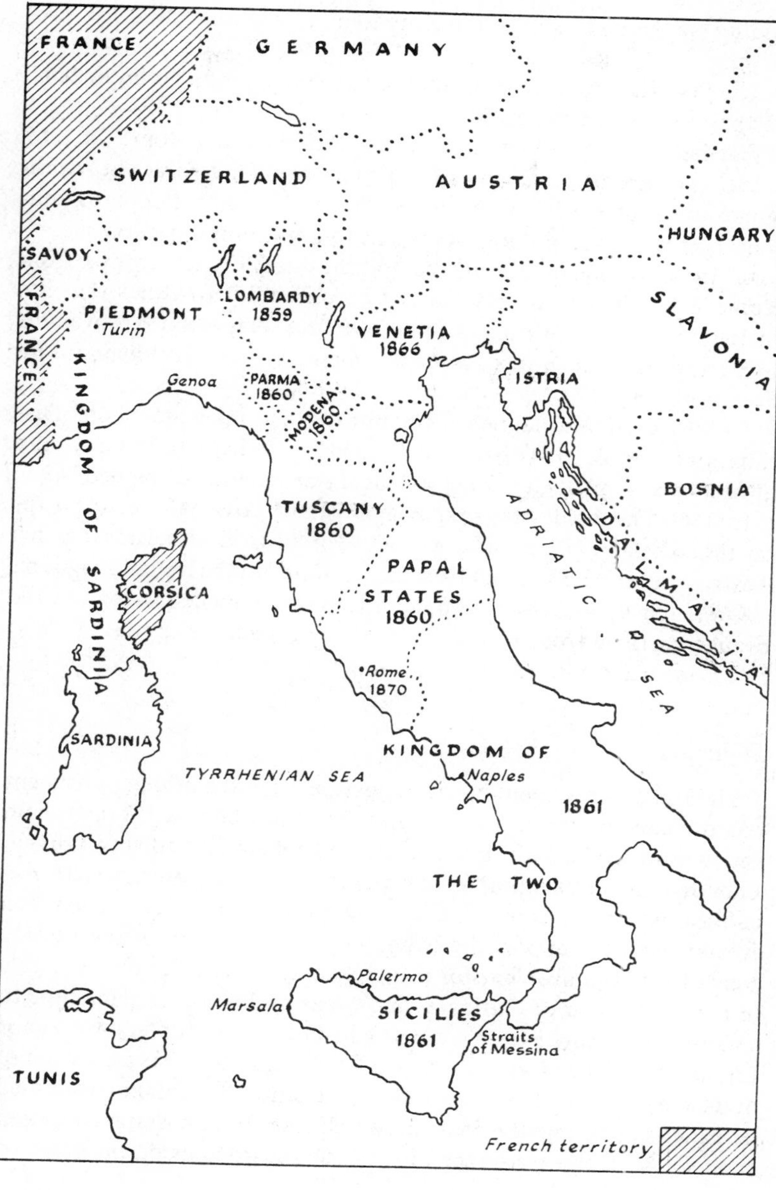
FRANCE
GERMANY
SWITZERLAND
AUSTRIA
HUNGARY
SAVOY
FRANCE
LOMBARDY 1859
PIEDMONT
Turin
VENETIA 1866
SLAVONIA
KINGDOM OF SARDINIA
Genoa
PARMA 1860
MODENA 1860
ISTRIA
BOSNIA
TUSCANY 1860
ADRIATIC SEA
DALMATIA
PAPAL STATES 1860
CORSICA
Rome 1870
SARDINIA
KINGDOM OF
TYRRHENIAN SEA
Naples
1861
THE TWO
Palermo
Marsala
SICILIES 1861
Straits of Messina
TUNIS
French territory

adding Naples and Sicily to the Kingdom of Italy which was now proclaimed.

The first Italian parliament met in the **first capital, Turin, in 1861.** In that year also Cavour died.

Garibaldi continued to wage war for the seizure of Rome. In 1862 his second expedition *from Sicily* was met by Italian forces at **Aspromonte** south of Rome, where he was taken prisoner. Popular agitation, however, forced the government to grant him a pardon.

In **1864,** Napoleon III agreed to withdraw French troops from Rome when the Italian government promised not to attack the city. In 1865 the capital of Italy became Florence. Napoleon removed his French forces, but in fact *the Pope's forces were still commanded by French officers.*

In 1867 Garibaldi launched his third attack on Rome from Tuscany, but Napoleon III had sent French forces back to the city, and at **Mentana,** Garibaldi's force was again defeated, and he fled.

In 1866 Garibaldi had fought against the Austrians in the Alps on the occasion of the alliance between Prussia and Italy against Austria. Venetia was at that time incorporated in the Italian kingdom.

On August 19th, 1870, Napoleon III was compelled to remove the French garrison from Rome, which then became the capital of Italy. The Pope was confined to the Vatican.

Summary

The Italian movement had diverse aspects, and a united movement was difficult to attain. Mazzini and Garibaldi opposed foreign help and denounced both the alliance with Napoleon III and with Prussia. They had strong support in the poverty-stricken south, where Republicanism was strong, while in the north the middle class had every reason to support the Monarchy. The position of the Papacy created extreme problems of principle and tactics. Cavour was able to use the fervour of Garibaldi and Mazzini, but at the same time to counter their more extreme aims. This policy was pursued by Victor Emmanuel II after Cavour's death. The Italian state was a creation of numerous differing lines of thought and action. Mazzini himself died in exile, lamenting the way in which the Italian state had been created—with the assistance of those he regarded as despots.

Dates

1815	**Vienna settlement of Italy.**
1820	**Rising in Naples.**
1821	**Rising in Piedmont.**
1830	**Risings in Parma, Modena, and the Papal States.**
1831	**Young Italy society founded by Mazzini.**
1833	**Mazzini's attempted rising in Piedmont.**
1846	**Accession of Pope Pius IX.**
1848	**Charles Albert defeated at Custozza.**
1849	**Charles Albert defeated at Novara.**
	Roman Republic defeated.
	Victor Emmanuel II succeeds Charles Albert.
1852	**Cavour Prime Minister.**
1854–56	**Sardinia participates in Crimean War.**
1858	**Orsini attempts assassination of Napoleon III.**
	Compact of Plombières.
1859	**Napoleon III enters war against Austria. Magenta, Solferino.**
	Truce of Villafranca.
1860	**Garibaldi and the Redshirts.**
1861	**First Italian Parliament at Turin.**
	Cavour gains control of Papal States.
1862	**Garibaldi attempts to liberate Rome but is defeated at Aspromonte.**
1865	**Florence the capital of Italian Kingdom.**
1866	**Italy supports Prussia against Austria. Venetia gained.**
1867	**Garibaldi's third expedition. Battle of Mentana.**
1870	**Rome becomes the capital of Italy.**

QUESTIONS

1. Why did the Italian revolutionary movements fail between 1815 and 1830?

2. Explain the importance of Mazzini in the struggle for Italian unification.

3. Explain the importance of Garibaldi in the Italian struggle.

4. What were the main causes of Italian failure in the movement of 1848–1849?

5. How did Cavour overcome the problems he faced in the struggle for Italian unification and independence?

CHAPTER NINE

GERMANY, 1815–1870

Germany after the Congress of Vienna

THE Vienna settlement created *thirty-nine German states.* An Assembly or Diet was set up for the German confederation into which these states were grouped. It met at Frankfort and consisted of seventeen members. The larger states had a majority and Metternich secured the permanent presidency of the Diet for Austria.

Two elements especially were discontented with the settlement: (*a*) the **Nationalists** who wanted a completely united Germany and (*b*) the **Liberals** who wanted elected parliaments and responsible government in each state and also a parliament for a united Germany. In four states only was there anything approaching a liberal constitution—in Baden, Bavaria, Wurtemburg and Saxe-Weimar. The majority of the population was not interested in liberalism in 1815. Its main support came from the ranks of the professions, and the universities, where the **Gymnastic Clubs** and **Burschenschaften (Students' Unions)** often had liberal sympathies. At the **Wartburg Festival of 1817,** Prussian jackboots and also an effigy of Metternich were burnt. Metternich was able to exploit these incidents and the murder of Kotzebue in 1819 to persuade the princes of Germany to accept the **Carlsbad Decrees.** The Decrees imposed strict supervision of the universities by a permanent investigating committee set up at Mainz.

The revolution of 1830 in France against Charles X had repercussions in Germany, where liberal demonstrations occurred very widely. These were not co-ordinated movements, and Metternich secured a complete ban on all political meetings. Repression in all its forms became more severe.

The Zollverein

By 1834, Prussia had established a Customs Union with almost all the German states except Austria. This meant that the German states could trade more freely within the boundaries of the Union or **Zollverein.** It also encouraged the idea of German unification and many German states began to look to Prussia for leadership rather than Austria.

Frederick William IV of Prussia, however, disappointed the liberal hopes of the growing middle class whose prosperity developed as the Zollverein was extended. Unrest developed in Prussia in the early years of his reign.

The revolution of 1848 in France against Louis Philippe had a deep effect on Germany. At this point most of the rulers of the German states were forced to grant liberal constitutions involving *elected parliaments, freedom of the press and of speech, and trial by jury*.

Unrest in Prussia developed quickly in 1848 and the liberal and national discontent previously suppressed now came to the surface. In Berlin itself there was a rapidly growing working class which had many grievances, which had been earlier inflamed by the military suppression of a Silesian weavers' revolt. Demonstrations in Berlin between March 12th and 17th forced the King to proclaim freedom of the press and of speech and to order the meeting of the Prussian Diet to establish a new constitution. He himself withdrew from the turbulence of Berlin to the royal palace at Potsdam.

The Liberal Movement in Prussia, 1848

A Constituent Assembly met in Berlin in May, 1848. The King, however, refused to accept demands for a government responsible to an elected parliament. In the Assembly his most violent supporters were a group of *junkers* of whom Bismarck was a member. The King played for time, especially when a rift appeared between the extreme Left, which wanted a Republic, and the more cautious, liberal middle-class elements, who would be satisfied with a limited monarchy.

The King and his advisers at Potsdam were able to take advantage of these differences. He was also aided by the fact that: (*a*) his army, officered by the aristocracy, was still loyal; (*b*) the revolutions in

Austria and Italy were collapsing; (*c*) the Berlin Assembly, afraid of Republicanism and Communism, had failed to produce a fighting force, demanded by the Left, which could have challenged the royal forces. On November 9th, 1848, the Prussian forces re-entered Berlin and the Assembly was dissolved a month later.

The *Prussian Constitution of 1850* was the creation of the monarchy and not the people. A *Lower House* was to be elected, and a *House of Lords* was to be partly hereditary and partly nominated by the King, who could introduce laws and appoint his government without reference to parliament. The government was responsible to him alone. Voters were divided into three classes and the wealthier had a greater proportion of votes. Open voting replaced the secret ballot.

The King, with the aid of the 'junkers', the army and the Prussian state officials, had won the day.

The Frankfort Parliament, 1848–1849

Meanwhile, the Nationalists had attempted to unify Germany. In 1847, the representatives of the Zollverein states met to discuss the union of Germany, and in 1848 a *Vorparlament* (Preliminary Parliament), of 600 delegates, arranged popular elections to a German parliament which met at **Frankfort-on-Main** on May 18th, **1848**. It consisted of 831 members, the majority of whom were 'intellectuals' with little previous political experience. After long discussions on human rights and the form a united Germany was to take, the following events occurred:

1. The position of Regent of a united Germany was offered to the **Archduke John of Austria,** who was acceptable to the princes.
2. The German parts of Schleswig-Holstein demanded union with Germany. Frederick William IV supported them, but his army was beaten by the Danes and the Great Powers forced him to make peace.
3. The parliament next proposed that a united Germany should contain the *German part of Austria*, but the Austrians refused this proposal. The parliament then decided to exclude Austria altogether, and the Austrian delegates withdrew.
4. The throne of a united Germany was now offered to Frederick William IV whose hatred of popular control led to his refusal; he

would not 'pick a crown out of the gutter'. The Prussian delegates then withdrew.

Soon afterwards the Prussian army was used to suppress the Frankfort parliament, having already suppressed the revolution at home.

The Prussian League

Frederick William IV now attempted to create a Prussian League consisting of Hanover, Saxony, Hesse and some other small states. The parliament of the League met at **Erfurt** in **1850,** but under Austrian pressure some states soon seceded. When a popular revolution in Hesse sought Frederick William's support, the Austrians mobilized against him and he abandoned the idea of the Prussian League by the **Treaty of Olmütz** with Austria, **1850.** Austria then restored the 1815 Confederation, and both Nationalism and Liberalism were defeated.

Summary

1. The Frankfort parliament had failed partly through dissensions in its ranks—some were Nationalists supporting Prussia, others were Liberal Nationalists opposed to Prussian leadership; some were divided between Prussia and Austria, and the extreme Left demanded an armed Republic.

2. The parliament did not create an armed force independent of both Austria and Prussia.

3. The Schleswig-Holstein failure weakened the national position of the parliament.

4. The general turn of the tide against the European liberal and national revolutions isolated the Frankfort parliament. It could only have succeeded in better general conditions.

5. The parliament was narrowly based in its class composition.

6. The failures of the parliament led to popular demonstrations against it, which were partly stimulated by the new **Communist League** of **Karl Marx (1818–1883)** and his supporters. The proletarian elements were in opposition to the middle-class elements of the parliament from the start.

German Unification under Prussia, 1850–1870

This was essentially the achievement of the 'Junker' Prince Otto von Bismarck and his aristocratic supporters who detested liberalism and democracy. After his pro-monarchist part in the Prussian parliament (see p. 80) he was regarded with favour by Frederick William IV. In 1851 he became Prussian representative in the revived German Confederation. He was ambassador to Russia, 1859–1862, and to France, 1862.

In 1861 the strongly anti-liberal **William I** became King of Prussia. He was also determined to strengthen Prussia against Austria who had imposed the humiliation of Olmütz on Prussia. He appointed **von Roon** Minister of War, and **von Moltke** Chief of the General Staff. When they demanded increased taxation to expand the army by 250,000 men, the liberals in the Prussian parliament, who wished to control the royal finances, opposed the proposals. William, who hesitated, was persuaded by von Roon to recall Bismarck from France and make him Minister-President. His ruthlessness could be counted upon. Bismarck, who despised the liberal opposition he had seen in Berlin and Frankfort, knew he could rely on the Prussian army. He at once imposed a newspaper censorship and purged the civil service of liberals. The taxes were then collected with little resistance.

Foreign Policy: War against Denmark

In 1863 the Danish government attempted to incorporate Schleswig completely into Denmark. This aroused the opposition of the Germans in Schleswig and the German majority in Holstein. Bismarck saw this dispute as the opportunity to gain the support of the German Nationalists and at the same time to use the dispute ultimately as a means of humiliating Austria and gaining the leadership of the German states for Prussia. He, therefore, ensured that Austria would have no allies by (*a*) supporting Russia against the Poles in 1863 and sending back Polish refugees from the Prussian borders; (*b*) vaguely promising (only verbally through the Prussian ambassador in Paris) concessions to Napoleon III along the Rhine.

Bismarck now co-operated with Austria against Denmark, who refused to accept a European conference to settle the question of the duchies. The combined attack on Denmark led to her defeat and the **Convention of Gastein, 1865,** by which Prussia was to administer Schleswig and Austria, Holstein. Throughout this period Bismarck had successfully 'called Palmerston's bluff' and accurately estimated that, despite sympathy with Denmark, Britain would not intervene alone.

Defeat of Austria: The Seven Weeks' War, 1866

Bismarck now exploited the Schleswig-Holstein situation to drive Austria from the German Confederation. In October, 1865, he held the *Biarritz meeting with Napoleon III.* There was no written agreement, but it appears that, in return for his neutrality in any Austro-Prussian struggle, Napoleon III was led to believe that concessions would be made to France in the Rhineland.

Bismarck now secured the alliance of the new Kingdom of Italy by promising to give Venetia to Italy.

In Schleswig-Holstein Austria continued to support the claims of the **Duke of Augustenburg** to rule the duchies. Bismarck opposed this and also accused Austria of stirring up anti-Prussian sentiment in Schleswig. To attempt to gain Liberal support Bismarck also, at this time, proposed the formation of a National German parliament based on universal suffrage. In June, 1866, Prussian forces took control of Holstein. In the German Diet Austria gained the support of most of the German states, but the already mobilized Prussian army moved rapidly against the North German states and having defeated them went on to defeat the Austrian main armies at the battle of **Sadowa, 1866.**

The reasons for Bismarck's success were principally: (1) his preliminary diplomacy which isolated Austria; (2) the Italian alliance, which was important, for although the Italians suffered defeats in their own fight for independence, 150,000 Austrian troops were needed in Italy to keep order; (3) efficient preparations by Prussia for war and superior armaments (the breech-loading rifle was particularly effective); (4) the Austrians used the old muzzle-loading rifles; (5) there was unrest in the Austrian Empire, especially in Hungary; (6) the Prussian armies were purely German, but the Austrian armies consisted of nationalities of doubtful loyalty; (7) Austrian finances were in a bad state, but Prussian financial preparation for the war had been thorough.

By the **Treaty of Prague, 1866,** Bismarck secured Schleswig-Holstein for Prussia. The North German states which had supported Austria (e.g. Hanover) were taken over. Prussia thus gained about 4,000,000 new inhabitants. Venetia was handed to Italy as promised. Bismarck refused to annex Austrian territory or impose other vindictive conditions. He was anxious not to make Austria a permanent enemy.

General Results of the War

Bismarck now formed the **North German Confederation** of states north of the Main. Most of the defeated states (e.g. Saxony) were forced to enter. The President was the King of Prussia and the Chancellor was Bismarck. *The member armies and foreign policy were controlled by Prussia*, but most other powers were left to the states. Bismarck showed great astuteness. This was not outright annexation by Prussia, and in the Federal Council, or **Bundesrat,** Prussia could actually be out-voted.

Both by the moderate Treaty of Prague and the way in which the North German Confederation was formed, Bismarck showed wise statesmanship in pursuance of his aim of securing the Prussian domination of all Germans, except those in the Austrian Empire. In the inevitable contest with Napoleon III he needed all the support he could muster.

Prussia and France, 1866–1870

In 1866 Bismarck received renewed demands from Napoleon III for concessions on the Rhine, especially at the expense of Bavaria. These demands he published and was able to sway the South German states towards him. They accepted an arrangement by which, in case of war, their armies would be controlled by Prussia. He also brought about a customs agreement between the North German Confederation and the South German states.

In 1867, Napoleon III renewed demands for Luxembourg and

Belgium. Bismarck's reply was to secure a European Conference which guaranteed the neutrality of Luxembourg.

France's position was weakening, especially after the quick result of the Austro-Prussian War, which had been against all Napoleon's hopes, and after the Mexican fiasco. Napoleon's attempts to gain allies were now frustrated by Bismarck's diplomacy. Bismarck promised to support Russia's repudiation of the Black Sea clauses of the Peace of Paris, 1856; Italy was grateful for Venetia and resentful of the French garrison in Rome; Austria had been leniently treated and was now involved in internal reforms leading to the 'Ausgleich' (see p. 67). Prussian preparations by von Roon and von Moltke were being pushed ahead rapidly.

The Spanish Succession, 1869

In 1869 a complication convenient to Bismarck occurred over the vacant Spanish throne. On the withdrawal, under French pressure, of the candidature of **Prince Leopold** of **Hohenzollern-Sigmaringen,** Napoleon III demanded that the German candidature should never be renewed. William I refused this and sent from **Ems** the famous telegram to Bismarck stating the facts. Bismarck so altered the wording for publication that it appeared that William had insulted the French ambassador by refusing to see him. War hysteria in France was the result (as Bismarck had estimated) and France declared war on July 14th, 1870. The disastrous results we have already seen in the section on France (p. 60).

The **German Empire** was proclaimed by Bismarck at Versailles in **1871.**

Summary

By suppression of internal liberalism, by active military preparation, by a clever and moderate diplomacy, Bismarck had gained German support, isolated France and, with ruthless determination, created a German Empire on Prussia's terms. He had not planned every step in advance, but, with German unification and German domination of Europe as his long-term aims, he seized every opportunity that presented itself.

Dates

1815	**German Confederation established.**
1817	**The Wartburg Festival.**
1819	**Murder of Kotzebue.**
	Carlsbad Decrees.
1830	**Revolts in German states.**
	Revolution against Charles X, France.
1847	**Meeting of representatives of Zollverein states.**
1848	**German 'Vorparlament'.**
	Constituent Assembly, Berlin.
	Meeting of Frankfort Parliament. May 18th.
	Prussian troops reoccupy Berlin. November.
1849	**Frankfort parliament suppressed by Prussian troops.**
1850	**Prussian Constitution.**
	Treaty of Olmütz.
	The German Confederation of 1815 re-established.
1861	**William I, King of Prussia.**
	Bismarck's defeat of Prussian liberals.
1863	**Polish revolt. Prussia aids suppression.**
1864	**Prussian defeat of Denmark.**
1865	**Convention of Gastein.**
1866	**The Seven Weeks' War.**
	Treaty of Prague.
	North German Confederation formed.
1869	**Spanish Succession question.**
1870–71	**Franco-Prussian War.**
1871	**German Empire proclaimed at Versailles.**

QUESTIONS

1. Why was Metternich able to suppress revolutionary movements before 1848?

2. Why did the revolution of 1848 in Prussia fail?

3. What problems faced the Frankfort parliament, and how did it attempt to deal with them?

4. For what reasons did the Frankfort parliament fail?

5. *Show how Bismarck's diplomacy led to German unification.*

6. *Write notes on three of the following:* (a) *the Treaty of Olmütz;* (b) *the Prussian Constitution, 1850;* (c) *the Convention of Gastein;* (d) *the Ems telegram.*

CHAPTER TEN

THE GERMAN EMPIRE UNDER BISMARCK, 1870–1890

The Imperial Constitution, 1871

1. The **Bundesrat** consisted of 58 members nominated by the rulers of the states. This was the main law-making body. But a vote of 14 against any measure could secure its rejection, and there were 17 Prussian votes.
2. The **Reichstag** was elected by manhood suffrage, with about 400 members, half of whom were Prussian. Ministers were not responsible to it, but to the Emperor alone. It could only debate laws put before it by the Bundesrat, and it could be dissolved by the Emperor at will. Its consent to internal taxation was needed.
3. The armed forces were controlled by the Emperor, who also appointed all principal officials and the Chancellor.
4. The individual states were left many powers, but the army, navy, foreign affairs, taxation, trade and railways were controlled by the Imperial goverment.

It was not a truly democratic constitution, for real popular control did not exist. In many ways it was an extension of the Prussian constitution of 1850.

Bismarck's Internal Problems

Bismarck had some formidable opponents in the Reichstag, and the task that faced him was to manage the party system so that he could counter any challenge to his ideas on the future of Germany. The Roman Catholic Church and the Socialists gave him immediate problems.

In 1870 the proclamation of the dogma of *Papal Infallibility* caused a crisis in the Catholic Church in Germany. The dissenting minority of Catholics were excommunicated by the bishops, and similar action against dissenting Catholic university professors and teachers was also threatened. Bismarck regarded these actions of the Church as an interference with the internal affairs of the state, especially where education was concerned. He attacked the pro-Papal **Centre Party,** and in **1872** the **May Laws** were introduced to undermine Papal authority. The Jesuit Society was expelled from Germany, priests could no longer inspect schools, and Catholic colleges were compelled to accept state examinations. Many resisting priests and bishops were imprisoned. This struggle was known as the *Kulturkampf* or 'struggle for civilization' and was waged around the question of whether the Church should be independent, or subordinate to the state as Bismarck wanted. Bismarck also threw down another challenge to the Church by making civil marriage legal.

Despite the campaign of Bismarck and his supporters, the Centre Party increased its representation in the Reichstag at the next elections. In 1878 Pius IX died and was succeeded by Leo XIII who was more inclined to compromise. The May Laws were largely rescinded, except that the Jesuits were still outlawed and the Church lost its right to inspect schools. On the other hand, various religious orders were allowed to function, and the Church regained the right to control the education of its own priesthood.

Bismarck's willingness to compromise with the Church arose in part from the growing strength of Socialism in Germany. Its main organization was the **Social Democratic Party** founded in **1869** by a disciple of **Karl Marx,** the founder of modern Communism. In 1847 Marx had established in Germany the **Communist League** during the upheavals leading to the Frankfort parliament of 1848 (see p. 81). With his collaborator **Friedrich Engels (1820–1895**) he produced the **Communist Manifesto** in **1848**. In this they propounded the basic theory that history is the history of class struggles in which new and rising classes throw off the shackles of the old. The final revolution was to be that of the workers or proletariat against the capitalist system. Marx's economics were developed in detail in his famous analysis of Capitalism, **'Das Kapital'**, the first volume of which was published in 1867.

To Bismarck Socialism was another challenge to the German state, although the Social Democratic Party did not strictly follow Marx's idea of the violent overthrow of Capitalism, but was prepared to work through the parliamentary system. In 1877 the Social Democrats returned 12 members to the Reichstag and Bismarck determined to challenge the movement before it grew stronger. His campaign against Socialism was as violent as the earlier campaign against the Church. He unscrupulously blamed the socialist movement for an attempted assassination of the Emperor in 1878. In that year Bismarck's allies in the Bundesrat secured the passing of the *Exceptional Law* which outlawed the Social Democratic Party. Many of its supporters were imprisoned or exiled and its newspapers suppressed. But Socialism itself could no more be suppressed than the Catholic supporters of the Pope, and in **1890** the Socialists polled a million and a half votes. After Bismarck's fall a number of the old restrictions were removed and by 1914 the socialist vote was over 4,000,000.

Bismarck had hoped to counteract Socialism by introducing an *unemployment and sickness insurance system*, but this was not satisfactory to a movement which demanded the fundamental transformation of the State from a capitalist to a socialist system.

Economic Policies and Industrial Development

Under Bismarck Germany made remarkable industrial progress. Although he failed to get the support of all the states for a nationalised railway system, in Prussia the railways became state-owned; fares and freight were reduced—to the great benefit of trade. He also gave direct government support to shipping lines, which enabled them to compete with Britain and made easier the founding of colonies. The tonnage of German steamships rose from 100,000 tons in 1871 to 2,000,000 tons in 1905. The value of German overseas trade trebled between 1891 and 1906, and between 1871 and 1906 coal consumption rose by five times. Germany became a great industrial state whose population had increased from 41,000,000 in 1871 to 65,000,000 by the outbreak of the Great War. This made her a formidable competitor against the United States, Britain, and France.

Bismarck and Tariffs

In 1879 Bismarck turned from free trade to a new tariff system to protect and expand German industry. Protection against agricultural imports also aided German agriculture. The income from this taxation of imports went directly to the government, and enabled Bismarck to gain *independence of the Reichstag*, whose consent to internal taxation was necessary under the constitution. This new source of revenue enabled Bismarck to counteract the influence of the free-trade **National Liberal Party** whom he had supported for some years.

Protection was linked to a new attitude towards colonies. Bismarck had been anti-colonial up to 1879, but the protected industries also wanted new sources of raw materials and outlets for their exports. Bismarck had to take into account the value of colonies as a means of easing the growing pressure of population in Germany. He hoped, by emigration, to reduce labour agitation and the influence of Socialism.

German Foreign Policy under Bismarck

Bismarck's aim was to keep control of European diplomacy, continue the *isolation of France*, and maintain peace by a policy of German strength and domination. For these purposes it was necessary above all to maintain good relations with both Austria and Russia.

Much to his surprise and alarm France had paid her indemnity by 1873 and German troops were withdrawn from France, who now had a reserve army of 2,000,000 men. Only the intervention of Queen Victoria and the **Czar Alexander II** prevented Bismarck from taking military action once again against France.

The DreiKaiserbund

In **1872** Bismarck arranged a treaty of friendship between Germany, Austria and Russia—the **DreiKaiserbund** or **League of the Three Emperors.** They agreed on their unity against socialist revolution and arranged to consult one another on all important international questions.

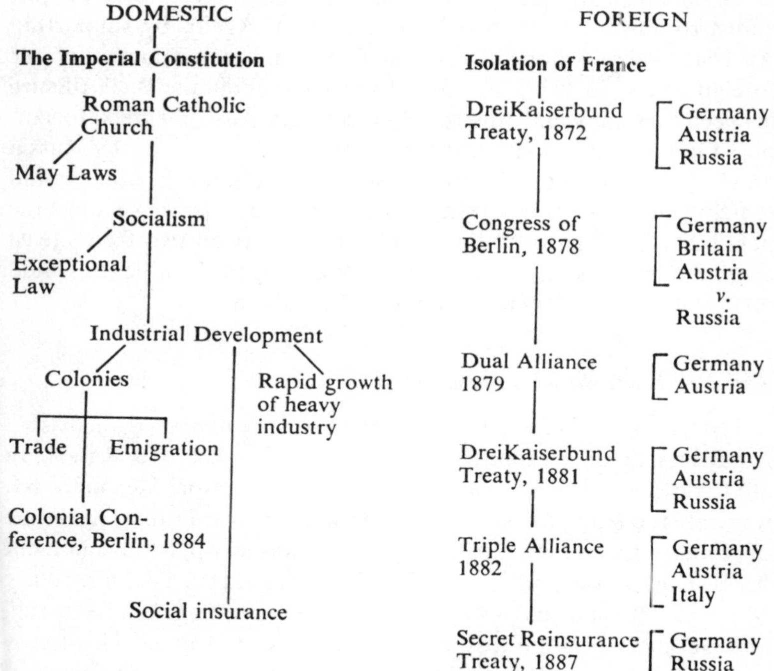

The Congress of Berlin, 1878

In consequence of revolts in Serbia and Montenegro in 1875 and in Bulgaria in 1876, the Turkish Empire was once again in turmoil. This led to Russian intervention against Turkey, to the latter's defeat and the creation of the 'Big Bulgaria' by the **Treaty of San Stefano, 1878** (see notes on Eastern Question). Britain disliked this Russian advance, and **Disraeli** succeeded in securing the meeting of the Great Powers at the **Congress of Berlin, 1878.**

At the Congress, presided over by Bismarck, the latter came out in support of Britain and Austria as against Russia. His reasons were perfectly logical in the situation then existing—if he supported Russia, Britain might well seek support from France. Both Austria and Britain had a common interest in keeping Russian influence from expanding in the Balkan peninsular and the Middle East, and Bismarck could not afford to alienate both Austria and Britain. Again, by supporting Austria, Bismarck hoped to be able to continue some control of her foreign policy. In **1879,** therefore, he brought about the **Dual Alliance** between Germany and Austria. By this treaty Austria agreed to support Germany if a combined attack was made upon her by Russia and France, but if either was at war with France alone the other would remain neutral. By this agreement Bismarck was guarding against the possibility of Germany being involved in a war on two fronts (east and west) by herself. At the same time he hoped the alliance would further promote German interests in the Balkans.

The DreiKaiserbund Treaty, 1881

The treaty of 1872 was now worthless and the danger again existed for Bismarck of a rapprochement between France and Russia. In 1881 Alexander II was assassinated and his successor, **Alexander III,** was only too ready to listen to Bismarck's views on France, the home of revolution and the hated democracy. It was an opportune moment for Bismarck to convert the old DreiKaiserbund into a definite treaty by which Russia would not support France in a war against Germany, and Germany would not support France against Russia. This treaty was renewed in **1884**. Bismarck also conceded the right to Russia of establishing the Big Bulgaria when she chose, and Russia agreed that Austria should take complete control of Bosnia and Herzegovina.

The Triple Alliance, 1882

In **1882** Bismarck brought Italy into the alliance with Germany and Austria by encouraging French seizure of Tunisia, to the great annoyance of Italy (as well as Britain). This created the **Triple Alliance** of Germany, Austria and Italy. They agreed to support one another if any one of them were attacked by two powers (i.e. France and Russia). Germany and Austria would support Italy against France, and Italy would assist Germany against France. By this treaty *the isolation of France was deepened.* Italy made the reservation, however, that the alliance should never be directed against Britain.

The Secret Reinsurance Treaty, 1887

In 1885 the **Big Bulgaria** was created by a revolt against the Turks in Eastern Rumelia which led to the union of that territory with Bulgaria. But the Bulgarians expelled their Russian advisers, much to the delight of Britain, Austria and Germany. Russia refused to recognize the new **Prince of Bulgaria, Ferdinand of Saxe-Coburg,** and also refused to renew the DreiKaiserbund Treaty. At the same time **General Boulanger** in France was demanding an alliance between Russia and France, and there were similar demands in Russia.

For Bismarck the situation was again dangerous. He dealt with it by means of the **Secret Reinsurance Treaty of 1887**, in which he promised German neutrality in the circumstances of a war between Austria and Russia. On the other hand, Russia would remain neutral if Germany were attacked by France. The secrecy of the treaty was dictated by the fact that Germany was prepared to desert Austria in certain circumstances.

Summary

Bismarck had effectively maintained the isolation of France and had kept on reasonably friendly relations with Russia, but the secrecy of the Reinsurance Treaty of 1887 showed how difficult it was to preserve the system, especially when the interests of Russia and Austria clashed in the Balkans.

As we shall see in the notes on the origins of the **Great War** of **1914–1918,** the dismissal of Bismarck by the **Kaiser William II** in **1890** was the beginning of the end of the stability which Bismarck had achieved in international affairs.

In his domestic policy he had produced a constitution which satisfied the different states, but which was fundamentally undemocratic. His battle with Roman Catholicism and Socialism was only partially successful, but his policy of partial compromise was extremely astute. His later modification of colonial and trading policy brought Germany into the world imperialist struggle for power based on military and economic strength, but he was not prepared to move with the speed required by the Kaiser William II and his supporters.

Dates

Domestic History

1869 **Social Democratic Party founded.**
1870 **Dogma of Papal Infallibility.**
1871 **The Empire and Constitution proclaimed.**
1872 **The May Laws.**
1877 **Twelve Social Democrats elected to Reichstag.**
1878 **Death of Pope Pius IX.**
'Exceptional Law' passed.
1879 **German tariff system introduced.**
Colonial policy adopted.
1881–89 **Introduction of German National Insurance system.**
1884 **Berlin Colonial Conference.**
1889 **Most of the May Laws rescinded by this date.**

Foreign Policy

1872 **The DreiKaiserbund.**
1873 **German troops withdrawn from France.**
1878 **Congress of Berlin.**
1879 **Dual Alliance of Germany and Austria.**
1881 **The DreiKaiserbund Treaty.**
1882 **Triple Alliance of Germany, Austria and Italy.**
1887 **Secret Reinsurance Treaty.**
1888 **Accession of William II.**
1890 **Dismissal of Bismarck.**

QUESTIONS

1. Describe the structure of the German Imperial Constitution.

2. How did the conflict between Bismarck and the Roman Catholic Church arise?

3. Why was Bismarck opposed to Socialism and how did he attempt to combat it?

4. Why did Bismarck change his policies on tariffs and colonies?

5. Show how German industry and trade developed in the period 1870–1914.

6. What were the aims of Bismarck's foreign policy and what difficulties had he to face?

CHAPTER ELEVEN

THE EASTERN QUESTION, 1815–1878

Introduction

FROM the time of the Turkish conquest of **Constantinople** in **1453,** the Turks had attempted to expand towards Europe. They had managed to gain control of the Balkan peninsula but their last serious threat to Europe was in 1683 when they were repulsed after the **Siege of Vienna.** During the eighteenth century their power declined and movements of revolt took place among their subject peoples. The *Eastern Question* in the nineteenth century is normally considered to mean the problems created by this decline of Turkey in the Balkan peninsula and the Middle East.

In **1804** a Serbian revolt was led by **Kara George,** but Serbia was reconquered by the Turks in **1813.** A further revolt in **1815** under **Milosch Obrenovitch** gained him the title of **Prince of the Serbians,** but the Turkish overlordship continued. The Czar Alexander I encouraged these revolts, and by the **Treaty of Bucharest** in **1812,** Russia obtained Bessarabia and brought her boundaries down to the River Pruth. The old policy of Russian expansion at the expense of Turkey was thus continuing, and Russia regarded herself as the protector of the **Orthodox Christians** and of the Slav race.

The Greek War of Independence, 1821–1827

The Greeks enjoyed privileges under the Turks, especially freedom from compulsory military service and religious freedom under their own Patriarch. But nevertheless they were a subject people very much at the mercy of the Turkish governors who ruled almost independently of the Sultan. Rule was corrupt and taxation heavy. The Greeks were always conscious of being ruled by aliens, and in the early nineteenth century the development of a new literary language helped to break down the barriers between different Greek dialects, thus enhancing the idea of national unity and feeling. This led to a revival of interest in the glories of ancient Greece, encouraged by their own national poets and others (e.g. **Lord Byron**). The **Society of Friends (Hetairia Philiké)**, set up secretly in **1814**, encouraged the growth of these interests in preparation for action against Turkey.

In 1821 conditions appeared favourable for a revolt. **Ali Pasha, Sultan of Janina,** was gaining control of **Albania,** and in Egypt **Mehemet Ali** was virtually independent of the Sultan. The Czar Alexander was employing Greek advisers, notably **Capodistria** and **Prince Hypsilanti.** The latter in 1821 attempted a rising of the Moldavians against the Turks, but his soldiers disgraced themselves by massacring the Moslems, and Alexander disowned him. The real beginning of the war against Turkey was the **revolt in the Morea** in southern Greece, in **1821.** The Greeks massacred Moslems and in retaliation the Turks massacred Greeks in Thessaly, Macedonia and the Aegean Islands. The **Greek Patriarch** was hanged in Constantinople on **Easter Day, 1822,** as a retaliation by the Turks.

The Great Powers

The Great Powers could not stand aside. Their interests were involved, and there was also wide public support in Europe for the Greeks. Volunteers from numerous countries went to their aid, and Byron himself died in **1824** at the **Siege of Missolonghi.** The decisive change which brought intervention from the Great Powers was the calling in by the Sultan of **Mehemet Ali (1769–1849)**. The latter's son, **Ibrahim,** invaded the Morea in **1825** and began to treat the Greeks with brutal ferocity. The new Czar, Nicholas I, now prepared to intervene. To prevent unilateral Russian action, the British Foreign Secretary, George Canning, achieved the **Treaty of London, 1827,** between England, Russia and France by which Greece was to be independent except for an annual payment of tribute to the Turks. The Sultan refused these terms, and a joint British, Russian and French naval force blockaded the Greek coast to prevent Ibrahim receiving supplies and reinforcements. This led to the destruction of the Turkish Fleet at the **Battle of Navarino, October, 1827.** Ibrahim was forced out of the Morea. The Russians, however, continued their pressure against Turkey and invaded Moldavia and Wallachia. They forced the Turks to sign the **Treaty of Adrianople, 1829,** by which Turkey recognized Greek independence, although tribute was still to be paid. Moldavia and Wallachia gained similar rights. Russian influence had clearly been decisive, and the tribute clauses might justify her further intervention at a later time. The British and Austrian reply was to demand the complete independence of the Greeks, free of tribute, and this was achieved in **1832.** Thus the very differences of motives between the Great Powers had facilitated Greek independence.

Mehemet Ali and the Middle East

The second phase of the Eastern Question involved the ambitions of Mehemet Ali, to whom the Sultan had promised both the Morea and Crete, as well as Syria, for his services against the Greeks. When the Sultan refused Mehemet Ali's renewed demands for these concessions, the latter sent his son, Ibrahim, into Syria, which he conquered, and later that year he defeated the Turks again at **Koniah, 1831.**

At this point Nicholas I offered Russian help to the Sultan and Russian troops were sent to Constantinople. This alarmed the Western powers. Palmerston's reply was to secure the despatch of a joint British and French naval force to the Aegean to 'persuade' the Sultan to hand over Syria, Damascus and Palestine to Mehemet Ali. This made Russian help useless and forestalled Nicholas to a certain extent. However, by the **Treaty of Unkiar-Skelessi, July, 1833,** Russia and Turkey secretly agreed that the Dardanelles Straits could be closed to the warships of all nations on Russia's request. In a conflict between Russia and the Western powers this would enable the Russian Navy to act in the Mediterranean and then withdraw into safe cover in the Black Sea. Palmerston soon came to know of this secret clause, and determined to counteract it as quickly as possible.

The Sultan and Mehemet Ali

In 1839 the **Sultan Mahmoud II,** whose armies had been reorganized by Prussian advisers, attacked Syria to regain it from Mehemet

Ali. But the latter's forces had also been reorganized by the French, and the Sultan's forces were crushed. His navy deserted to Mehemet Ali. Palmerston now aimed: (*a*) To forestall Russian intervention and (*b*) to defeat the imperialist aims of Thiers and the French in the Middle East. He called the **Conference of London, 1840,** deliberately omitting France. Britain, Russia and Austria now offered the southern part of Syria to Mehemet Ali, and when he refused, a British fleet sailed to Alexandria and British troops captured **Acre** in Syria. Russian forces also moved against Mehemet. He capitulated, gave up his claims to Crete and Syria, but was confirmed as hereditary ruler of Egypt. Thiers, whose policy had failed and nearly brought war between Britain and France, was dismissed by Louis Philippe. At the **Second Conference of London** France was therefore represented.

The Straits Convention, 1841

Palmerston having secured the defeat of Mehemet Ali was in a strong bargaining position with the Sultan. By the **Straits Convention** he counteracted Unkiar-Skelessi. The Sultan agreed that in time of peace the Dardanelles and Bosphorus would be closed to the warships of *all* nations. This was a distinct setback for Russian policy.

The Crimean War, 1853–1856

The war arose from the ambitions of Nicholas I, of Napoleon III and the determination of Britain to maintain the *integrity* of Turkey as a protection for Britain's imperial interests in the Mediterranean, the Middle East and India.

Before 1853 Nicholas I had approached Britain on two occasions with suggestions that they should settle the problem of Turkey between them. Turkey was, he said, *the sick man of Europe*. He proposed that Britain should take over Egypt and Crete and Russia should occupy Constantinople. At the same time the Great Powers should guarantee the independence of Wallachia and Moldavia, of Bulgaria and Serbia. Britain distrusted the Czar's motives.

The immediate causes of the Crimean War were in the Middle

East. Napoleon III revived the French Catholic claims to the *guardianship of the Holy Places* in Palestine. The present guardians, the Russian Greek Orthodox Church, resisted these claims with the support of the Czar. The Czar repeated the old claim that Russia should be recognized as the protector of all Orthodox Christians in the Turkish Empire. The British Ambassador, **Lord Stratford de Redcliffe,** persuaded the Sultan to refuse these demands. The British Prime Minister, **Lord Aberdeen,** despite differences in his cabinet, supported Redcliffe. The Russians moved troops into Moldavia and Wallachia in 1853 and refused to withdraw. Turkish armies moved against the Russians; England and France sent a naval force into the Dardanelles, and the Russians then destroyed the Turkish fleet at **Sinope, 1853.** Turkey having already declared war, Britain and France also declared war against Russia in 1854.

The motives for the war were reasonably clear, but scarcely justified it. Napoleon III wanted military glory; he wanted to intervene in the Middle East more successfully than Louis Philippe had, and for this he received the support of Catholicism in France; Napoleon also wanted to defeat the old enemy of 1812. He hoped to show his support for nationality by the redrawing of the European map on a national basis, so erasing the memory of the 1815 Vienna settlement associated with the defeat of Napoleon I. Britain was concerned to maintain the Turkish Empire as a bulwark against Russia. The Czar pressed on, falsely encouraged by divisions in the British government of Aberdeen.

In the West there was much popular support for the war against Nicholas I, who was regarded as the arch tyrant who had recently (1849) suppressed Hungarian liberties.

The war itself was one of confusion and ineptitude, the only redeeming feature being the great work of **Florence Nightingale.** Through delays and misunderstandings on the allied side, **Todleben,** the Russian engineer, was able to strengthen **Sebastopol** and prolong the war. The ghastly folly of the **Charge of the Light Brigade** showed inept command at its worst. After the long-delayed allied victories of **Inkerman** and **Balaclava (1854), Sebastopol** was stormed in September, **1855.** Nicholas I had died in March, and his successor, Alexander II, made terms with the allies.

The Treaty of Paris, 1856

No warships or arsenals were allowed within the bounds of the Black Sea, and Russia was forbidden to build military or naval fortifications in the area. The Black Sea was to be free to the merchant ships of all nations and the Danube was internationalized. Serbia, Wallachia and Moldavia were declared independent, but Turkish overlordship was still recognized. The Sultan promised equality of treatment for Christians and Moslems, and Russia abandoned her claim to protect the Orthodox Christians.

Russia had been checked, but was able to repudiate the Black Sea clauses in 1870. The Sultan's promises proved worthless.

The Eastern Question from 1856 to the Congress of Berlin, 1878

In these years the Turkish Empire was further weakened by (*a*) the struggle of the various nationalities for real independence, (*b*) the internal mismanagement and corruption of the Turkish Empire.

(*a*) In Serbia an intense feud developed for control between the Obrenovich and Karageorgeovich dynasties. **Michael Obrenovich** secured the withdrawal of all Turkish forces in **1868**, but was soon afterwards assassinated. In **1861** the separate assemblies of Moldavia and Wallachia, allowed by the Paris treaty of 1856, were united under **Alexander I of Rumania** into the state of Rumania. Alexander was forced to abdicate in **1866** and was succeeded by **Prince Charles of Hohenzollern-Sigmaringen,** which brought Rumania more under German than Russian influence. The **Montenegrins** also increased their independence after **1856.** Only Bulgaria had no real element of independence.

(*b*) The Turkish government failed to give equality to Christians and Moslems. Taxation became crushing, but the revenue was misspent. The government tried to stave off bankruptcy by borrowing huge sums from its Western backers, but this money went the way of all the rest.

This was the state of Turkey when the **revolt of Bosnia and Herzegovina** (the southern part of Bosnia) broke out in **1875.** Conditions in these provinces, inhabited by Serbs, were very bad. Serfdom still existed, and taxation of the Christians was crippling. Both Montenegro and Serbia joined the rising and were soon followed by Bulgaria. The Sultan, **Abdul Hamid II,** appropriately known as the 'red Sultan', waged a war of the utmost brutality against the Bulgarians—massacres of men, women and children—atrocities on a wide scale which aroused the horror of Europe.

Disraeli summoned a *conference of the Great Powers at Constantinople.* The Sultan was forced to restore the frontiers of Serbia and he was required to guarantee the independence of Bulgaria, Herzegovina

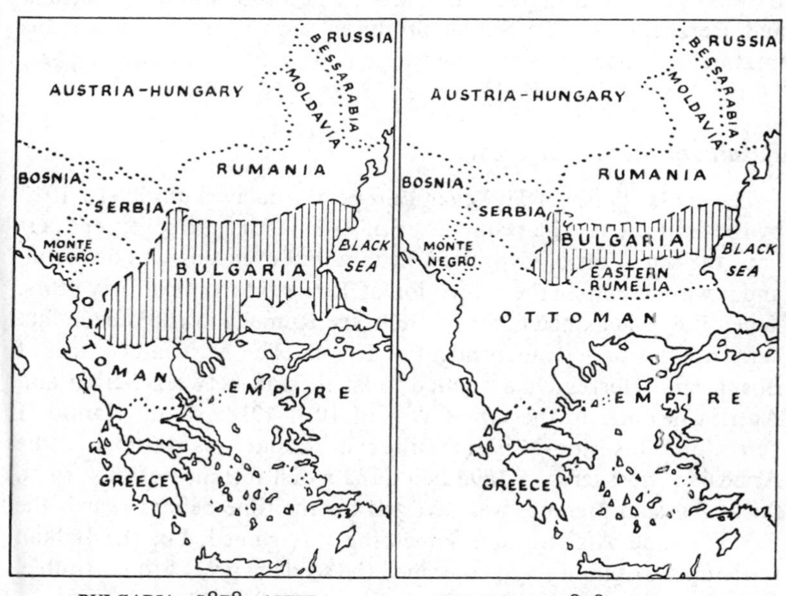

BULGARIA, 1878, AFTER SAN STEFANO

BULGARIA, 1878, AFTER THE CONGRESS OF BERLIN

and Bosnia and to reduce his armed forces as a sign of good faith. When these demands were refused, Russia declared war on Turkey and was quickly joined by Montenegro, Rumania and Bulgaria. The Russians reached Adrianople, and at this point Disraeli ordered the British fleet to the Dardanelles. Russia then concluded the Treaty of **San Stefano** with Turkey, March, **1878.** The creation of the 'Big Bulgaria', stretching across the Balkans, was the cause of further trouble. Both Britain and Austria were alarmed at the creation of what might become a formidable Russian satellite. Russia would, it was feared, dominate the Balkan peninsula. When Bismarck came down on the side of Britain and Austria, Russia agreed to the Congress of Berlin, 1878, which modified the San Stefano Treaty. The Congress divided Bulgaria in three, the northern part being virtually independent. The central part, Eastern Rumelia, was given a Christian Governor-General, but was still under Turkish control. The southern part, including Macedonia, was returned to Turkey. Britain gained **Cyprus** by a separate agreement and Austria was to administer Bosnia and Herzegovina. The Sultan promised once again to reform his treatment of his Christian subjects.

Results of the Berlin Treaty

The final collapse of Turkey in Europe was delayed until 1912–1913 by the settlement. The results were of little lasting value, except perhaps the retention of Cyprus by Britain, but even this was doubtful, and it was no help in the protection of Turkey in the next forty years. When Bulgaria gained control of Eastern Rumelia in **1885** she in fact carried out a policy independent of Russia. The Austrian control of Bosnia and Herzegovina created great tension between Serbia and Austria, leading to the Great War of 1914–1918. Abdul Hamid II persecuted his non-Moslem subjects, despite his promises, the **Armenian Massacres** of **1896** being the worst instance of this. In so far as Russian pressure was diverted for the time being towards the Far East and Afghanistan, something was gained, but the Balkan settlement was flimsy and contained the seeds of great future trouble. (See notes on origins of the Great War, pp. 127–129.)

Summary

The Eastern Question particularly involved the relationship between Russia and the other Great Powers. Russian expansionist aims were involved in the Greek War of Independence, the Mehemet Ali episodes, the Treaty of Unkiar-Skelessi, the Crimean War, and the Treaty of San Stefano leading to the Congress of Berlin, 1878.

Thus the struggles of the Balkan peoples for freedom from Turkey involved the interests of the Great Powers. In general, the interests of Austria and Britain and (later) the Germany of Bismarck were aligned against Russia.

Russian reverses in Europe caused her to look to the Far East. Before 1914, however, she had settled her main differences with Great Britain, and the **Triple Entente** of **1907** was the outcome of this development.

Dates

1812	**Treaty of Bucharest.**
1814	**'Hetairia Philiké' established.**
1821	**Hypsilanti's expedition.**
	Revolt in the Morea. Greek War of Independence begins.
1822	**Greek Patriarch executed at Constantinople.**
1825	**Ibrahim Pasha invades the Morea.**
1827	**Treaty of London.**
	Battle of Navarino.
1829	**Treaty of Adrianople.**
1831	**Ibrahim defeats Turks at Koniah.**
1832	**Greek independence gained.**
1833	**Treaty of Unkiar-Skelessi.**
1839	**Mehemet Ali defeats the Turks.**
	French give assistance to Mehemet Ali.
1840	**Palmerston calls the Conference of London.**
1841	**The Straits Convention.**
1853	**The Russians occupy Moldavia and Wallachia.**
1853–56	**Crimean War.**
1856	**Treaty of Paris.**
1866	**Serbia secures withdrawal of all Turkish forces.**
1875	**Revolts in Bosnia and Herzegovina.**
	The Bulgarian atrocities.
1878	**Treaty of San Stefano.**
	The Congress of Berlin.

QUESTIONS

1. What were the causes of the Greek War of Independence, and why were the Greeks successful?

2. What international complications did the career of Mehemet Ali produce?

3. What were the causes of the Crimean War?

4. Write notes on four of the following: (a) *the Straits Convention, 1841;* (b) *Rumania;* (c) *the Bulgarian atrocities;* (d) *the Treaty of San Stefano.*

CHAPTER TWELVE

FRANCE, 1870–1914

The Position in 1870–1871

Léon Gambetta attempted to organize further resistance to the Prussians after the defeat at Metz, October, 1870, but his efforts failed. The Prussians laid siege to Paris. After the armistice of January, 1871, elections were held for a *National Assembly* which met at Bordeaux. Adolphe Thiers was head of the provisional government. The Bordeaux Assembly moved to Versailles, the home of the Kings of France from the age of Louis XIV to the Revolution of 1789. In May, 1871, the German peace terms, including the cession of Alsace-Lorraine, were accepted.

The Paris Commune

The people of Paris were hostile to the Versailles Assembly, which was monarchist in outlook. In Paris the revolutionary Republican tradition was strong. Paris feared a royalist restoration by the Versailles government. The German victory parade through Paris in March, 1871, was another humiliation brought about by the unpopular terms of peace. During the Prussian siege of Paris the government had suspended the payment of all debts, but in March, 1871, the Versailles government ordered the payment of all arrears and the disbandment of the National Guard. Negotiators sent by the Versailles government were murdered, and Paris then set up its own local government or commune. The **Commune** was mainly composed of anti-Versailles Republicans and had working- and lower-middle-class support. Communes were also set up in other important French cities at this time.

Thiers gave **Marshal MacMahon** command of the Versailles forces sent against Paris, and the Germans stood aside. The civil war went on for seven weeks, with 20,000 casualties. Many thousands of Communards were deported after their defeat. Large areas of Paris were in ruins after MacMahon's bombardment with incendiary shells.

The Commune left a permanent effect on the politics of France. From it arose the opposition forces of the extreme Left under the guidance of Marxism. The sharp division between *the proletarian Left and the extreme Right* was made even more bitter than in the past.

However, with the Commune suppressed, the position of Thiers was strong. The wealthier classes had sufficient confidence in him to subscribe so heavily to special loans that the German indemnity was paid off in three years and the German army of occupation withdrawn.

Establishment of the Republic

Thiers was President from 1871 to 1873, but royalist influence secured the election of MacMahon in 1873. At this time there were three candidates for the throne of France—the **Comte de Paris** (grandson of Louis Philippe), the **Comte de Chambord** (representing the Bourbon line) and the **Prince Imperial,** son of Napoleon III. Only the first two were seriously considered, but after an arrangement had been made by which the Comte de Chambord would be elected and then adopt the Comte de Paris as his heir, the former refused to accept the tricolor flag in place of the white flag of the Bourbons. This led to unseemly bickerings between the two royal claimants which aided the Republican cause, energetically taken up by Gambetta and his supporters. In June, 1875, the Assembly voted for a Republic by a majority of one vote. MacMahon, using various powers given him as President, did all he could to get this decision reversed, but failed. By 1879 there was a clear republican majority in the Assembly and the Senate. At this point MacMahon resigned.

The Constitution of 1875 remained substantially in force until the German occupation of France in 1940. Elections for the Chamber of Deputies were held every four years, and all men over 20 had the vote. The Senate was elected for nine years by the electoral colleges of the Departments. The ministers of the government were directly responsible to the Chamber and the Senate. The President was elected for seven years.

Principal Events of the Years 1880–1914

One of the most important Prime Ministers of this period was **Jules Ferry** (1880–1881 and 1883–1885). He attempted to heal the political and social wounds left by the Commune. The exiles were permitted to return, trade unions were legalized and the censorship of the press removed. The French system of schools for all between the ages of 6 and 16 was established. Ferry was anti-clerical and put severe restrictions on the Church. Members of various Catholic orders were not allowed to teach in State schools, while Catholic colleges lost their university status. The new secondary schools or 'lycées' were established, with science occupying a more important place in the curriculum than hitherto. Much discontent was expressed by the Church, and there was a tendency for some sections of Catholics to support movements aimed at overthrowing the Republic.

Ferry also undertook a *strong colonial policy* partly to compensate for France's weakened position in Europe. France seized Tunis in 1881 and Madagascar in 1885. In Indochina French control was greatly increased. The French commercial and financial interests were pleased, but the extreme Left denounced Ferry's policy of imperialism.

General Boulanger

A number of serious crises shook the French Republic between 1870 and 1914. The first of these, after the attempted royalist restoration, was the Boulangist crisis. The General's aim was to revise the constitution and give greatly increased powers to the President. He advocated an aggressive foreign policy and the recovery of Alsace-Lorraine. He also advocated an alliance between France and Russia directed against Germany. In 1888 he was elected for six French constituencies and his popularity appeared to be gathering strength. There is little doubt that he planned a Napoleon-type 'coup d'état' to overthrow the constitution, and this led the extreme Left and the liberal Republicans to combine forces against him. Their charges of treason forced the government to order Boulanger's arrest and trial. However, his nerve failed, he fled to Belgium and committed suicide in 1891.

The Panama Scandal, 1888–1892

The Panama scandal caused no less a stir. **Ferdinand de Lesseps,** the successful promoter of the Suez Canal scheme, floated a company to construct a canal across the Isthmus of Panama. Due to a variety of causes, the scheme failed. This led to official investigations of the company's finances, which disclosed that *members of the Chamber of Deputies had been bribed to support the scheme.* There had also been great extravagance and much fraud. De Lesseps was sentenced to five years' imprisonment.

The combined effects of the Boulanger affair and the Panama scandal was to shake public confidence in the Republic, but the Dreyfus case was even more severe in its results.

The Dreyfus Case

Captain Dreyfus, a Jew and a French officer, was accused of selling military secrets to Germany. His committal to Devil's Island roused immense public controversy. A campaign to clear his name was undertaken by a number of leading French citizens, the most notable of whom was the great novelist, **Émile Zola.** After the suicide of one of the accusers, **Colonel Henry,** it became clear to many that Dreyfus had been victimized in order to cover up the real malefactors in the French Foreign Office. He was pardoned in 1899, but it was not until 1906 that his commission was restored.

The Dreyfus case showed unpleasant anti-semitic (anti-Jewish) trends in France, and at the same time gave a further jolt to public confidence in the French political system. It also embittered even further the struggle between the Left parties who had supported Dreyfus (Socialists, Communists, Republicans) and the Right-wing parties supported by the Church.

The Separation Law, 1905

The Socialists had achieved a substantial representation in the Chamber of Deputies in 1890 (fifty members) and, especially after the Dreyfus affair, their influence increased. From 1899 to 1905 a number of moderate Socialists served in government posts and took a leading part in further restrictions placed on the Catholic Church. All religious orders were compelled to submit their rules for government approval and all teachers came under state supervision. By the **Separation Law of 1905** (i.e. the separation of Church and State) the Church lost all support from state funds, and special committees, known as *Associations Culturelles*, were set up to administer Church property.

Socialist influence was seen in the achievement of a working day of 9½ hours and the setting up in 1901 of arbitration boards to settle wage disputes. There was also an increase of militant action by workers under syndicalist leadership, and large-scale strikes were frequent just before the Great War.

Summary

The outstandingly important events of the years 1870 to 1914 in France were the defeat in 1871 of the Paris Commune; the struggle to establish Republican institutions as against attempted royalist restoration; the crises (especially Boulanger, Panama, and Dreyfus) which shook the Republic and embittered the contest between Left and Right; the separation of Church and State; and the development of new socialist forces which led to increasing conflict between capital and labour before 1914.

Dates

1870	**Defeat of France.**
1871	**Treaty of Frankfort.**
	Paris Commune.
	Thiers elected President.
1873	**MacMahon—President.**
1875	**Establishment of Third Republic.**
1880	**Jules Ferry—Prime Minister.**
1886	**General Boulanger—Minister of War.**
1888–92	**Panama Scandal.**
1894–1906	**Dreyfus case.**
1905	**Separation Law.**

QUESTIONS

1. What events led to the rise of the Paris Commune?

2. Why did it take nearly ten years to establish the republican form of government in France?

3. What was the importance of Jules Ferry?

4. Write notes on three of the following: (a) *Boulanger;* (b) *the Panama scandal;* (c) *the Dreyfus case;* (d) *the Separation Law, 1905.*

CHAPTER THIRTEEN

RUSSIA TO 1914

Introduction

IT was **Peter the Great** who did most to bring Russia into closer contact with Europe (1682–1725). He reformed his country on western lines and built his new capital of St. Petersburg as a westward-looking city. He greatly strengthened the Russian army with the help of foreign advisers and with it enlarged the boundaries of Russia by defeating Sweden and acquiring Latvia, Estonia, Karelia, Ingria and part of Finland. Peter's policies were continued by **Catherine the Great (1762–1796).** She gained the Crimea from the Turks and took full advantage of the internal chaos of Poland to secure control of more than half that country by 1795.

Alexander I, 1801–1825

He was the grandson of Catherine, and one of the most enigmatic and interesting of the Russian Czars. He continued the policy of Russian expansion. The famous *Treaty of Tilsit* made with Napoleon in 1807 (see p. 29) enabled him to acquire Bessarabia from Turkey and the whole of Finland in 1809. After the defeat of Napoleon's Moscow campaign in 1812, he saw himself as having a 'divine mission'. He entered an intensely religious phase as well as a liberal one. He played with the idea of liberal reforms in despotic Russia and appointed liberal advisers. His father's special police were suppressed, torture was forbidden, exiles recalled from Siberia, new universities set up. Even 50,000 serfs were liberated. He continued to support national revolts against the Turks in the Balkan peninsula, a policy which also aided Russian expansion. However, he was forced by the Russian gentry to dismiss the liberal reformer Speransky who proposed to give the peasants some voice in elections to a national assembly.

In Poland, Alexander introduced a liberal constitution, granted freedom of speech and religion, introduced a new code of laws, and founded the University of Warsaw. Polish citizens alone were acceptable in the Civil Service and Polish was made the official language.

Reactionary Period of Alexander I

However, in the period 1819–1825 Alexander turned sharply away from liberalism. The murder of Kotzebue in 1819 (see p. 43) enabled Metternich to gain decisive influence with the Czar. The revolutions in Spain (1818) and Naples (1820) were used by Metternich to draw Alexander completely away from liberalism. Alexander now introduced a censorship of all school books, abandoned his schemes for liberating the serfs, and gave the Russian Orthodox Church control of education. Alexander died in 1825 and was succeeded by his son Nicholas I. The latter's brother Constantine had already renounced the throne in favour of Nicholas, but a liberal plot aided by some of the guards regiments in St. Petersburg attempted to place Constantine on the throne. The plot failed.

Nicholas I, 1825–1855

The **Decembrist Revolt** (above) hardened Nicholas still further against liberalism. He re-established the secret police, increased the censorship, restricted Alexander's new secondary schools to the children of the gentry, used police spies in the universities, where the teaching of 'dangerous' subjects was forbidden. In 1849 he assisted the Austrian Emperor to quell the Hungarian liberal rising under Kossuth. He feared above all the Russian intellectuals, many of whom were exiled to Siberia during his reign.

In foreign policy Nicholas continued the expansionist policies of Peter, Catherine and Alexander I. In the Far East he gained territory from China on the Amur River, and in the Balkans he supported the Greeks. The Treaty of Unkiar-Skelessi with Turkey was a triumph (see p. 99), but this was counteracted by Palmerston in the Straits Convention of 1841 (see p. 100). He attempted to break up the Turkish

Empire in conjunction with Britain, but failed. His attempt to act alone against Turkey led to the Crimean War. He died in 1855, before the end of the war.

In Poland he reversed Alexander's liberal policy. Russian officials replaced Polish, and in 1828 he closed down the Polish parliament altogether. In *1830 Polish troops in Warsaw rose in revolt*, Poland was declared independent, and Nicholas deposed. Nicholas despatched 120,000 troops against Warsaw and the revolt was crushed. Among the Poles themselves there were differences between the Whites and the more extreme Reds, disputes over military strategy, and lack of real peasant support. Nicholas abolished Alexander's constitution of 1815, closed Warsaw University, and ruled the country through Russian officials. Nicholas was probably the *most despotic of the Czars* of the nineteenth century and was hated throughout Europe by liberal sympathizers.

Alexander II, 1855–1881

The new Czar, whose autocratic position had been weakened by defeat in war, wished to reform a number of obvious abuses. His first great effort was the **Edict of Emancipation, 1861,** which freed all the serfs. They were given about half the landlords' estates and were now grouped in village communities or *mirs* under village Elders. Compensation to the landlords was to be paid in annual payments spread over 49 years. But the payments proved too burdensome to the peasantry who tended to drift to the towns. Little improvement in agricultural methods occurred. This limited the good effects of emancipation to a minority of the peasantry.

Another important reform was the introduction of the *Zemstvos* in 1864. They were local councils at district and provincial levels. Previously the nobility had dominated local government, but now townsmen and peasants had the right to elect members of the District Zemstvos, who then elected the Provincial Zemstvos. While limited, this was an attempt to widen and improve local government.

Alexander encouraged *law reform*, and judges and magistrates were made independent of other government departments. Equality of all before the law was proclaimed (though its application was very limited), and trial by jury was introduced.

An important *military reform* of 1874 declared all classes liable to military service—a liability also reduced from 25 to 15 years.

Alexander also allowed *greater freedom of the press*, and the number of newspapers and journals greatly increased during his reign.

Discontent in the Reign of Alexander II

The Liberal and Socialist reformers regarded these changes as slight and unsatisfactory. For instance, the provincial governors could still over-ride the Zemstvos. Again, *political offenders* were not given jury trial. The peasants were still dealt with in special courts, and the secret police could still arrest people at will. The peasants were discontented with the working of the Emancipation Edict, and were still too impoverished to obtain sufficient land and cultivate it well.

Discontent led to the growth of *nihilism* among many of the younger generation in Russia. Their aim was to sweep away everything, including the Czar himself, which was not based on reason and science. A nihilist attempt to assassinate Alexander II in 1866 failed, and resulted in harsher rule. Between 1863 and 1874 over 150,000 persons were exiled to Siberia.

The socialist movement also developed strength, linked to the Socialist International with its headquarters in Switzerland. Young Socialists went into the countryside to spread their propaganda, but found the peasantry too ignorant and oppressed to challenge their 'little father', the Czar. At this time the anarchist, **Michael Bakunin,** was also preaching the need of a peasant revolution. Terrorism, aimed at destroying the Czar and leading officials, became the creed of a few determined fanatics.

There was also trouble in Poland. Alexander had re-opened Warsaw University, restored Polish as the official language, and began to displace Russian officials in favour of the Poles. However, these reforms were not the same as independence, and in *1863 another uprising occurred.* This was defeated for much the same reasons as in 1830, and the Czar also received indirect support from Bismarck (see p. 83). Alexander then divided Poland into provinces under

Russian governors and the central government was transferred to St. Petersburg.

Alexander II was assassinated in 1881.

Alexander III, 1881–1894

The policy of despotism was strengthened in the reign of Alexander III. The old measures of repression were again revived—police control of the universities, suppression of newspapers, and entry to secondary schools restricted to the upper classes. Special *Land Captains* were appointed to control both local officials and the Zemstvos. Candidates for the Zemstvos were carefully selected in order to prevent the election of anti-Czarist elements. In the Baltic provinces and in Poland the Russian language was made compulsory in the educational system and for official purposes. The Russian Orthodox Church gained increased privileges, and with this there occurred increasing persecution of religious minorities, especially the Jews. All this showed the worst aspects of Czarism, and Alexander III, fearful of assassination, shut himself away in the royal palace surrounded by special guards.

Nicholas II, 1894–1917

Nicholas II was the last of the Czars. In outlook he was a complete autocrat determined to sustain all the old despotic powers of his predecessors. He was murdered by the Bolsheviks in 1918.

The revolutionary and reforming movements had achieved very little success among the peasantry. It became almost a Socialist article of faith that *Russia needed big industrial development*, the growth of large-scale cities with a working class or proletariat who could be organized for the overthrow of the Czarist and Capitalist system. This was already occurring. The alliance with France in 1893 provided Russia with capital for industrial development. By 1914 Russia was fifth among the industrial nations of the world. The Czar's minister who was most responsible for this development was **Sergei Witte,** appointed Minister of Finance and Commerce in 1892. The **Trans-Siberian Railway** was begun in 1892 and completed ten years later. The industries of cotton, wool, coal, iron and steel developed rapidly.

Movements of Opposition in the Early Twentieth Century

The Russian **Social Democratic Labour Party** was formed in **1898,** its most important leaders being **Lenin** and **Trotsky.** Their whole programme was based on the doctrines of Karl Marx (see p. 90). Owing to police activity against it, the party was organized from abroad. Lenin edited the revolutionary paper **'Iskra'** ('The Spark') which was printed in Britain for illegal distribution in Russia. The movement aimed at a revolution led by the industrial proletariat. The strike weapon became the method for taking up immediate grievances of the workers and for preparing the day of revolution. In 1903 serious division appeared in the party between the **Mensheviks** (Minority) who wanted a wide recruitment of both active and non-active members and the **Bolsheviks** (Majority) who wanted selection of dedicated activists and rigid control by the Central Committee.

Another movement of opposition to Czarism was that of the **Liberals,** who aimed at a parliamentary system for Russia on western lines. They were influential in the Zemstvos and among the professional middle class of the towns.

The Social Revolutionaries still pinned their faith on a peasant uprising, and also used the weapon of terror against the Czarist system.

These various movements were making considerable headway by the time of the Russo-Japanese War.

The Russo-Japanese War, 1904–1905

In 1895 Japan had defeated China and taken over Korea and Port Arthur. Russia then formed an agreement with France and Germany which forced Japan to give up Port Arthur. In reply the Japanese built up their armed forces for an eventual challenge to Russia, and in **1902** made the alliance with Britain by which the latter would remain neutral if Japan were at war with one power only, and would support Japan in the event of a war against two powers. In the meantime Russia had leased Port Arthur from China, and also increased her armies in Manchuria and Korea. When she refused to withdraw them, the Japanese declared war, which ended in the defeat of Russia on land at the **Battle of Mukden** and on the sea at the **Battle of**

Tsushima in May, 1905. These disasters had shown the weakness and bad leadership of the Russian forces, and by the **Treaty of Portsmouth** (New Hampshire, U.S.A.), **1905,** Japan gained Port Arthur and Korea, and Russia was forced to withdraw her troops from Manchuria.

Effects of the Defeat in Russia

Great discontent followed. The Zemstvos put forward demands for an elected parliament, and a wave of strikes broke out under the influence of the Social Democratic Party and the Social Revolutionaries. Disorder broke out in the countryside. **Father Gapon,** a priest who was regarded by many as a government agent, led a procession on January 22, 1905, **Red Sunday,** to the Czar's Winter Palace in St. Petersburg demanding political freedom and improvements in working conditions. The procession was mown down by volleys from the guards. Gapon escaped, but was later murdered by revolutionaries. The results of this affair were the spread of strikes and the increasing influence of the Marxists over the workers.

The Social Democrats called a general strike, and *Workers' Councils* (*Soviets*) were set up in many cities. However, in December, 1905, an armed uprising by the Soviets was suppressed by the Czarist troops. But conditions of general turmoil existed.

Nicholas II was now compelled to promise an elected parliament (**October Manifesto, 1905**), but he clung obstinately to control of the armed forces and foreign policy. The system of election was so elaborate that overwhelming weight was given to the wealthier classes. The **First Duma** or Parliament met in May, **1906,** but when the members attempted to gain control of all affairs of state, Nicholas dissolved it and ordered new elections. The **Second Duma** met in **1907,** but the Minister of the Interior, **Stolypin,** had organized a weeding-out of undesirable candidates, many voters were disfranchised, and the Jews threatened with retaliation if they voted. The Social Democrats had succeeded, despite this, in winning fifty seats, and the Czar, regarding them as unfit for membership of the Duma, ordered further elections. In these the Social Democrats were prohibited altogether, and in the **Third Duma,** the Czar's supporters were in a majority. Thus the Third Duma was the result of election-rigging and intimidation, and it gave point to the declaration of Lenin that the Duma experiments were a fraud against the workers.

The Prime Minister was now Stolypin. His policies were highly oppressive to his opponents. There occurred numerous peasant revolts, dealt with ruthlessly by military courts and executions. He now attempted to end the old Russian commune or 'mir' and create a class of wealthier peasants, who would support the Czar. Compact farms took the place of many still run on the old strip system, and Stolypin provided government help for the renting or purchase of land by the peasants from the gentry. This new class of *kulaks* became the backbone of resistance to Communism after the Bolshevik Revolution of 1917. Stolypin was assassinated in 1911.

In 1914 Russia possessed only the feeblest shadow of a parliamentary democratic system, totally unsatisfactory to large sections both of the working and middle classes. The Czar still exercised a despotic control, only slightly disguised.

Summary

Czarist policies within Russia continued to fluctuate throughout the nineteenth century between cautious, half-liberal measures and outright repression. Alexander I, liberal, then reactionary, Nicholas I, reactionary, Alexander II, reforming, Alexander III, reactionary, Nicholas II, autocratic and with no real intention of introducing liberal democracy, as was shown by the limitations and failure of the Duma experiments after 1905. Movements of opposition to Czarism were Liberal, Socialist, Terroristic and Marxist. The latter forces won the day in 1917, aided by the existence of a town proletariat which had developed with Russian industrialization.

Russian expansionist policy received a serious setback with the Crimean War and the Congress of Berlin, 1878. Russian expansionism looked more towards the east after this, but her defeat by the Japanese in 1905 showed the weakness of Russian imperialism and it produced great internal unrest.

Dates

1812–19 Alexander I's liberal phase.
1819–25 Alexander's reactionary phase.

1825	**Decembrist revolt.**
	Accession of Nicholas I.
1828	**Closure of Polish parliament.**
1830	**Polish revolt.**
1833	**Treaty of Unkiar-Skelessi.**
1841	**The Straits Convention.**
1849	**Nicholas intervenes against Hungarian revolution.**
1853	**Crimean War begins.**
1855	**Death of Nicholas I and accession of Alexander II.**
1861	**Edict of Emancipation.**
1863	**Polish rising.**
1881	**Assassination of Alexander II and accession of Alexander III.**
1892	**Sergei Witte—Minister of Commerce.**
	Trans-Siberian Railway begun.
1894	**Accession of Nicholas II.**
1898	**Russian Social Democratic Labour Party founded.**
1903	**Bolshevik–Menshevik differences.**
1904–5	**Russo-Japanese war.**
	'Red Sunday' (Father Gapon)
	Workers' councils or Soviets suppressed.
	The Czar's October Manifesto.
1906	**First Duma.**
1907	**Second Duma.**
	Third Duma (to 1912).
1907–11	**Stolypin's internal policies. The 'kulaks'.**

QUESTIONS

1. *Explain the reasons for Alexander I's liberal phase and his later anti-liberal policies.*

2. *Describe the domestic or foreign policy of Nicholas I.*

3. *What reforms were attempted in Russia in the reign of Alexander II?*

4. *What forms did social and political unrest take in Russia up to 1914?*

5. *Write notes on four of the following:* (a) *the Land Captains;* (b) *Sergei Witte;* (c) *'Iskra';* (d) *Father Gapon;* (e) *the October Manifesto, 1905;* (f) *Stolypin.*

CHAPTER FOURTEEN

THE ORIGINS OF THE GREAT WAR, 1914–1918

The Colonization of Africa

ECONOMIC changes in Europe in the second half of the nineteenth century produced larger business concerns which sought new markets and sources of raw materials. These concerns were directly aided by governments, and this increased the competition for colonies between the European states. The activities of explorers and missionaries were therefore encouraged. Great improvements in communications, especially railways and steamships, aided these developments.

In Africa above all there were many sources of foodstuffs and raw materials required by Europe. Britain's exploitation of Africa was for many years ahead of other states. Britain gained an important stake in the Suez Canal in 1875 and took *control of Egypt in 1881.* The French, pushed out of Egypt, looked elsewhere and took control of Tunis in 1881 (see also p. 109). France had disliked Britain's control of Egypt and, after the conquest of the French Congo, they reached the Nile at **Fashoda** in **1898. Kitchener** and **Major Marchand** faced each other with their troops, there was nearly war, but the French retired. The **British East Africa Company** also opened up Kenya and Uganda, the **Niger Company** gained control of the palm-oil product of Nigeria, and the **South Africa Company** under **Cecil Rhodes** laid the foundation of Rhodesia.

Bismarck's change of attitude to colonies was partly due to the pressure of German trading interests and the **German Colonial League.** Germany occupied South-West Africa, Togoland and the Cameroons in 1884 and German East Africa and Tanganyika in 1885. The Berlin Colonial Conference in 1884 laid down a number of rules for colonization and the division of Africa by friendly agreements was decided upon. The Congo Free State was also established under Belgian control.

The Italians were defeated by the Abyssinians at **Adowa in 1896,** but before 1900 they had succeeded in occupying Eritrea and Somaliland.

There had been little conflict between the Great Powers over the division of the huge continent of Africa, where there was room for all imperialist powers. The Berlin Conference had settled the main 'spheres of influence', and had attempted to work out a code of fair trading practices and treatment of the natives. There were, however, many unfair practices and considerable ruthlessness in the treatment of the native populations.

Imperialism in the Far East

The principal countries involved were Britain, Germany, Russia, the U.S.A., France and Japan. Palmerston gained for Britain a lease of Hong Kong and trading rights in the five Chinese Treaty Ports. In 1874 Britain occupied the Fiji Islands. Germany and the U.S.A. partitioned Samoa, and the former also gained New Guinea and the Caroline Islands. After the Congress of Berlin, 1878 (see p. 104), Russia turned eastward, and built the Trans-Siberian Railway, 1892–1902. She also expanded her trade with Manchuria and North China. Japan had introduced a form of government based in part on the Bismarckian model for the German Empire, and she became an expansionist power. Russia had assisted China against Japan, but Japan defeated Russia in 1905 and seized Port Arthur (see p. 119). Thus there had been more open conflict in the Far East than in the case of Africa.

General Comments

The only major colonial clashes up to 1905 were between Japan and Russia and between Britain and the Boers in South Africa. In general, the Western powers had avoided military conflict, but nevertheless the fierce competition for markets, for raw materials, and for the shipping business became more intense between 1900 and

1914. A system of alliances and counter-alliances developed which showed this increasing clash. In Europe, Bismarck's most difficult problem had been to keep on good terms with Russia and prevent any alliance between that country and France. His dismissal by Kaiser William II in 1890 set Germany on the 'new course' which increased the tensions between the Great Powers.

The Dual Alliance of France and Russia, 1893

The alliance pledged Russia and France to assist one another if attacked by a third party. This change was due to *the increasing antagonism of Germany and Russia* over the Balkan question, the dismissal of Bismarck by the Kaiser, who made little effort to keep on good terms with Russia, the refusal of Germany to assist Sergei Witte's economic programme in Russia and the willingness of the French to give that assistance.

Britain's 'Splendid Isolation' Removed

The Dual Alliance of France and Russia had emphasized even more Britain's diplomatic isolation. Britain could only remonstrate against Turkey on the occasion of the Armenian massacres in 1896, and in the **Boer War, 1899–1902,** Continental opinion was against Britain. The Kaiser gave the Boers considerable support. Thus in 1900 Germany, France and Russia were all antagonistic to Britain. **Joseph Chamberlain** advocated a British-German alliance, but the Kaiser was not particularly interested. In fact, he proceeded to enlarge the German navy, promote plans for the Berlin–Baghdad Railway and, in connection with the Boer War, aroused much hatred of Britain in Germany. An early effect of this German campaign was the Anglo-Japanese Alliance of 1902 which gave Britain an ally against Russia and Germany in the Far East. As the danger to both France and Britain from Germany became more obvious, the two powers came closer together, especially after the death of Queen Victoria (who had been very pro-German) and the accession of Edward VII who distrusted the Kaiser and admired the French. By the **Entente Cordiale** of **1904** France recognized Britain's occupation of Egypt and Britain agreed to support French policy in Morocco. Regular consultations were to be held on military and naval matters, and special consultation in case of the danger of attack from another power. This was an understanding, not a binding alliance.

The First Moroccan Crisis and the Triple Entente

The Moroccan clause of the 'Entente Cordiale' was secret, but the *Kaiser* gained knowledge of it and *visited Tangier in 1905*, where he assured the Sultan of German support for the independence of Morocco. He demanded a European Conference on Morocco, and when **Delcassé,** the French Foreign Minister, resisted this, he was dismissed through German pressure. The **Conference of Algeciras** met in January, **1906**. It was decided that France and Spain should police Morocco, and France should control the customs and arms supply. Germany gained an equal control with France, Spain and Britain in the Moroccan state bank. German attempts to exclude French interests in Morocco had failed, largely because of the joint opposition of Britain, France and Russia, who were thus drawn closer together.

The French, especially through Delcassé's influence, had been attempting for some time to bring about agreement between Russia and Britain, and the Russian Foreign Minister, **Izvolsky,** came to support this. He made an agreement between Russia and Japan in 1907 by which they both guaranteed the integrity of China, and this eased British fears of Russian aims in the Far East. The defeat of Russia in 1905 had also reduced British fears of Russian power in the Far East. Both Britain and Russia were opposed to the German scheme of a Berlin–Baghdad Railway. The Balkan states were now apparently independent of Russia, and it was the Germans who were now seeking influence with Turkey. All these factors helped to bring about an agreement between Britain and Russia in 1907 by which Britain gained control of Afghanistan's foreign policy, but Russia had equal trading rights there with Britain. Persia was divided into clearly defined zones of Russian and British influence. Thus by **1907** the **Triple Entente** of **Britain, France and Russia** was in existence as a clear counterweight to Germany and her allies.

The Second Moroccan Crisis, 1911

In 1911 the French occupied the capital, Fez, in order to suppress a revolution against the pro-French Sultan. Thereupon the *Kaiser despatched the gunboat 'Panther' to Agadir,* ostensibly to protect German interests. War preparations were made, but eventually the Kaiser abandoned his Moroccan interests in exchange for approximately half the French Congo. The general situation in Europe had, however, been tense and dangerous.

Crises in the Balkans

The Great War really began in the Balkan peninsula. In 1908 the **Young Turk** movement secured by rebellion a parliamentary system of government from Abdul Hamid II. This internal discord encouraged Bulgaria to declare her independence. Austria now completely occupied Bosnia and Herzegovina in order to strengthen her Balkan position against Serbia, the centre of anti-Austrian movements in the Balkans. Russia wished to support Serbian aims of a united Slav state in the Balkans, but the Kaiser declared that if Austria were attacked 'a knight in shining armour would be found by her side'. Thus the Great Powers were once again being dangerously drawn into Balkan complications.

Turkey was further weakened by the war with Italy and Italy gained possession of Tripoli (1911–1912). The weakened Turkey was attacked in 1912 by the **Balkan League** comprising Greece, Serbia, Montenegro and Bulgaria. The league was victorious, and by the Treaty of London, Turkey lost nearly all her territory in Europe. However, the victors then quarrelled among themselves, and the Bulgarians, claiming a part of Macedonia taken by Serbia, attacked the latter. Serbia was supported by Rumania and Turkey, and they overwhelmed the Bulgarians. Turkey recovered Adrianople for her services in this, the **Second Balkan War.**

Effects of the First and Second Balkan Wars

The Balkan wars had a generally unsettling effect on European affairs. They especially *increased the antagonism between Austria and Serbia.* Austria, seeing the dangers of a break-up of the Turkish Empire, had occupied Bosnia and Herzegovina in order to block Serbia's expansionism. Austria had also demanded the formation of an independent Albania, thus preventing the Serbs reaching the Adriatic in that direction. Propaganda from within Serbia for the union of all the Balkan Slavs now intensified, while the Austrians wished to wipe Serbia off the map and thus gain a continuous territory across the peninsula.

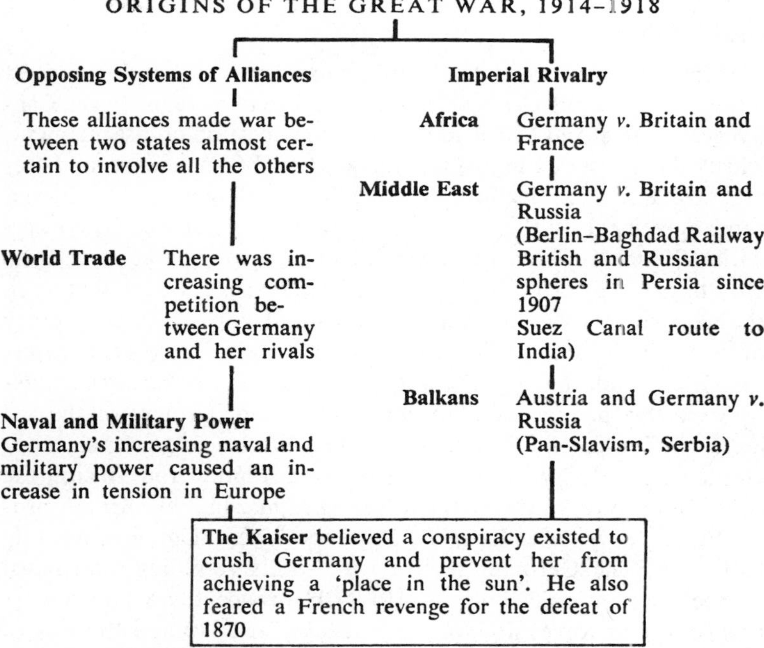

This was the situation when the **Archduke Ferdinand** was assassinated at **Sarajevo**, capital of Bosnia, on **June 28th, 1914.** The Austrian ultimatum to Serbia of July 23rd demanded the suppression of all anti-Austrian societies, the dismissal of officials to whom Austria objected, and the entry into Serbia of Austrian police to supervise these measures. Serbia accepted the first two, but not the third. Austria declared war on Serbia on July 28th, despite the wish of the Kaiser that she should accept Serbia's reply. Russia then mobilized.

The German **Schlieffen Plan** had been devised to give Germany quick victory in the west by a rapid thrust to the Channel ports and Paris. This would avoid the dreaded war on two fronts. Russian mobilization, therefore, made war almost inevitable and Germany declared war on France on August 3rd when the latter refused neutrality. The German **invasion of Belgium** on August 4th brought the hesitating British government squarely down on the side of France, and Britain declared war on Germany on August 4th, 1914.

General Points

Many movements had developed opposed to war, but they proved incapable of halting the course of events. The two **Hague Peace Conferences of 1899** and **1907** had failed on the question of disarmament, which the Kaiser (and many others) thought an absurd and impracticable aim for the Great Powers. The conferences had achieved some agreement on the 'humanizing' of the rules of war. The International Socialist movement, which had pledged itself as recently as 1911 to halt the outbreak of war by a general strike, was caught up in the national aims of the various states and only a small minority of its members came out in opposition to the war. There were aggressive forces in all the major powers. The speed of *German naval building since 1898* had increased the tension between Germany on the one hand and Britain and France on the other. The leading campaigner in Germany for the great German navy was **Admiral von Tirpitz,** the controlling spirit of the **German Navy League**. In 1906 Britain produced the new **'Dreadnought',** more powerful than any existing battleship. The Germans replied with similar building, and naval competition intensified up to 1914. In France there had always existed strong forces advocating *révanche* for 1870 and the loss of Alsace-Lorraine.

Summary of Causes of Great War, 1914–1918

The following considerations must be taken into account as causes leading to the war:

1. Colonial and trade rivalry throughout the world.
2. **The growth of naval rivalry and Germany's efforts to overtake Britain.**

3. The clash of interests between Germany and Russia in the Balkans and elsewhere (Pan-Germanism *v.* Pan-Slavism).

4. Increasing conflict over Africa, especially in Morocco.

5. The alarm caused to both Britain and Russia by the Berlin–Baghdad Railway project of Germany. This would affect radically their interests in the Balkans and the Middle East.

6. The Kaiser's often expressed wish for more colonies, which meant the abandonment of some by other powers. His 'place in the sun' declaration expressed this attitude.

7. The severe clash of interests between Austria and Serbia in the Balkans.

8. The desire of many elements in France to regain Alsace-Lorraine and wipe out the disgrace of 1870.

9. The pre-war system of alliances was designed to give security, yet incurred the risk of general war. The German Schlieffen Plan meant that if Russia mobilized, war was almost inevitable, for Russia and France were allies.

Dates

1875	**Britain's interest in Suez Canal.**
1881	**Britain gains control of Egypt.**
1884	**German occupation of South-West Africa, Togoland and the Cameroons.**
	Berlin Colonial Conference.
1893	**Dual Alliance of France and Russia.**
1898	**German naval programme.**
1902	**Anglo-Japanese alliance.**
1904	**'Entente Cordiale'.**
1904–5	**Russo-Japanese War.**
1905	**The Kaiser visits Tangier.**
1906	**First Moroccan crisis.**
	Conference of Algeciras.
	Britain produces the 'Dreadnought'.
1907	**Izvolsky secures agreement between Russia and Japan.**
	Triple Entente formed.
1908	**Young Turk revolution.**
1911	**Second Moroccan crisis.**

1912	**Balkan League attacks Turkey.**
1913	**Second Balkan War.**
1914	
June 28th	**Sarajevo assassination.**
July 28th	**Austria declares war on Serbia.**
August 4th	**Britain declares war on Germany.**

QUESTIONS

1. Why did no major war occur between the European powers between 1870 and 1914?

2. How and why did the international situation become more strained after 1900?

3. What were the main causes of the Great War?

4. Explain in what circumstances the following understanding or alliances were made: (a) *Dual Alliance of France and Russia;* (b) *the Anglo-Japanese alliance;* (c) *the Triple Entente.*

CHAPTER FIFTEEN

THE GREAT WAR, 1914–1918

The Great War became the *first total war* in modern times. As it proceeded, it affected the whole populations of the warring states. Every possible man and woman was mobilized for the war effort. Bombardment of civilian populations by airships, guns and aeroplanes developed.

The German Plan

The Schlieffen Plan, devised ten years earlier, was put into operation by the Germans. The general aim was a lightning defeat of France and then a turn eastward against Russia. The first stage was an attack through Belgium and northern France and then in a wide sweep towards Paris. However, Belgian delaying tactics gave time for a British force under **Sir John French** to reach Belgium. At the **Battle of Mons** the British delayed the German advance but were forced to retreat. The whole front was driven back by the Germans and Belgium was over-run in three weeks. Then the Germans *changed the direction of their advance*, moving down from the north in a more direct line towards Paris. This change has mystified military experts and seemed to show a fault in the strategy of the German High Command. However, the Germans reached the Marne and shelled Paris from twenty miles. At this point the French Commander-in-Chief, **General Joffre,** brought out every available reserve from Paris itself and between September 6th and 10th the Germans were thrust back to the Aisne in the **First Battle of the Marne.** Paris and the whole front had been saved. The war now became static, and a trench system developed which ultimately ran from the Belgian frontier down to Switzerland.

The Eastern Front in 1914—Tannenberg

The Russians were defeated by Hindenburg and Ludendorf at **Tannenberg, August, 1914.** This saved the Germans the need to send troops from the west. The Russians, however, defeated the Austrians in Galicia and the Serbs reoccupied Belgrade.

In general, the first two months of the war had not developed as the German High Command had planned. The quick victory in the west had not been obtained.

Turkey and Bulgaria join Germany

A serious development for the western allies was the *entry of Turkey into the war* on the side of Germany, November, 1914. Bulgaria also joined Germany in 1915. (This was counteracted to a certain extent by Italy joining Britain and France in 1915 on being promised the Tyrol and Trentino.) Turkey had a population of 21,000,000 and controlled most of the Middle East. Turkey could also open the Dardanelles to warships operating against Russia in the Black Sea.

The Naval War in 1914—Falkland Islands

Britain's naval superiority told in her favour. The navy won the **Battle of the Falkland Islands** in **December, 1914,** and soon all German warships outside German ports had been eliminated except the lone raider, the warship **'Emden'.** The Japanese occupied the German Far Eastern port of Kiauchau. The main results were to isolate the German colonies, most of which were quickly over-run. The transfer of Allied troops and supplies to the Western Front went on without hindrance.

The Year 1915—Ypres and Gallipoli

The year 1915 was one of stalemate, accompanied by colossal casualties on both sides. In March a British attack at **Neuve Chapelle** came to nothing. In April, the German attack at **Ypres,** aided by *poison gas,* also came to a halt after some headway. This situation led to the replacement of Joffre, and also of Sir John French by **General Haig.**

The Germans revived their 1914 policy in reverse and attempted to defeat Russia before again turning west. Under **Hindenburg** and **Mackensen,** they won the **Battle of the Masurian Lakes** in February, **1915,** drove the Russians out of Galicia, Lithuania and Courland and captured Warsaw. It was those successes which brought Bulgaria into the war on the side of Germany. Although the Russians had lost nearly 2,000,000 men killed, wounded or captured, they were still in the war.

Allied failures on both the western and eastern fronts gave rise in Britain to a demand, voiced strongly by **Lloyd George,** Chancellor of the Exchequer, and by **Winston Churchill,** First Lord of the Admiralty, for action against Turkey. The aim was to defeat Turkey, gain the alliance of the Balkan states, and open the Dardanelles to allied shipping in order to aid Russia in the Black Sea. The plan had merit, but was badly executed. In March the British and French fleets attempted to run through the Dardanelles, but suffered disaster from Turkish shore batteries. This gave the Turks time to reinforce their defences, and when the **Anzacs** under **General Sir Ian Hamilton** landed on the **Gallipoli** peninsula they were immediately tied down. The same fate befell the landing at **Suvla Bay** in August, **1915.** After heavy casualties and appalling general conditions, the whole force was evacuated in December–January, 1915–1916.

The Year 1916—Siege of Verdun, Battles of the Somme and Jutland

Both sides now developed new weapons and methods. Poison gas, *aerial bombardment* and *the tank* (first used by the British) now became integral parts of the war effort. In Britain *conscription* was introduced, for the old armies of 1914 and 1915 had been destroyed. Lloyd George replaced **Asquith** as Prime Minister.

The year 1916 on the western front saw the siege of **Verdun** and the **Battle of the Somme.** The Germans decided to concentrate their main attack against Verdun, the fortress which was the hub of the French defensive system on the western front. By drawing the French forces into Verdun and destroying them they hoped eventually to break through to victory. The French under Pétain held Verdun for six months, and this gave time for the British to strengthen their forces considerably. Verdun was a great defensive victory for the French.

The Battle of the Somme, launched by the Allies, was, however, a ghastly failure. 60,000 men were lost on the first day of the offensive, July 1st. By October the British had suffered 450,000 casualties, the French 340,000 and the Germans 530,000. The Germans were now compelled to dig and to build a great defensive system which became known as the **Hindenburg line.**

At sea the **Battle of Jutland** took place on May 31st, **1916,** between the British Fleet under **Jellicoe** and the German Grand Fleet under **von Speer** which emerged from Kiel. Although the German fleet inflicted more damage than it received, it made for harbour and remained there during the rest of the war. The naval supremacy of Britain, although severely challenged, was thus maintained.

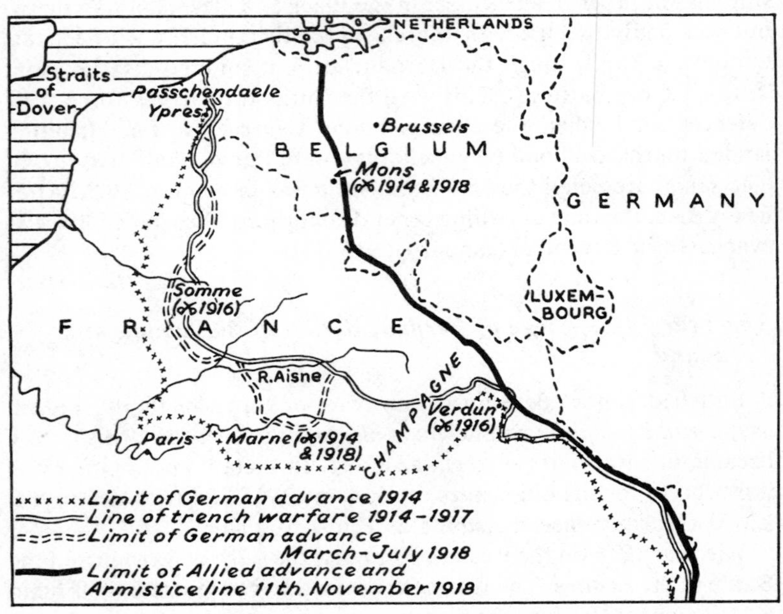

MAIN AREA OF WAR ON THE WESTERN FRONT, 1914–1918

The War in 1917—the Russian Revolution

The war in the west continued much as before. A British offensive at **Arras** was held by the Germans, although **Vimy Ridge,** in the

Hindenburg line, was captured. A French offensive launched by General **Nivelle** against the Hindenburg line also failed and suffered enormous casualties. Unrest developed in the French army, and Nivelle was replaced by **Pétain.** The British offensive at **Passchendaele** (July–December) was based on a preliminary bombardment of such intensity that the ground became unmanageable, and in the miry conditions produced, the offensive became bogged down, at a cost of 300,000 British casualties. General Haig was heavily criticized for the conduct of the battle. Despondency now affected the morale of the British forces. *The Revolution in Russia took that country out of the war.* Further British attacks with tanks at Ypres and Cambrai also failed, while in Italy the Austrians won the **Battle of Caporetto.** Allied forces had to be moved from the western front to assist the Italians.

The United States enters the War

The war at sea produced a most menacing situation for the Allies. The Germans now made a determined effort to starve Britain out before the British naval blockade starved Germany. *The U-boat menace* grew speedily. In May, **1915,** the **'Lusitania'** had been sunk off Ireland, and among the victims were over 100 American passengers. In March, **1916,** the **'Sussex'** was sunk, and this also carried American passengers. In 1917 the Germans began *unrestricted submarine warfare*, and any vessels trading with Britain were liable to be sunk without warning. In 1917 Britain lost 2,000,000 tons more of shipping than were constructed. The effect of the German offensive was *to bring America into the war* under **President Wilson,** and in Britain, Lloyd George introduced a rationing system and also a convoy system to protect shipping. Armed trawlers and Q-boats, disguised to look like ordinary traders, began to take effective toll of the German submarines. In general, the year 1917 had been the blackest for the Allies so far.

The Year 1918—the last German Offensive

The first campaigns of the British in the Middle East against the Turks in 1914–1915 had been utterly disastrous. But in **1917 T. E. Lawrence** had succeeded in arousing Arab revolt against the Turks, and **General Allenby's** forces entered Jerusalem in December, **1917.** This was an important allied gain, but on the western front the year 1918 began as gloomily as any other. The German High Command decided to strike before substantial American forces could arrive. From March to July their offensive along the whole front took them once again within striking distance of Paris (40 miles). But their casualties had been about 500,000; they were exhausted by their efforts and serious lack of food, and could not press home the advantage. The 'flu epidemic of 1918 also struck them rather more violently than it did the Allies. 700,000 American troops arrived in June, and **Marshal Foch,** now Supreme Allied Commander, began a number of partial offensives. The British under Haig, using masses of tanks, drove well into the Hindenburg line. In September, the partial offensives were converted into a general offensive, in which the Americans played a most important part in the **Argonnes** forest. In the Balkans the British forces at **Salonica** took the offensive against Bulgaria, which was knocked out of the war, and the Austrians also capitulated. *Mutinies occurred in the German navy* at Kiel and in *the Germany army.* President Wilson had already acquainted Germany with the famous **Fourteen Points.** Germany accepted an armistice on **November 11th, 1918,** and Kaiser William II fled to Holland.

Some Reasons for the German Defeat

The following points should be considered:

1. Much depended for Germany on quick victory. Her defeat at the Marne in 1914 was a serious setback at the start. The change of direction of her main attack (see p. 131) seems to have proved an error.

2. Despite her eventual abandonment of the war, Russia remained in it far longer than the Germans expected.

3. British naval control of the seas in the first two years maintained her own food supplies and at the same time removed all contact between Germany and her colonies. The naval blockade of Germany produced a much more serious food situation for Germany than for the Allies. This, in part, accounted for the exhaustion of her last great offensive in 1918. British naval supremacy also made it easy for Britain to open a new front in the Middle East.

4. British control of the Mediterranean was further enhanced by the fact that Italy joined the Allies in 1915.

5. The German gamble of unrestricted submarine warfare brought America into the war.

6. The 'ramshackle Empire' of Austria, with its many discontented nationalities, proved only a partially effective ally for Germany. The early Austrian defeats by the Russians were a considerable setback for Germany, and German troops had to be used to strengthen the Austrian front. British imperial unity contrasted very favourably with this.

7. The German invasion of Belgium was used to end doubts in Britain and to bring Britain in on the side of France. The invasion was a mistake, based on military considerations rather than political ones.

Dates

1914 **Battle of Mons.**
First Battle of the Marne.
Russians defeated at Tannenberg.
Russians defeat Austrians in Galicia.
Turkey joins Germany.
Battle of the Falkland Islands.
1915 **Battle of Neuve Chapelle.**
German attack at Ypres.
Russians defeated in Battle of the Masurian Lakes.
Dardanelles Campaign.
1916 **Lloyd George British Prime Minister.**
Conscription in Britain.
Siege of Verdun.
Battle of the Somme.
Battle of Jutland.
1917 **Vimy Ridge captured.**
Battle of Passchendaele.
Revolution in Russia.
Battle of Ypres.
Battle of Cambrai.
Battle of Caporetto.

Unrestricted submarine warfare by Germany.
U.S.A. enters the war.
1918 **Turks defeated in Middle East.**
Second Battle of the Marne.
British campaign from Salonica—Bulgaria out of war.
700,000 American troops arrive.
Austria capitulates.
Allied counter-offensive on western front.
Naval revolt at Kiel.
November 11th, Armistice.

QUESTIONS

1. *Why did Germany fail to win the war by 1916?*

2. *What were the main reasons for Germany's defeat?*

3. *Write notes on* **four** *of the following:* (a) *the Schlieffen Plan;* (b) *Gallipoli;* (c) *the 'Lusitania';* (d) *Passchendaele;* (e) *the Battle of Jutland.*

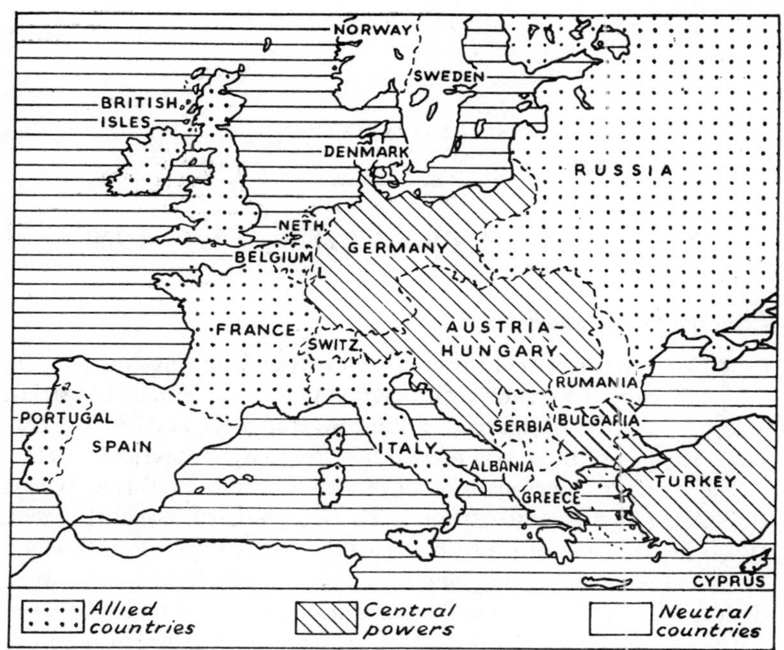

Above: EUROPE, 1914–1918 *Below:* EUROPE, 1919–1923

CHAPTER SIXTEEN

THE PEACE TREATIES, 1919–1920

Principal Personalities

THE peace settlement consisted of the following treaties: the Treaty of **Versailles** with Germany, of **St. Germain** (Austria), of **Neuilly** (Bulgaria), of **Trianon** (Hungary), and **Sèvres** (Turkey). The last of these was revised by the **Treaty of Lausanne, 1923.**

The principal personalities at Versailles were **President Wilson** (U.S.A.), **Lloyd George** (Britain) and **Georges Clemenceau** (France). Wilson wished the peace to be based on the Fourteen Points which he had already elaborated, and which included the demand for open diplomacy; freedom of the seas; abolition of tariff barriers between nations; and the establishment of an international organization to guarantee peace. Clemenceau's main consideration was *the safety of France* and his attitude towards Germany was extremely severe. Lloyd George attempted to achieve *a middle course* between Wilson's idealism and Clemenceau's anti-German attitudes. The main decisions were arrived at by the *Council of Ten*, and these were then ratified by the whole Conference.

Germany

Clemenceau demanded a French frontier on the Rhine. Lloyd George and Wilson opposed this, but the **Saar** was put under international control for 15 years and then a plebiscite was to be held to decide its future. Germany lost all her colonies, was declared guilty of provoking the war, and was to pay £6,500,000,000 in reparations by instalments in money and kind. **Alsace-Lorraine** was returned to France. Germany was permitted an army of only 100,000, no air force, no submarines and only six second-class battleships. She lost the Danish part of **Schleswig to Denmark, Danzig** became a **Free City** under the **League of Nations.** The industrial part of **Upper Silesia** went to **Poland,** as also did the province of **Posen.** Poland was now given a land corridor running to the sea, *thus dividing East Prussia from the remainder of Germany.* The Rhineland was demilitarized in deference to French demands for security.

Eastern Europe

Austria was reduced to a country of 6,500,000 people only, with the capital, Vienna, containing one-third of these. Italy gained Istria (which was mainly Italian), while Austria lost Bosnia, Herzegovina and Dalmatia to the new state of **Yugoslavia,** whose centre was the old kingdom of Serbia. Austrian Bohemia and Moravia were now incorporated in the new state of **Czechoslovakia,** while Austrian **Galicia** went to **Poland.** Hungary lost **Croatia** to Yugoslavia. Turkey retained Constantinople and a narrow strip of territory to the north of the Sea of Marmora. Turkish **Thrace** went to Greece, and Rumania received **Transylvania, Bukowina** and **Bessarabia.** In northern Europe the new Baltic states of **Latvia, Estonia** and **Lithuania** were formed from the old Russian Empire. Finland gained complete independence. The Turkish Empire in Asia also gave way to **Arab states,** some under a League of Nations mandate.

These arrangements were the results of the *break-up of the old empires of Germany, Austria, Russia and Turkey.* In the main the principle of natural boundaries according to language, race and general culture were reasonably adhered to in the formation of the new states. But there were faults leading to future trouble.

General Criticism

In Russia, civil war had broken out between the Whites (anti-revolutionaries) and the Bolsheviks. The Whites refused an invitation to Versailles, but Wilson would not accept a Bolshevik deputation. This *absence of any contact with Russia* was bad and was to have an adverse effect on the future.

The idea of truly national frontiers was not entirely carried out, e.g. Italy gained the Lower Tyrol, containing 250,000 Germans. In Poland there were 10,000,000 who were not Poles, including 2,500,000 Germans. This presented opportunities of anti-Polish propaganda in the later Nazi period in Germany.

In regard to Czechoslovakia, it could be argued that to leave a large German population in the **Sudeten** area was asking for future trouble with Germany, which arose in the time of Hitler. But the Sudeten Mountains gave Czechoslovakia a much more defendable frontier and the Sudeten Germans were of great importance industrially to the new state. On the other hand, the Treaty of Trianon, which settled the frontiers of Hungary, transferred half a million Hungarians to Czechoslovakia, included in Slovakia itself. Later Hitler was able to play off this minority against the Czech majority and after the conquest of Czechoslovakia he was able to form a puppet state in Slovakia.

Austria was left as a German-speaking state, excluded from Germany. She was economically unbalanced, having a great capital in the midst of a mainly agricultural country. In later years Austria became dependent on foreign states for support and became a victim of the Nazi take-over under Hitler. Austrian instability was the cause of constant intrigue in eastern Europe. The reparation clauses were unrealistic. Germany could not pay and this was to create great international tension in the future.

Wilson's Fourteen Points and the Extent to which they were Carried Out at Versailles

1. All negotiations between states to be conducted openly.

(This was not carried out even at the Conference itself.)

2. Absolute freedom of navigation in both peace and war, except in territorial waters.

(Lloyd George refused to accept this. Britain's own maritime and naval interests counted here.)

3. Abolition of tariff barriers between nations.

(Discussed at the Conference, but tariffs became a regular feature of the new national states created.)

4. Nations to agree to disarm to the 'lowest point consistent with domestic safety'.

(Nothing came of it. The point was disregarded at the Conference.)

5. Interests of the colonial peoples, placed under mandates, should be regarded as equal to those of the mandatory power.

(Partially applied under the mandates system, but most mandates continued to be ruled essentially in the interests of the mandatory powers. Trouble quickly developed (see p. 144).)

6. Evacuation of all Russian territory and assistance to be given to Russia.

(The outbreak of war between the Bolsheviks and the Whites led to difficulties here. The United States herself became one of the states intervening against the Bolshevik government of Lenin.)

7. Belgium to be completely liberated.

(This was accepted.)

8. France to receive back Alsace-Lorraine.

(Accepted.)

9. Italy to receive her proper national frontiers.

(Not entirely carried out—for example, Italy gained the Lower Tyrol having 250,000 Germans and the Istrian Peninsula containing 400,000 Yugoslavs.)

10. Peoples of Austria-Hungary to be given the opportunity of an independent existence.

(This was carried out in the main.)

11. Rumania, Serbia and Montenegro to be evacuated and Serbia to be given access to the sea.

(The creation of Yugoslavia ensured that this was done.)

12. Peoples under Turkish rule to be independent and the Dardnelles to be open to all nations.

(This was arranged.)

13. An independent Poland to be created, inhabited by 'indisputably Polish populations'.

(Not really carried out. 10,000,000 non-Poles in Poland.)

14. An international organization to be formed to guarantee the independence of all states.

(**The League of Nations** was the outcome, incorporated in the Treaty of Versailles.)

The League of Nations

Wilson's idea was achieved and a new international organization established (as part of the Versailles Peace) to maintain world peace.

The League of Nations had its headquarters in Geneva. It comprised a Council and an Assembly. The Council consisted of representatives of five major powers and four lesser ones. The Council was to meet at least once a year. The Assembly consisted of representatives of all member states.

The *Covenant of the League* bound its members 'not to resort to war' to settle disputes, to accept the rules of international law as operated by the **International Court at The Hague,** to respect treaties and to publish them, to do everything they could to improve labour and social conditions in their territories. The most important clause was *Article XVI*—the *Sanctions clause.* By this clause economic and, if necessary, military action was to be taken against any member committing aggression. A little later an **International Labour Organization (ILO)** was set up to secure international agreements on wages, conditions of labour and general social conditions.

The Covenant set up the *Mandates* system for the control of the colonies of the defeated states. Rather than return to the old colonial system, the colonies were entrusted to the supervision of various mandatory powers who were expected to govern them with the interests of the people as the primary objective. The mandatory powers were answerable to the League.

The mandatory system worked reasonably well in the former African colonies of Germany, but there were many difficulties. In Syria the French were regarded as mere colonialists and there was great national opposition. Britain also soon abandoned her mandate over Iraq. The British mandate in Palestine was opposed by the new Arab states which had been created as the result of British promises in the era of Lawrence of Arabia. The mandates over Turkish territory in the Near East (held by Britain, France and Italy) had to be abandoned by 1923.

The general effectiveness or otherwise of the League will be dealt with in the notes on developments in the years 1919–1939.

Modern Turkey and the Treaty of Sèvres, 1920

By the Treaty of Sèvres, 1920, Turkey in Asia was divided into allied spheres of influence. **Smyrna (Izmir),** which was assigned to the Greeks, was an early centre of disturbance, when the Greeks began a violent persecution of the Turkish inhabitants. As a result of these events, **Mustapha Kemal** came to the fore as the leader of the new Nationalist Party to oppose the Sèvres treaty. **Ankara** was proclaimed the new capital, the Sultan deposed, and Kemal became **President** of the **Turkish Republic.** Smyrna was recaptured, and when Kemal's forces faced the British at **Chanak,** Britain decided to abandon the Treaty of Sèvres. The French and Italians followed suit, and by the *Treaty of Lausanne, 1923,* Turkey regained control of Asia Minor and **Istanbul** (Constantinople).

Mustapha Kemal *radically changed life in Turkey*—women were accorded the vote in 1929, and encouraged to take part in public life, the fez was abandoned, the alphabet westernized and a system of state schools established.

In respect of Turkey the peace settlement of 1920 proved unwise and unworkable and was the first arrangement to be overthrown.

Summary

The Versailles settlement was an honest attempt to settle European problems on the basis of the rights of peoples to self-determination, as urged by President Wilson. Perfection could not be expected, and the principle was not altogether carried out—a number of 'minority' problems were, in fact, created. The severe attitude to Germany has been criticized, but the fears of France can well be understood. The creation of the League of Nations was a great advance, unfortunately weakened by the rejection of Wilson in the U.S.A. who refused to guarantee the peace treaties or enter the League.

QUESTIONS

1. What criticisms can be made of the Versailles settlement?

2. Describe the aims and organization of the League of Nations.

3. Write notes on four of the following: (a) *Wilson's Fourteen Points;* (b) *the Polish Corridor;* (c) *the Treaty of Sèvres;* (d) *the Mandates system;* (e) *Austria after 1919.*

CHAPTER SEVENTEEN

RUSSIA, 1914–1939

THE Great War was disastrous for Russia. To make matters worse the Czar Nicholas II came under the strange influence of the monk **Rasputin,** who advised him on many state matters. Rasputin was murdered by plotters in 1916 in the hope that this would improve Russia's position in the war and her political and social condition at home. But little improvement resulted, and casualties at the front mounted through inadequate supplies of arms, and poor leadership.

Revolution of February, 1917

Scarcity of food, unemployment and huge casualties at the front led to a *general strike in Petrograd*, and the Czar's Cossack regiments proved unreliable. *Workers' Committees or Soviets* were set up with the inclusion of soldier representatives. The Russian Duma refused to end its session as the Czar demanded, and on March 15th, 1917, he abdicated.

A Provisional Government was now formed by the Duma under **Prince Lvov,** a Liberal. It decreed freedom of speech, the right to strike, and released political prisoners. It arranged for a Constituent Assembly to be elected to organise a democratic parliamentary system for Russia.

However, the **Petrograd Soviet** continued its activities parallel with the Duma and the Provisional Government. It declared its own control of the armed forces in the capital, and demanded the acceptance of the Provisional Government's actions only if approved by the Soviet.

The government of Lvov decided to continue the war and attempt to honour its commitments to its allies. But casualties against the Germans continued on an enormous scale, widespread desertion took place and *soldiers' councils* were formed at the front.

The Bolsheviks demanded an end to the war at all costs. **Kerensky** (a Social Revolutionary) was now Minister of War, and Bolshevik propaganda was directed violently against him.

The Return of Lenin, April, 1917

Lenin returned from his exile in Switzerland, a journey facilitated by the Germans to get Russia out of the war, and arrived in Petrograd on April 16th, 1917. At this time both **Stalin** and **Trotsky** had returned from exile. Lenin demanded an end to the war and the seizure of power by the Soviets. However, a workers' rising in July was a failure, Stalin and Trotsky were both arrested, and Lenin fled in disguise to Finland.

Kerensky became Prime Minister in July, but a new offensive at the front proved a failure. Much more widespread unrest now developed. **General Kornilov,** Russian Supreme Commander, now began to move troops towards Moscow and Petrograd to prevent a revolution. The Bolsheviks (Lenin had now returned from Finland) decided to move first, and Trotsky was appointed chairman of the *Revolutionary Committee.* On November 6th (or October under the old calendar) the forces under the control of the Petrograd Soviet seized with comparative ease all key points in the city. In Moscow similar action took place and the Soviets achieved success after about a week's fighting against troops loyal to the Provisional Government.

A Bolshevik government was now formed under Lenin, and Trotsky became Commissar for Foreign Affairs. The second or **October Revolution** (the 'proletarian' revolution) had succeeded in its first stages.

Reasons for the Bolshevik Success

The Bolshevik Party, which numbered probably not more than 60,000 members throughout Russia, had evolved *a highly efficient and disciplined organization* of devoted activists. By 1905 the Bolshevik (majority) of the Russian Social Democratic Labour Party had won its ideological battle against the Mensheviks (minority). This victory meant highly centralized control of the party machine and the rejection of the idea of a loosely democratic party of the western type with large numbers of non-active members. The Bolsheviks were aided by the great mistakes of their opponents, the worst of which was the attempt to continue the war in hopeless circumstances. Kerensky, the very symbol to masses of workers of the ineffective 'bourgeois' approach to the problems of the hour, was rapidly discredited by Bolshevik propaganda and he also failed to settle the land problem. Another important factor to be considered is the broader historical one of the real failure of attempts to introduce a western parliamentary system since 1905. This helped to open the way to the 'proletarian' revolution. Lenin also stressed the *international nature of the revolution* and prophesied the spread of revolution which would prevent the isolation of the Russian movement.

Bolshevik Rule, 1918–1927

In peace negotiations with the Germans, Trotsky refused their demands, but Lenin insisted on the acceptance of the terms laid down by the **Treaty of Brest-Litovsk, March, 1918.** Russia lost nearly one-third of her population, nine-tenths of her coal production, and the Ukraine became independent, but was really under German control. Finland also gained her complete independence.

The Social Revolutionaries were opposed to *peace at any price*, and they also encouraged a number of peasant risings to oppose the Communist agents in the countryside. Lenin himself was wounded by a would-be assassin. Bolshevik control now became more severe, and the secret police, the **Cheka,** was enlarged. *The Social Revolutionary Party was now suppressed.* In July, **1918,** the Czar and his family, held prisoners at **Ekaterinburg,** were murdered. Intervention by foreign powers against the Bolsheviks now began. Britain, America, France, Poland and Japan sent forces against the Bolsheviks, the British occupying Archangel, as well as parts of the Trans-Siberian Railway. The Russian Whites were now under the command of **Admiral Kolchak.**

Allied intervention failed. After two years, Kolchak was captured by the Red Army and shot. Other interventionist forces were withdrawn, partly on account of labour opposition in their own countries. A serious mutiny also broke out in the French navy in the Black Sea. Léon Trotsky had proved a most effective organizer of the new Red Army, while the Whites made themselves unpopular by their ruthless requisitioning of the peasants' food supplies.

The new Polish National Government also sent its troops into the Ukraine and occupied Kiev. The Red Army drove them back and marched on Warsaw. At this point, **Pilsudski,** the Polish commander, received western help in the form of arms, and defeated the Red Army. Lenin was then compelled to make the **Treaty of Riga** with Poland by which 4,000,000 Russians and Ukrainians came under Polish rule. This peace between Poland and Russia ended all hopes the Whites had of success.

Internal Development of Russia

Until the changes of 1936, the main national assembly was the *Congress of Soviets,* consisting of delegates from the local Soviets throughout Russia. The main work of government was carried out under the close direction of the Communist Party, and the Congress in the main was expected to accept the decisions of the central planners. After the Civil War foreign aid was obtained, and American, German and British experts were called in for advice on the great technical problems facing a devastated country.

Lenin faced great difficulties. A mutiny broke out among the sailors at **Kronstadt,** while the *kulaks* murdered Communist agents in the countryside. Lenin produced what became known as the *New Economic Policy* (*NEP*). This was essentially a temporary compromise with Capitalism and private ownership. (1) A grain tax was substituted for the forced requisitioning of food from the peasants to supply the needs of the towns. (2) Peasants were allowed to sell a portion of their produce on the free market. (3) Small-scale industry and trade was allowed to function for private profit. (4) The major industries—coal, steel, railways, etc.—were controlled by the Soviets—in other words, were nationalized. To secure the acceptance of this policy Lenin had to fight strongly against the more rigid Communists who demanded immediate socialism. He regarded the NEP as the most effective way of getting the country's economy working again.

On the death of Lenin in January, 1924—a great blow to Russia and world Communism—Joseph Stalin kept *the key position of Secretary of the Russian Communist Party*, which he had occupied since 1922.

Stalin v. *Trotsky*

Differences developed between Stalin and Trotsky on the future of Communism. Trotsky regarded Russia as the springboard for world revolution—the theory of *permanent revolution.* Stalin advocated the achievement of *socialism in one country* alone as the immediate task. These differences led to violent controversy within the Communist Party, and Stalin won the day. In 1927 several of Trotsky's supporters were expelled from the Party and he himself was banished to Turkestan, and later from Russia. From abroad in Mexico he continued his criticism of Stalin's aims and methods until assassinated there in 1940.

The Five-year Plans

With Trotsky defeated, Stalin's path was cleared. His aims were: (1) the rapid building of heavy industry in Russia as the first priority; (2) the collectivization of agriculture and the ending of individual peasant farming. This involved the production and application of great quantities of agricultural machinery.

The *First Five-year Plan* of *1927* laid down production targets to which most luxuries of life were to be sacrificed. The greatest trouble occurred with the peasants under 'kulak' control. Strife and murder broke out in the countryside, there was loss of production and widespread starvation. Stalin was forced to slow down the pace of collectivization. But by 1939 the collective farm or *kolkhoz* had become the dominant feature of the countryside, with peasant ownership of small private plots also allowed. There existed also an adequate supply of tractors.

Industrial production increased rapidly. Magnitogorsk and Stalingrad grew into huge new industrial centres, and the great **Dnieper Dam** began the electrification of Russia—one of Lenin's economic aims. The Moscow-Volga Canal was also completed. In 1938 coal production was four times that of 1913 and steel production six times. *In 1937 Russia was the largest producer of agricultural machinery in the world*—and it was possible in 1935 to end the food rationing which had existed since the Revolution. Electric power was nearly forty times greater than in 1913. This development was ruthlessly pushed forward by Stalin—Magnitogorsk was built by a combination of ardent Communists and convicted kulaks, saboteurs and peasants, in the harshest conditions of life. By 1939 (the second year of the Third Five-year Plan) the main aims of Stalin had been achieved.

Political Developments under Stalin

In 1936 a Soviet Parliament was established for the first time, with a separate House to represent the nationalities. The vote by secret ballot was introduced for all over eighteen. Party and non-party candidates were permitted.

Although no other parties than the Communist were allowed to exist, internal tensions developed after 1934, when **Kirov,** a leading Communist, was assassinated. As the result of investigations, an opposition group was discovered and a widespread **purge** of those suspected of anti-Stalinism was undertaken. Plots were unearthed in the army, and leading men were executed or sent to the forced labour camp at Vorkhuta in the north. These purges extended over the years 1934–1938. By 1939 Stalin had removed most of the 'Old Guard' of the 1917 revolution. Conditions of terror existed, and Stalin achieved an almost complete personal dictatorship. There was rigid control of the press, of the arts (where *Socialist realism* was alone tolerated in respect of new works and the interpretation of old ones) and of social life in general. The origins and nature of these policies have been the subject of constant controversy and investigation since, and in recent years have been *denounced in the Soviet Union itself.*

Summary

The disaster of Russia in the Great War produced a situation in which the highly disciplined and effective Bolshevik Party could seize power. The policy pursued by Lvov and Kerensky of continuing Russian participation in the war proved a disastrous failure. Foreign intervention in support of the Whites also proved a disaster and increased labour sympathy in the West for the Revolution. Lenin's NEP proved effective in improving food supplies and in gradually reviving industrial production. With the exile of Trotsky, Stalin proceeded on the lines of Socialism in one country, and the Five-year Plans, commenced in 1927, were carried through with a ruthless determination which rapidly increased industrial production. Great difficulties were encountered in the countryside, but early mistakes were corrected (after widespread suffering), and by 1939 the economic position of Russia was strong. The pre-war 'purges' led to a rigid social system in which terror played a part and much injustice and suffering were caused. However, by 1939 Russia was a great industrial power, her strength as a state was increasing, and has rapidly increased since.

Dates

1917

February **First (or 'bourgeois') Revolution.**
Petrograd Soviet established.
April **Lenin returns to Russia.**
July **Kerensky Prime Minister.**
October **Bolshevik (or 'proletarian') Revolution.**

1918

March **Treaty of Brest-Litovsk.**
July **Czar and his family assassinated.**
1918–22 **Failure of Allied intervention against the Revolution.**
1923 **New Economic Policy.**
1924 **Death of Lenin.**
1927 **Exile of Trotsky.**
First Five-year Plan.
1936 **New Constitution.**
1937 **Pre-war purges reach their peak.**

QUESTIONS

1. What were the main reasons for Bolshevik success in 1917?

2. What were the main lines of Lenin's internal and foreign policies?

3. What were the main reasons for the conflict between Stalin and Trotsky?

4. What can be said for and against Stalin's policies in the 1930's?

CHAPTER EIGHTEEN

GERMANY AND ITALY, 1919–1935

Germany

IN 1918 workers and soldiers' councils (soviets) were widely created. It seemed that events in Germany might well follow the Russian pattern. But the Socialist Chancellor, **Ebert,** and the Minister of the Interior, **Noske,** continued to work with the old imperial officials. The German Officers' Corps, the Free Corps, was also allowed to function. The Socialist leaders in Germany were prepared to use the Free Corps against Communism.

In June, 1919, the **Spartacists,** the leading Communist movement in Berlin, attempted to seize control of the city, under the leadership of **Karl Liebknecht** and **Rosa Luxemburg.** The Free Corps was called in to suppress the attempted Communist revolution, and both Karl Liebknecht and Rosa Luxemburg were murdered. The Socialist government had used the Kaiser's officer corps to suppress the Communists. This was the beginning of that post-war division between Socialists and Communists which prevented their union against Hitler.

The Weimar Republic

A German parliament was now elected by manhood suffrage. The largest party was the **Social Democrats** (Socialists), but the **Nationalists** (representing the Prussian junkers and sections of big industry) returned 42 members. Thus the old forces favouring militarism and dictatorship were still much alive and were later to join forces with Hitler.

The new German constitution was far more democratic than that of Bismarck and the Kaiser. The Chancellor and the government were now completely accountable to the **Reichstag.** The latter at last gained *complete control over taxation.* The Upper House or **Reichsrat,** representing the German states, could not delay any laws which had a two-thirds majority in the Reichstag. However, the President's powers were considerable and (as was shown in the case of Hitler) could be dangerous to liberty. He could dissolve the Reichstag, order new elections, and could use the armed forces to restore law and order. The **Weimar Republic** (so named after the town where the national assembly formulated the new constitution) had an uncertain start. Attempts to overthrow it continued for some years. Communist risings occurred in the Ruhr and at Munich. These were suppressed by armed force on the orders of President Ebert. Then the Free Corps attempted a Right-wing revolution in March, 1920, when they seized control of Berlin. This effort was defeated mainly by working-class resistance. But in the elections of 1920 the Nationalists on the Right, and the Communists on the extreme Left, made gains.

General State of Germany

The general condition of Germany was bad. There was widespread unemployment, and the huge Allied demand for reparations led to financial complications. *French forces occupied the Ruhr* to guarantee German payments, and this led to a strike by the German workers supported by their government. German currency lost its value, and everyone suffered, especially the middle and professional classes depending on salaries, interest, insurance and pensions.

Policy of Stresemann, 1923–1929

The situation was partly retrieved by **Stresemann** (People's Party) who was German Foreign Minister in 1923, and Chancellor. The bad social situation had led to Fascist violence in Munich under **Hitler** (see also p. 156) and to strong Communist action in Saxony. Stresemann revalued the German currency and persuaded the French to accept easier reparations payment with the promise to pay more later. The French then withdrew from the Ruhr. He also brought Germany into the League of Nations in 1926. By the **Locarno Treaty of 1925,** he achieved a guarantee of the western frontier of Germany from France, and Franco-German relations greatly improved. By 1929 German industry and employment had greatly revived and the parties of the extreme Right (Nationalists) and Left (Communists) had lost ground. Under the **Dawes Plan** (put forward by the American General Dawes) Stresemann had also negotiated loans from America to assist German recovery and the payment of reparations.

Then in 1929 circumstances took a tragic turn for the worse.

The Great Industrial Depression, 1929–1931, and the Rise of Adolf Hitler

The **Nazi** or **National Socialist Party** was founded in Munich in 1921. Adolf Hitler became its president.

The disturbed state of Germany after the war aided the Nazi movement to a certain extent. Hitler concentrated on denouncing the Versailles Treaty and at the same time used the argument that Germany was not defeated in the Great War but had been *stabbed in the back* by Jews, Communists, Socialists and Pacifists.

Hitler launched a particularly violent attack on Stresemann for his compromise with France and the acceptance of reparations. On November 8th, 1923, Hitler attempted his *Munich 'putsch'* and declared himself President of Germany. This attempt was suppressed and Hitler was sentenced to five years' imprisonment, of which he served only nine months. During his imprisonment he began the writing of the Nazi bible, '**Mein Kampf**' ('My Struggle'), in which, besides the arguments mentioned above, he elaborated the *theory of the superiority of the so-called 'Aryan race'*, of which true Germans were the leading people. This concept of *racial superiority* was used to justify the anti-Jewish policies of the Nazis. It led also to general 'colour prejudice'.

Hitler soon decided that he needed the support of the German army and the big industrialists of Germany. Nevertheless, the Nazis organized their own 'para-military' forces, the **Brownshirts,** under **Captain Roehm.**

Economic Crisis

In 1929 the panic on Wall Street brought world economic crisis, with *mass unemployment affecting all the great states.* By 1931 there were 6,000,000 unemployed in Germany. Hitler now stepped up the campaign against the Versailles Treaty and reparations, and against Jews, Socialists, etc. The **Storm Troopers,** now numbering over 400,000, carried out violent attacks on their political opponents. Hitler gained considerable support from those who feared Communism and genuinely thought that Versailles was the cause of Germany's troubles. In 1932 Hitler polled 11,000,000 votes for the Presidency and the Nazis gained 230 seats in the Reichstag.

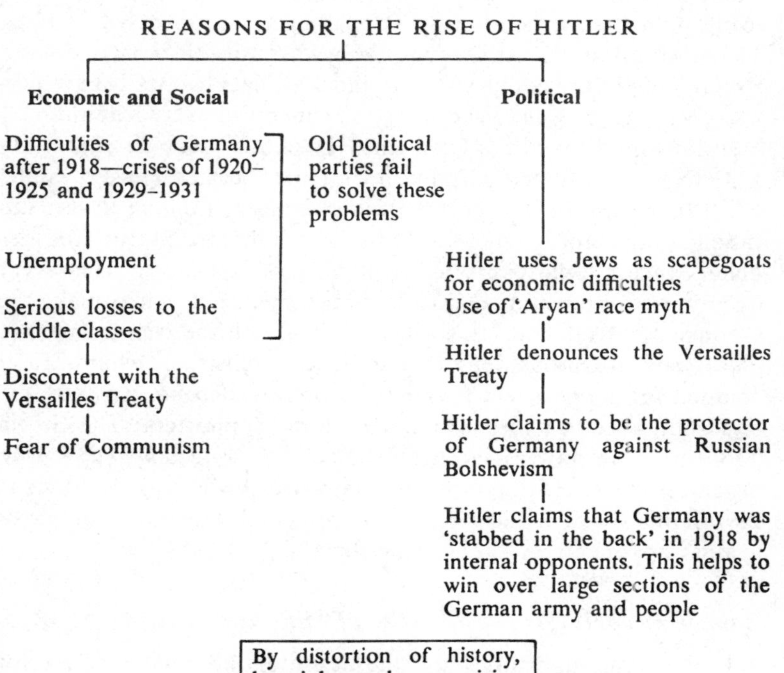

The Reichstag Fire

Hitler was appointed Chancellor by Hindenburg in January, 1933.

On February 27th, 1933, the Reichstag was burnt to the ground and the Communists accused by Hitler of this outrage. Despite a reign of terror the Nazis only gained a bare majority in the elections of March, 1933. Nevertheless, the Reichstag gave Hitler powers to rule for four years without its control. The opposition German parties were declared illegal, many of their leaders imprisoned, and the trade unions similarly treated. **Dr. Goebbels** was appointed Minister of Propaganda, **General Goering** organized the Secret Police or **Gestapo** which was later taken over by **Heinrich Himmler.** *Concentration camps for Nazi opponents* and the Jews were now commenced, and millions were to die in them under conditions of appalling ill-treatment before 1945. The most notorious was **Dachau.** Everywhere the Nazi party dominated the life of the country—every block of flats had its Nazi supervisor, whose task was to check the movements of everyone in it.

In 1934 on the death of President Hindenburg (who had agreed in 1933 to Hitler becoming Chancellor), Hitler became Head of State.

On June 30th, 1934, occurred the *liquidation of Captain Roehm* and the end of the Storm Troopers. Hitler feared that the Storm Troopers under Roehm, who expressed a number of 'socialistic' ideas very openly, would not only control the movement but would make the German army reluctant to throw in its lot with the Nazis. Roehm's ideas were also obnoxious to the big Capitalists on whom Hitler counted for support. On a variety of pretexts Roehm was arrested and shot, together with a number of his supporters. The Storm Troopers were now replaced by the *S.S. or protection squads* who organized the security police and controlled the leading positions in the German army. They were the principal organizers of terror against opponents of the Nazi system.

Some Considerations on the Rise of Hitlerism

1. Economic difficulties and the desire of the middle classes for 'order' and stability played into Hitler's hands.

2. The denunciation of the Versailles Treaty was popular.

3. Hitler claimed to be the protector of Europe against Communism, and this gained him much support from German Capitalists.

4. Hitler was able, in the bewilderment of the times, to create a sense of purpose, especially among the unemployed enrolled in his semi-military organizations under the swastika flag.

5. His preaching of German superiority over other peoples on account of their pure Aryan race (a complete fallacy) was a revival of attitudes which had existed in the Kaiser's Germany and appealed to many Germans.

6. Many army leaders saw in Hitler the means of ending the Versailles Treaty and re-forming a great German army. This process of re-arming went on rapidly after 1934.

7. Hitler's occupation of the Rhineland in 1936 in complete defiance of both the Versailles settlement and the League of Nations strengthened his position in Germany.

8. Germany was not freed in 1919 from the old militaristic cliques and officers who had supported the Kaiser (such as the Free Corps already mentioned). These groups, waiting for a determined lead, finally threw in their lot with Hitler. It was Hindenburg himself who handed over power to Hitler.

9. The Leftist forces in Germany (especially the Communists and Socialists) were deeply divided and were unable effectively to unite against Hitler.

10. Hitler's hysterical oratory exercised a powerful influence over his audiences. It aroused, for Nazi purposes, the utmost violence of emotion, which was a dangerous expression of the frustrations felt by so many Germans after 1919. Hitler convinced millions of Germans by sheer emotion and the use of the 'Aryan myth', that every opponent of the Nazis had something to do with the sufferings of Germany after 1919. This was really a preparation for violence on an international scale.

Italy after 1919: The Rise of Mussolini

In 1919 conditions in Italy were bad—unemployment in the northern cities and peasant poverty in the south. Italy had gained little from the war at a cost of 600,000 casualties. Various extremist movements developed, and in the northern towns Soviets on the Russian and German model were set up under Communist leadership. Against the Socialist and Communist movements Fascism developed.

The name Fascism was derived from the 'fasces' or bundle of rods which symbolized the magistrates' powers in ancient Rome. **Benito Mussolini,** formerly a member of the Italian Socialist Party, became leader of the Milan 'fascio' in 1919. In 1921 the **National Fascist Party** was formed with the blackshirt uniform and the Roman salute. The new party gained 22 seats in Parliament and demanded representation in the government. Much confusion prevailed—a number of parties being evenly balanced and making stable government difficult. On October 28th, 1922, occurred the fascist 'march on Rome', which they entered unopposed. **King Victor Emmanuel III** asked Mussolini to form a government. Neither the army nor the King had opposed Mussolini.

From 1922 to 1925 Mussolini governed in collaboration with some other parties, and his government contained only a minority of outright Fascists. However, fascist violence against their opponents greatly increased during these years. In June, 1924, **Matteotti,** the much-respected leader of the Socialist Party, was murdered by Fascists. Opposition to Mussolini increased as a result of this crime, and demands for his resignation arose on all sides. Mussolini's answer was to intensify the terror against his opponents, who were arrested in their hundreds. Newspapers were closed down and opposition meetings attacked by armed Fascists. The leading figure in this development was **Farinacci,** secretary-general of the National Fascist Party. Mussolini in this way created his dictatorship, and neither the King nor the army opposed him.

In considering the reasons for Mussolini's success in establishing the fascist dictatorship, the following points must be considered:

1. The support he gained from many of the wealthier classes who saw Fascism as a real protection against Socialism and Communism.
2. The monarchy, the army and the police were strongly anti-Socialist and fell readily into line with Mussolini's policies.
3. The difficulties of the Italian parliamentary system played into Mussolini's hands. A variety of conflicting parties, unable to form stable governments, weakened Italian democracy. Mussolini's demands for 'order' and 'discipline' seemed to many Italians a way out of this impasse.
4. **He healed the breach with the Papacy by the Lateran Treaty of 1929 which created the Vatican City State.**

The Corporate State

As in the case of Hitler's Germany, the traditional workers' trade unions were abolished and industries organized in *corporations* in which representatives of workers, employers, the government and fascist party decided matters relating to wages, hours and general conditions of work. Strikes were made illegal, and a government department, the **Ministry of Corporations,** supervised the whole structure.

In 1938 the Italian Parliament was abandoned altogether and the country ruled by representatives of the industrial corporations in an **Assembly of Corporations.**

The idea of the State, with **Il Duce** (the Leader) Mussolini at the summit, now became the dominant line of fascist propaganda, which was organized, as in Germany, by a government department.

The military outlook was encouraged, and schoolchildren, also as in Hitler's Germany, were organized in semi-military formations. Mussolini himself praised warfare as the highest of man's endeavours, while discipline and sacrifice were preached incessantly.

Mussolini's most dangerous opponents were sent to close confinement on the Lipari Islands.

Under Mussolini, Italian industry made considerable progress, and unemployment was eased by public work schemes such as the extensive drainage of swamp land for the improvement of agriculture. The Italians were proud of the fact that at last their 'trains ran on time' and, like Hitler's 'autobahnen', the new system of communications was used to propagate the idea of fascist efficiency.

Summary

Both in Germany and in Italy the post-war period was one of economic crisis and mass unemployment. In these circumstances the parties of the extreme Right and Left made considerable progress. Agitation from both extremes became violent. In Germany there was a period of recovery under Stresemann, but the economic crisis beginning with the Wall Street crash of 1929 ended these stable conditions. Hitler's movement made rapid progress, and Communists and Socialists failed to unite effectively against him.

In Italy the King, the civil service, the police and armed forces, supported by the wealthy, welcomed Mussolini as their protector against Communism and Socialism. In Germany, also, big industry began to support Hitler, and the army gradually threw in its lot with the Nazi movement.

The fascist cult of violence resulted in the complete suppression of opposition both in Germany and Italy, the ending of the independent trade unions, the use of anti-semitism (less in Italy), the creation of the most barbarous institution known to history—the concentration camp—for the extermination under sadistic torture of Jews and opponents of the fascist system.

Dates

1919 **The Weimar Republic established.**
Spartacist movement in Berlin.
1920 **Attempted 'coup' by the Free Corps.**
1921 **National Fascist Party formed in Italy.**
1922 **Fascist 'March on Rome'.**
1923 **French troops occupy the Ruhr.**
Hitler's Munich 'putsch'.
1924 **Murder of Matteotti.**
Mussolini seizes power.
1926 **Stresemann brings Germany into League of Nations.**
1930 **Storm troops organized by Captain Roehm.**
1931 **Six million unemployed in Germany.**
1932 **Hitler polls 11,000,000 votes for President.**
Nazis gain 230 seats in Reichstag.
1933 **Hitler appointed Chancellor by Hindenburg.**
Reichstag fire.
1934 **Roehm and many of his followers liquidated.**

QUESTIONS

1. What was the condition of Germany in the years 1919–1924?

2. What were the aims and achievements of Stresemann?

3. What were the main reasons for the rise to power of Hitler?

4. How do you account for the rise to power of Mussolini?

5. What were the main stages by which Hitler overthrew the Versailles Settlement as it applied to Germany?

CHAPTER NINETEEN

INTERNATIONAL POLITICS, 1919–1939

France and Germany

THE main aims of French policy were to keep Germany in isolation and to exact every ounce of reparations. This policy was typified by **Poincaré,** Prime Minister in 1922. France proceeded to build a *system of alliances surrounding Germany*. She made defensive treaties with Belgium and Poland and encouraged the formation of the *Little Entente* (1920–1923) between Czechoslovakia, Rumania and Yugoslavia. With the 'Little Entente' powers, France made a defensive agreement to maintain the Versailles settlements.

The Reparations Problem

Germany fell behind in her payment of reparations, and in 1923 Poincaré sent French troops to occupy the Ruhr as a guarantee of payment. The German workers went on strike, German industry slumped terribly and the German *mark* became worthless. Stresemann secured the withdrawal of French forces on the promise to pay. The French electors turned out Poincaré in favour of **Aristide Briand** who wished to work with Stresemann for healthier relations between Germany and France.

The League of Nations

The League achieved some important results during the 1920's. (1) It secured loans to Austria to develop her industries. (2) It settled a dispute between Finland and Sweden by which the Aaland Islands went to Finland. (3) It settled the complicated questions of the division of Upper Silesia between Germany and Poland, although the settlement never satisfied the extreme German nationalists. However, until the seizure of the whole of Silesia by Hitler in 1939, the arrangements made for industry and trade worked quite well. (4) A Yugoslav invasion of Albania in 1921 was stopped. (5) The Baltic port of Memel, which had been German before 1914, was placed under Allied control in 1919, but in 1923 Lithuania seized the port and compelled occupying French forces to withdraw. In 1924 the League secured a convention by which Memel was within Lithuanian territory, but had considerable rights of self-government. (6) In 1923 four Italians, who were engaged in settling the frontier between Albania and Greece, were murdered by Greeks. Mussolini bombarded and seized the island of Corfu as a reprisal. The League, working with the Allied Conference of Ambassadors, secured the withdrawal of Italian forces and the payment of compensation by Greece. (7) The League played an important part in settling the frontiers between Turkey and Iraq and the future of the great oil centre of Mosul. It was finally decided that Mosul should be in Iraq during the British mandate over that country, but at the same time important oil revenues went to Turkey. (8) Trouble in October, 1925, when Greek forces moved six miles into Bulgaria, was promptly settled by League envoys sent to the spot, and Greek forces were withdrawn.

Economic and Humanitarian Work of the League

1. It attempted to safeguard the rights of minorities in various countries. This presented great difficulties and was only partly successful.
2. It organized economic aid for both Austria and Hungary.
3. £10,000,000 was given to assist Greek refugees from Asia Minor. The fund was used mainly to assist their settlement on the land in Greece.
4. Similar assistance was rendered to Bulgarian refugees.
5. A strong effort was made to suppress the drug traffic.
6. The League did valuable work in limiting the effects of serious post-war epidemics—especially a serious typhus outbreak in Poland and in Soviet Russia. Special Epidemics Commissions were sent to the affected areas.

The Problem of Aggression

The Corfu incident and others led the League to attempt a clear and generally accepted *definition of aggression.* The **Geneva Protocol of 1924,** approved by the League Assembly, declared as an aggressor any state refusing arbitration and resorting to war.

The Locarno Treaty of 1925 was also important in strengthening the work of the League. By this treaty Britain, France, Italy, Germany and Belgium entered into an agreement to respect the frontiers of Belgium. France, Poland and Czechoslovakia also guaranteed one another against German aggression. Stresemann agreed to arbitration in cases of dispute between Germany and other powers. The Locarno Treaty and the entry of Germany into the League in 1926 greatly strengthened the League's work and standing in the years 1925–1929.

A League resolution of 1927 also led on to the **Kellogg Pact** of **1928,** signed by all the Great Powers (including Russia, still a non-member), renouncing war as an instrument of policy, except in 'self-defence'.

The Weakness of the League of Nations after 1930

As already noted, the economic crisis 1929–1931 aided the rise of the Nazis in Germany. In the Far East, Japan, heavily hit by unemployment, sought new sources of wealth and trade. In 1931, in defiance of all League principles, she attacked China and established the puppet state of **Manchukuo** (Manchuria). The League failed to act against Japan, and this was the real commencement of its decline.

In 1933 Japan, having been condemned over Manchuria, left the League, and in the same year Hitler also withdrew Germany from the League. In 1935, Mussolini launched his attack on Abyssinia. The League then proceeded to impose an embargo on the sale of arms to Italy, but the governments of two of its leading members, Britain and France, then proposed a division of Abyssinia (the **Hoare-Laval** plan) which would have given Italy the greater part. This was seen by many people as 'appeasement' of the worst kind, and further weakened the League, which failed with its economic sanctions to prevent the conquest of Abyssinia. In **1936** Hitler's forces occupied the **Rhineland** in contravention of the Versailles Treaty. Hitler and

Mussolini then established a closer understanding—the **Rome-Berlin Axis.** In 1937 Japan launched another successful attack on China, and by 1940 the **Rome-Berlin-Tokyo Axis** had been established.

The Spanish Civil War, 1936–1939

In **1936 General Franco,** in exile in the Canaries, raised a revolt against the Spanish government which had followed the overthrow of the Spanish monarchy in 1931. With Spanish Moroccan forces he invaded the mainland, but failed to capture Madrid. For two years the Republicans and Franco fought out the struggle, in which the International Brigade supported the Republicans. Russia gave support in the form of arms to the Republicans, and, despite a non-intervention agreement, Italy and to a lesser extent Germany sent forces into Spain to assist Franco. In 1939, the war was won by Franco.

Austria

Hitler demanded the union of Germany and Austria on the grounds that Austria was a Germanic state. The Austrian Nazis gained representation in the Austrian government, and in 1934 the Chancellor of Austria, **Dr. Dollfuss,** was murdered, but there was no Nazi take-over for Mussolini mobilized to prevent it. Successive Austrian Chancellors resisted Hitler's demands until 1938. By this time Mussolini had abandoned the understanding arrived at with Britain and France at Stresa (the Stresa front) in 1935, and he had thrown in his lot with Hitler. In March, 1938, German troops moved into Austria and, greeted by large numbers of the population, established their own government which controlled the country until 1945. Once again, aggression had been successful and neither the League nor the great powers made any other than verbal resistance.

Czechoslovakia

The **Sudetenland** contained a mainly German population of about 3,000,000. A movement for union with Germany had developed under the local Nazi leader **Henlein.** The Sudeten mountain defences were absolutely vital to Czech security and at the same time there was a strong national desire to resist German threats. In 1934 Russia and France had signed a treaty of mutual aid, while Russia also had a treaty with the Czechs. Russia, however, would not act to defend Czechoslovakia without action by France as well. In 1938 Hitler's propaganda pressure against Czechoslovakia was intensified, with violent attacks on the President, **Dr. Benesh.** War seemed imminent.

At this point occurred the notorious **Munich Agreement** of **September, 1938,** by which **Neville Chamberlain** for Britain, **Daladier** for France, and Hitler and Mussolini agreed to the German occupation of the Sudetenland. Hitler assured Chamberlain and Daladier that he had no further territorial claims to make. The non-fascist powers were completely deceived and the Czech people were betrayed. The German army now entered the Sudetenland after Chamberlain had returned to Britain declaring that Munich meant 'peace in our time'. Six months later in March, 1939, the Nazis occupied the whole of Czechoslovakia.

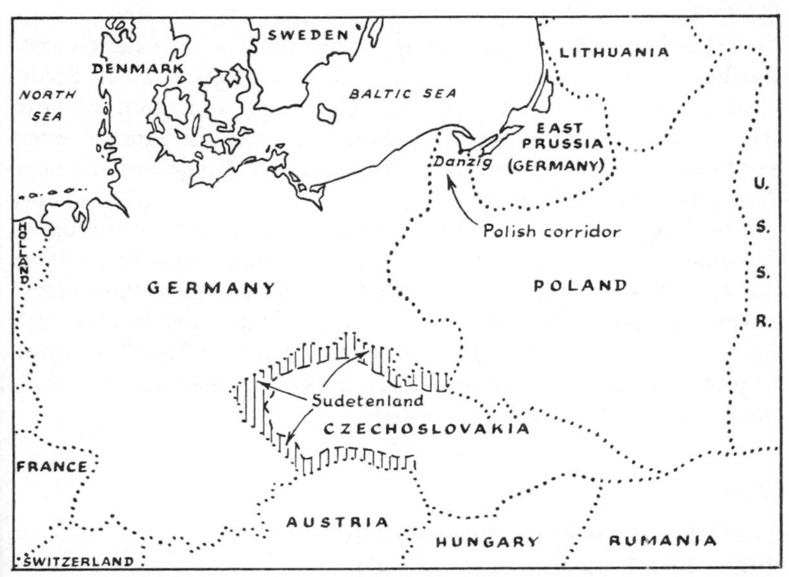

THE SUDETENLAND AND THE POLISH CORRIDOR

Poland

Hitler now intensified the Nazi campaign for the return to Germany of the **Polish Corridor** and **Danzig.** But Britain now signed a defensive treaty with Poland, and France did the same. However, negotiations between Britain and Russia, which had been proceeding for some months, broke down, and at that point Stalin made a treaty with Hitler known as the **Soviet-German Non-Aggression Pact.** On September 1, 1939, German panzer divisions invaded Poland and Warsaw was bombed from the air. On September 3, Britain and France, having received no reply to their demand for a cessation of hostilities, declared war on Germany.

Summary

Relations between France and Germany continued to be strained in the years 1919–1924, but Briand (France) and Stresemann (Germany) achieved a better understanding in the years 1925–1929. After 1929, however, the international situation deteriorated. Japan, Germany and Italy all pursued aggressive policies with success, and the League of Nations scarcely attempted to halt them. In Spain, Franco, with the help of Italy and Germany, won the Civil War. The Japanese made further inroads into China. The gains of international Fascism were very great by 1940, and the Rome-Berlin-Tokyo Axis had been established.

The League of Nations did valuable work immediately after its foundation, its most successful period being 1919–1929, when dangerous disputes were settled, and Germany entered the League. Several important treaties and pacts were signed, and the League's economic and humanitarian work was considerable. The world economic slump beginning in 1929, however, changed the whole international situation for the worse.

Dates

1920 Formation of the 'Little Entente'.
1923 French troops occupy the Ruhr.
The Corfu incident.

1924 The Geneva Protocol.
1925 League stops Greek incursion into Bulgaria.
The Locarno Treaty.
1928 The Kellogg Pact.
1929 World economic crisis begins.
1931 Japanese attack on China.
1935 Mussolini attacks Abyssinia.
1936 Hitler reoccupies the Rhineland.
Spanish Civil War begins.
1937 Second Japanese attack on China.
1938 Hitler occupies Austria.
The Munich Agreement (September).
1939 Franco in control of Spain.
Hitler occupies whole of Czechoslovakia (March).
Soviet-Nazi Pact.
Hitler attacks Poland.
Britain and France declare war on Germany (Sept. 3rd).

QUESTIONS

1. *Describe French foreign policy in the years 1919–1924.*
2. *Explain the work of the League of Nations in the years 1919–1929.*
3. *How would you account for the success of the League up to 1930 and its increasing failure afterwards?*
4. *By what stages of aggression was Hitler successful in the period 1934–1939?*

CHAPTER TWENTY

THE SECOND WORLD WAR, 1939–1945

Poland and Finland

HITLER invaded Poland, September 1st, 1939, and the German panzer divisions swept all before them. Warsaw was bombed, and capitulated on September 27th. Under the terms of the Soviet-German Pact, Russian forces occupied eastern Poland on September 17th.

The *phoney war* period extended from October, 1939, to April, 1940, when the war was almost completely static. The Allies continued their defence preparations, and Commonwealth troops began to arrive in Europe. In the defensive works of the **Maginot Line,** along the north-eastern frontier of France, French troops remained inactive. Stalin, failing to achieve by negotiation the rectification of the Finnish-Russian frontier in order to give further protection to Leningrad, attacked Finland and, after strong resistance from the Finns and the expressed sympathy of the Western powers, succeeded in defeating Finland.

The winter of 1939–1940 was extremely bad, and icy conditions in Europe delayed Hitler's plans. At the same time, rumours of an attempted negotiated peace were frequent.

Attack on Denmark and Norway

In April, 1940, Hitler attacked Denmark and Norway. Airborne troops seized all major positions in the two countries. Hitler's aim was to forestall a British landing and safeguard Norwegian iron-ore supplies to Germany. After much hesitation and confusion, a British force landed in northern Norway, but lacked air support and was forced to withdraw. The depressing Norwegian fiasco was the immediate *cause of the fall of Chamberlain* and his replacement by **Winston Churchill.**

The Collapse of France

In May, 1940, German armoured columns struck into Belgium, Rotterdam was subjected to a ferocious air blitz, and Holland was invaded and over-run.

German forces next struck at France on the Ardennes front. They cut through the French defences and moved towards the Channel coast, which they quickly reached at Abbéville. This isolated the northern Allied armies, which comprised the British Expeditionary Force under **Lord Gort,** the French First Army, and the Belgian forces. The Belgian King capitulated, and the British and French forces fought a determined rearguard action to delay the Germans and to reach the port of **Dunkirk.** From there 300,000 troops were evacuated to Great Britain from the beaches—one of the most astonishing achievements of the war in conditions that appeared hopeless. All equipment, however, was lost.

The French position became increasingly hopeless. Chaos and confusion reigned behind the front, and German armoured divisions advanced at a furious pace. Paris was entered and Marshal **Pétain,** now Prime Minister of France, capitulated to the Germans. **General de Gaulle** escaped to Britain, where he began the organization of the Free French forces.

Mussolini now entered the war in alliance with Hitler.

Pétain's fleet in North Africa, at **Oran,** was bombarded by the British navy and put out of action to prevent its use by Germany.

Britain was now alone against Nazi Germany. Churchill received Nazi peace offers, but declared his intention of continuing the struggle until Hitler was defeated.

The Battle of Britain

Hitler's main aim was to extend German power in the East, the old Teutonic aim of empire. Britain's position he regarded as now hopeless, and could not understand her refusal to capitulate. The invasion of Britain was prepared, but was unlikely to succeed against British naval power in the Channel. In May the **Home Guard** was formed to help repel invasion. The gaining of air superiority was essential to Germany, and the air **Battle of Britain** took place from August to September, 1940. German bombers attacked the airfields and the key points along the coast, but the British radar system (just completed) proved invaluable. London itself was bombed, and British aircraft replied with bomb-attacks on German concentrations in French and Belgian ports. By September, however, the British fighter pilots had inflicted such damage on Goering's air force that daylight attacks were abandoned, and at this point immediate invasion plans also appear to have been given up. The Battle of Britain had been won and was decisive for the future of the war.

The German *night blitz on Britain* now continued from September, 1940, to May, 1941. London suffered nightly raids, and the ordeal of the population was severe. Other great cities, such as Coventry, were attacked with typical Nazi thoroughness. Despite great civilian casualties, morale continued high, and British industrial production was not radically reduced. The R.A.F. also commenced reprisal bombing on German industrial towns.

During this time, the American President, **Franklin D. Roosevelt,** had secured the passing by Congress of the **Lend-Lease Act, 1941,** to supply Britain with food and armaments. Hitler now began a concerted submarine and air attack on British trans-Atlantic shipping, and losses became severe. The U.S.A. gave Britain fifty destroyers in exchange for British bases in the West Indies from which the U.S.A. could protect Panama.

British Victory in Cyrenaica

The war went badly for Mussolini from the start. British Commonwealth forces regained all territory lost in the first Italian attacks in North Africa. Italian forces were *driven from Egypt, Kenya, British Somaliland, the Sudan and the whole of Cyrenaica.* In 1940 Mussolini's attack on Greece was also repelled and the British navy destroyed a large part of his fleet at **Taranto.**

Rommel's First African Campaign

Hitler now came to Mussolini's aid. German forces attacked Greece and over-ran Yugoslavia (where the struggle against the Nazis took on the form of the guerrilla warfare which was eventually to be controlled and dominated by **Marshal Tito**). British forces were evacuated from Greece after the German attack. These forces had been sent from North Africa, where the consequent weakness of the British forces enabled **Rommel** and the **Afrika Corps** to sweep all before them right up to the frontiers of Egypt.

Hitler now prepared to carry out his eastern policy. Everything was favourable. Britain was alone and greatly weakened by her reverses. German forces were poised in North Africa to break through into the Middle East. The Balkans were under German control and would be a springboard for any movements against southern Russia.

Hitler Attacks Russia

On **June 22nd, 1941**, Hitler tore up the Soviet-German Pact, and *launched his forces against Russia.* The German advance eventually reached the outskirts of Leningrad in the north, within 100 miles of Moscow in the centre, and went deep into the southern Ukraine. But by 1942 the German advance had been held, and the swift victory on which Hitler had built his hopes had failed. Churchill had been quick to bring about an alliance with Russia (he had warned Stalin of the impending German attack). Supply convoys to Russia by the northern route were now organized, with considerable losses to the British from German submarines. In Africa, Italian East Africa was conquered by the British and German armour was once again forced back along the North African coast.

The Japanese now decided that the time was ripe for the creation of their great eastern empire. On **December 7th, 1941,** they launched their treacherous air attack on the United States navy at **Pearl Harbor,** destroying the greater part of the fleet. From Indochina, they launched an attack on Malaya and Siam. They quickly over-ran the ill-prepared British defences of **Singapore** and **Hong Kong,** and the Japanese army advanced towards India. The Americans were driven from the **Philippines,** and the Japanese occupied all the main Pacific islands in that area.

Germany and Italy declared war on the United States, while Roosevelt, immediately after Pearl Harbour, brought America into the war on the side of Britain and Russia.

The American navy succeeded in preventing the Japanese occupation of New Guinea by defeating them in the **Battle of the Coral Sea**—an early success in very difficult circumstances.

1942—Stalingrad and El Alamein

The year 1942 witnessed more German successes, but in the second half of the year Allied recovery began to take place. In North Africa, Rommel and the Italians forced the British back once more into Egypt, and in southern Russia the Germans continued their drive towards the Caucasian oilfields. But now at **Stalingrad,** the Russians made the heroic stand which helped to turn the tide. Hitler refused all suggestions of a German strategic withdrawal, and in consequence the German forces under **General von Paulus** were surrounded and forced to capitulate. 300,000 German soldiers were thus lost to the Nazis. In Europe the first *thousand-bomber raid on Cologne* took place in May.

In October, 1942, the **British Eighth Army** under **General Montgomery** struck back at Rommel's forces at the decisive battle of **El Alamein,** and the German-Italian forces were driven back into Tunisia. Here they finally capitulated under pressure from both Montgomery's forces and the Anglo-American forces under **General Eisenhower** which had landed further west. The Axis army in North Africa was thus destroyed.

El Alamein and Stalingrad were *the great turning-points of the war*. They showed increasing Allied strength and, above all, showed clearly that the vast power of the Axis could be defeated.

In 1943 the Germans were forced to raise the siege of Leningrad, which had suffered terribly. The Atlantic U-boats were suffering increasing losses from air attack, and Germany was being constantly bombed by the British and American air forces. In July, 1943, the Anglo-American forces *invaded Sicily* from North Africa, and the Germans retreated over the Straits of Messina to the mainland of Italy.

Mussolini's position was now increasingly precarious. He himself was imprisoned and replaced by **Marshal Badoglio,** who brought Italy on to the Allied side in October, 1943. However, Mussolini was rescued by German parachute troops, and set up his own government in northern Italy.

Allied Invasion of Italy

On September 3rd, 1943, Allied forces landed in southern Italy from Sicily, and began the long and bloody battle up the Italian peninsula—a terrain contested fiercely every inch of the way by the Germans. Their defence of **Monte Cassino** was a determined but useless bid to hold the Allies.

D-Day, June 6th, 1944

In the north, the **Second Front,** demanded by Stalin as early as 1942, was opened on **June 6th, 1944.** The total organization of **D-Day** was undertaken by General Eisenhower, with General Montgomery in command of the invasion land forces. A special oil pipe-line (Pluto) was laid across the Channel from the Isle of Wight, and two immense artificial harbours were constructed to be towed across the Channel. The air bombardment of German installations was intensified. The British navy was in complete command of the Channel and gave cover to the invasion forces, which landed on June 6th. The first objective was the Cherbourg Peninsula. Further troops were landed by gliders to establish a definite bridgehead. German resistance was stiff, but they had been deceived by the Allied intelligence as to the actual point of landing, which they expected to be in the Calais-Boulogne area. In August the Americans broke through German resistance, and the most important Allied success was the surrounding and destruction of large German forces in the **Falaise gap.**

Differences arose between Eisenhower and Montgomery on the strategy now to be employed. Montgomery wished to attack in force on a narrow front, drive into Germany and isolate the Ruhr. Eisenhower, however, employed the strategy of advance on a broad front—slower, but less risky to lines of communication. Northern and western France were over-run and Paris was liberated. The Allied forces then moved on towards Belgium and Holland. In the meantime the German *flying-bomb attacks* (*V 1s*) on Britain had ceased with the over-running of the sites in northern France, but the *V 2 rockets* were still falling on London from their sites in the Low Countries. Montgomery's attempt to capture **Arnhem** and establish a bridgehead over the Rhine by parachute attack failed. The Allies then concentrated on liberating Antwerp in order to get supplies through to the fronts more quickly. Antwerp was at last taken, and the V 2 attacks on London ceased.

German Counter-Offensive

Germany's position now deteriorated rapidly. *In July, an attempt to assassinate Hitler* had failed, and the officers concerned were executed. The Russians had now forced Bulgaria, Finland and Rumania out of the war and their forces had entered East Prussia, Poland, Czechoslovakia, Hungary and Yugoslavia. The air bombardment of Germany was intensified.

In December, 1944, in winter conditions, the Germans under **Rundstedt** made a sudden and powerful counter-attack in the **Ardennes,** and achieved some success, but were eventually thrown back. This was the last major German effort of the war.

Death of Hitler and Mussolini

In March, 1945, Eisenhower launched the Allied forces over the Rhine, and the Ruhr was captured. Russian and American forces met on the **River Elbe** on **April 25th.** By the end of April the Russians had occupied Berlin, and Hitler had committed suicide in the bunker of the Chancellory. In Italy Mussolini had already been shot by Italian partisans.

The Atomic Bomb

Hitler's successor, **Admiral Doenitz,** then accepted the terms of unconditional surrender which had become the agreed policy of the Allies, and an **armistice** was signed on **May 7th, 1945.**

In the Far East the Americans had recaptured by 1945 the Solomon

Islands, New Guinea and the Philippines. From India Allied forces had driven back the Japanese and had reached Rangoon. On **August 6th, 1945,** with the avowed purpose of bringing the far eastern war to a rapid end with the least possible Allied casualties, the first atomic bomb was dropped on **Hiroshima.** In one devastating blast the city was totally destroyed. Russia now declared war on Japan and invaded Manchuria. On **August 9th,** the second atomic bomb was dropped on **Nagasaki,** which was obliterated as Hiroshima had been. On **August 14th,** *the Japanese accepted unconditional surrender.*

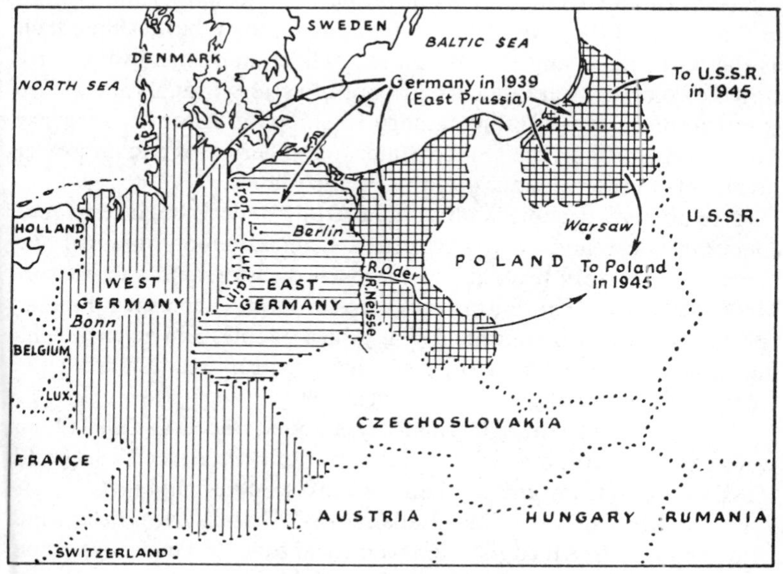

GERMANY AFTER 1945

Reasons for Germany's Defeat

The following points may be considered when discussing the reasons for Germany's defeat:

1. Britain's refusal to capitulate even after the complete success of Hitler in Europe. Churchill's leadership was a vital factor. Britain, as in the days of Napoleon, became the great rallying point of continued opposition.

2. The Battle of Britain assured the continued freedom of Britain from Nazi occupation.

3. The aggressive nature of world Fascism caused the attack of Germany on Russia and of Japan on the United States. This in itself created a new and powerful alliance against Nazi Germany.

4. Hitler's greatest error was the attack on Russia. He was really continuing a very old German policy of seeking 'lebensraum' at the expense of the Slav peoples. Churchill was quick to see the fatal implications of this policy for Hitler.

5. British and United States naval power were important factors in the defeat of the Axis. The few roaming German battleships, such as the **'Graf Spee'** and the **'Bismarck',** while dangerous in the early stages of the war, were quickly put out of action, though not before they had done considerable damage to shipping. After her recovery from Pearl Harbour, the United States found her naval and air power invaluable in the reconquest of the Pacific islands.

6. In all Nazi-occupied countries, a strong underground resistance encouraged by, and partly organized from London, harassed the Germans. The very brutality of the Nazi dictatorship, with its tortures, its ghastly concentration camps, roused increasing popular resistance as the war continued. The Allied peoples and governments had a genuine belief that their struggle was for freedom from the worst dictatorship the world had ever seen.

7. As in World War I, Germany was not equipped to fight a long war against the combined industrial power of Britain, the U.S.A. and Russia—a power far greater than the Fascists could mobilize.

8. The early defeat of the Italians was a liability to Hitler, and helped to sustain Allied morale at a critical time. German forces had to be deployed to prop up the weak Italian régime.

9. Hitler's persecutions had driven from Germany some of the most brilliant scientists of the age—e.g. Albert Einstein. This, in all probability, is why America produced the atomic bomb first and the Germans lagged far behind. Had Hitler gained this weapon first, he might still have retrieved the situation.

10. Air power gradually turned in favour of the Allies, and Hitler was forced to drain away much of his air power to the vast eastern front against Russia.

11. Hitler's increasing control of military affairs was fatal for

Germany. He refused to face realities, as in the case of Stalingrad. Even in 1945 as the Russians advanced on Berlin he was calling on non-existent German armies to resist.

Dates

1939–April, 1940	**The 'phoney war'.**
1940	**Hitler invades Denmark and Norway.**
	Churchill replaces Chamberlain.
	Holland and Belgium over-run.
	Dunkirk evacuation.
	Paris falls and Pétain capitulates.
	British bombard French fleet at Oran.
	Air Battle of Britain.
	Night blitz on Britain begins in September.
	British defeat Italians in Cyrenaica.
	Mussolini's attack on Greece repelled.
	Half Italian Battleships put out of action by British Fleet Air Arm at Taranto.
1941	**German invasion of Yugoslavia and Greece.**
	Rommel recaptures Cyrenaica from British.
	British naval victory against Italians.
	German capture of Crete.
June 22nd	**Hitler launches invasion of Russia.**
	British conquer Italian East Africa (November).
	British reconquer Cyrenaica (by January, 1942).
December 7th	**Japanese attack on U.S. Pacific Fleet at Pearl Harbour.**
1942	**Japanese occupy Indochina, Singapore, Hong Kong, Malaya and Siam, all main Pacific islands.**
	Battle of the Coral Sea.
	Rommel forces British back into Egypt.
	Russian victory at Stalingrad.
	British victory at El Alamein.
1943	**Germans raise siege of Leningrad.**
	British-American bomber attacks on Germany intensified.
	Allied forces occupy Sicily (July) and invade southern Italy (September).

	Mussolini imprisoned and Badoglio makes peace with the Allies.
	Mussolini liberated by German paratroops and sets up government in northern Italy.
	Russian counter-offensives make continuous headway.
1944	**V 1 attacks on Britain begin.**
June 6th	**Second Front opened. D-Day.**
	Fighting French forces with other Allied forces land in southern France.
	Battle of the Falaise gap, and Allied break-through in Normandy.
	Attempt to assassinate Hitler.
	Battle of Arnhem.
	V 2 rockets falling on London.
	German counter-offensive in the Ardennes fails.
1945	**Eisenhower's forces cross the Rhine.**
	Russians reach the Oder.
	Russians reach Vienna and Berlin.
April 25th	**American and Russian forces meet on the Elbe.**
	Mussolini shot by partisans.
April 30th	**Hitler commits suicide.**
	Liberation of the concentration camps.
May 7th	**Germans sign armistice.**
August 6th	**Atomic bomb on Hiroshima.**
August 8th	**Russia declares war on Japan and invades Manchuria.**
August 9th	**Atomic bomb on Nagasaki.**
August 14th	**Japan accepts unconditional surrender.**

QUESTIONS

1. *How would you account for the successes of Nazi Germany in the period 1939–1942?*
2. *What was the importance of the Battles of Stalingrad and El Alamein?*
3. *What mistakes were made by Hitler in the conduct of the war?*
4. *How would you account for the final defeat of the Axis powers?*

CHAPTER TWENTY-ONE

THE GREAT WAR-TIME CONFERENCES

The Atlantic Charter, 1941

THIS was the result of a meeting between Churchill and Roosevelt on a warship in the western Atlantic. Although the United States was not yet in the war, she was prepared to join with Britain in issuing a statement of the principles on which peace would be based after the war. *Its main point was that neither Britain nor the United States would seek any territory and that every people should be free to possess the government of its own free choice.* This statement was eventually accepted by all the states fighting against Hitler.

The Yalta Conference, February, 1945

This was attended by Roosevelt, Churchill and Stalin. The defeat of Germany was now imminent, and the conference surveyed the main problems relating to territories (especially those over-run by Russia). The conference agreed that Germany should be divided into *Allied occupation zones*, and that a new organization should be set up to replace the old League of Nations. The frontiers of Poland were also agreed, involving the inclusion in Poland of much German territory up to the Oder-Neisse line.

The San Francisco Conference, April–June, 1945

At this conference the **United Nations Organization** was established. It was to comprise (1) **The General Assembly**; (2) **The Security Council** which was to decide on any actions required, and which is the all-powerful element of UNO. Five permanent members of the Security Council were elected—Britain, France, Russia, U.S.A. and China (then under control of Chiang-Kai-shek). Six non-permanent members were to be elected by the General Assembly for two years. Any Council decisions *must have the support of all five permanent members*, any one of whom could thus *veto* proposed measures. The basic idea was that unless all the Great Powers agreed, little could really be achieved—real unity was necessary. Among other important organs of UNO were the International Court of Justice, and the Economic and Social Council. The main servant of UNO was the **Secretary-General.**

Other important departments of the United Nations are:

The Trusteeship Council (taking over a number of the old League mandates)
The International Labour Organization (ILO).
The Food and Agricultural Organization (FAO).
The World Health Organization (WHO).
The International Refugee Organization (IRO)
The Educational, Scientific and Cultural Organization (UNESCO).
The Atomic Energy Commission.
(See also Chapter 28.)

The Potsdam Conference, July, 1945

The war in Europe had ended, but not the far eastern war. Roosevelt had died in April, and **President Truman** represented the U.S.A. at the Potsdam Conference. The main problems arose from the defeat of Germany and the creation of four Allied zones of control in Germany as agreed upon in principle at Yalta. *Berlin itself was also divided into four zones.* Berlin, however, lay *within the Russian zone.*

In Berlin the four commanders-in-chief (American, British, French and Russian) were to constitute a Control Council for the city. The conference declared the purposes of the Allied occupation of Germany to be: (*a*) the complete disarmament of Germany; (*b*) to convince the German people of their responsibility for the war and to bring to trial the German war criminals; (*c*) to destroy finally the Nazi party and to prevent its revival in any form; (*d*) supervision of reparations to be paid by Germany in the form of industrial equipment which was to be removed from Germany; (*e*) to prepare the ground for the eventual creation of a democratic form of government for Germany.

In Britain the General Election had seen the defeat of **Mr. Churchill**, who was replaced as British representative at Potsdam by **Mr. Attlee.**

Summary

These principal conferences between the Allies raised all the main problems with which the immediate post-war period was faced: (1) the relations of Russia and the West; (2) the vast extension of Russian influence in eastern Europe, and especially the frontiers of the new Poland; (3) the difficulties arising from the peculiar position of Berlin within the Russian zone of occupation; (4) the importance of the new United Nations Organization, and the great power of veto given to each of the permanent members of the Council. (How would this veto be used in the post-war period?)

Dates

1941 **The Atlantic Charter.**
1945 **The Yalta Conference, February.**
The San Francisco Conference, April–June.
The Potsdam Conference, July.

QUESTIONS

1. What decisions were arrived at in the Yalta and Potsdam Conferences?

2. What problems affecting the post-war period were discussed by the war-time conferences?

CHAPTER TWENTY-TWO

THE POST-WAR WORLD, 1945–1953 —EASTERN EUROPE

BETWEEN 1945 and the death of Stalin, 1953, the history of Europe and a good deal of Asia was dominated by the political problems which arose between the Western powers and the Soviet Union. We see the development of the 'Cold War'. But after 1953 important changes occurred which it is more convenient to consider in Chapter 25.

The General Position at the End of World War II

In eastern Europe certain countries had achieved their own liberation from German occupation in the last stages of the war—namely, Yugoslavia, Albania and most of Greece. *Their resistance armies were led mainly by Communists.*

Russian armies occupied Poland, Hungary, Rumania, Bulgaria, about a third of Austria and Germany and most of Czechoslovakia.

Thus Communist influence in these countries was dominant, either with or without Russian armed support.

In North Africa, France now reoccupied her territories of Morocco and Tunisia. In the Middle East, however, independent governments took over from the French in Syria and Lebanon. Some British forces remained in Egypt, Iraq, Palestine and Transjordan.

In the Far East, American troops were in Japan and in the reconquered American Pacific islands. Russian forces were in Manchuria, and, by agreement, they occupied Northern Korea and the Americans occupied the South. Indochina was divided between British and Chinese forces. British forces had re-entered Burma and Malaya and were also in Indonesia.

All colonial countries occupied by the Axis powers during the war were anxious for complete independence. Russia wished to see forms of Communism arise in these countries, whereas the Western powers wished for various forms of liberal democracy. As in Europe, Communist parties in the Far East had played a considerable part in the struggle against the Japanese.

Eastern Europe

Stalin was determined to have friendly states on Russia's western frontiers. For this purpose it was necessary to have Communist or Communist-dominated governments in eastern Europe. *Communists gained key posts in many governments* and served in immediate post-war coalitions.

Poland. With Russian forces in Poland, the Soviet influence was decisive. Stalin had refused assistance to the revolt in Warsaw in 1944 initiated by the Polish Home Army which received its instructions from the Polish government in exile in Britain. Stalin set up a Polish government of his own supporters. The Polish People's Party, the main voice of the peasants, was eventually suppressed. Its leader, **Mikolajczyk,** fled from Poland in 1947. In that year Stalin's policy of collaboration with the returned exiles ended. Leaders of several non-Communist parties were imprisoned, and some executed.

Rumania. A coalition government containing Communists had taken over when the Germans left, but in 1945 Soviet pressure led to a Communist-controlled government being set up. The Peasant Party leader, **Maniu,** and others, were imprisoned.

Bulgaria. The Rumanian pattern was repeated in 1945 in Bulgaria.

Hungary. In 1947 the Hungarian Smallholders' Party was made illegal and its leader, **Bela Kovacs,** was arrested by Soviet police. Several parliamentary deputies of the party were arrested and tried, mostly on charges of treason.

Czechoslovakia. Here the native Communist Party was very powerful by 1945. As in other east European states, Communists had taken a leading part in anti-Nazi activities. They had also been strong in the pre-war period. They had the support of at least half the industrial workers. At first in 1945 the Communist Party of Czechoslovakia *adopted a policy of coalition* with other parties. The key ministries of the Interior (police) and of Information (radio, press) went to Communists. It also had highly placed officials in the Ministry of Defence. Its members effectively controlled the factories and trade unions. In the election of 1946 about a third of the electorate voted Communist. The Prime Minister was the Communist leader, **Klement Gottwald.** In February, 1948, twelve ministers of the government resigned because of the increase of Communists in key posts. The leader of the Czech Social Democratic Party, **Dr. Fierlinger,** was prepared to collaborate with the Communists and brought a considerable section of his party with him. This gave the Socialists and Communists a parliamentary majority and President Benesh confirmed Gottwald as Prime Minister. Communist Action Committees were now formed throughout the country, and the leaders of several other parties joined them. A 'purge' of the Civil Service was now undertaken to remove those elements who were accused of opposing the policy of collaboration with the Soviet Union. A **National Front Government** was formed composed mainly of Communists and Social Democrats, but containing members of other parties. Before the General Election of May, 1948, the government announced that a single list of candidates would be put forward by agreement between the parties, and voters could vote for the single list or cast a blank vote. Seven million out of eight million voters went to the polls and the National Front received 89 per cent of the votes cast. President Benesh resigned in June, 1948, and was succeeded by Gottwald. Communist control of Czechoslovakia, in collaboration with the Social Democratic Party and a number of smaller groups, had been achieved.

Yugoslavia. Soviet forces did not enter Yugoslavia at the end of the war, and Communist control was purely national. Here, as in Czechoslovakia, there had been much support for Communism in the town centres before the war. These educated elements had taken a leading part in the liberation struggle against the Nazis. **Marshal Tito** and the Communist Party had gained effective control of the Yugoslav Partisans and this was the basis of their post-war power. The supporters of the Yugoslav government in exile received the same severe treatment as in the case of Poland, and their principal spokesman in Yugoslavia, **Mihailovich,** was executed on the grounds that during the war forces under his command, the **Chetniks,** had not only fought to gain control from the Partisans, but had also collaborated with the Germans.

In 1948 Soviet relations with Yugoslavia suddenly deteriorated. The apparent cause of the quarrel was a Yugoslav charge that the Soviet Union was secretly negotiating with the Western powers to repudiate Yugoslavia's claims to the part of Austria known as Slovene Carinthia. The Soviet reply simply reversed the accusation, accusing the Yugoslavs of abandoning their fellow Slavs in Carinthia and attempting to put the blame on the Soviet Union. The latter then accused the Yugoslavs of brutal ill-treatment of arrested Soviet citizens in Yugoslavia, but Tito replied that these individuals were in fact 'white' Russians who had collaborated with the Germans. Eventually Russia denounced Tito as a collaborator with the Western Capitalists against the interests of Communism, and called for his overthrow. He and his party were expelled from the international Communist organization, the Cominform.

Effects of the Soviet-Yugoslav Quarrel

The Soviet Union's boycott of trade with Yugoslavia led to Tito receiving economic and financial aid from the Western powers, and especially the United States. It also led to a move away from Stalinism within the country. This meant less centralized control and the giving of more power to the Workers' Councils in the factories. It also meant that the production of consumer goods was encouraged in place of the typically Stalinist policy of sacrificing everything to the basic industries. In 1953 the peasants were permitted to leave the collective farms which Tito had enforced, and great numbers did so. These were all deviations from the strict Stalinist principles, and showed further the independence of Tito, which the Soviet Union had distrusted from the beginning.

Tito had, to a certain extent, taken a national rather than an international Communist line, and his policies were denounced by Russia as *nationalist deviation.* In the so-called satellite states of Russia, Tito had his supporters, and these were now denounced by those accepting the Stalinist line. In Hungary a leading Communist, **Laslo Rajk,** was tried and executed, as also was **Traicho Kostov** in Bulgaria. In Poland **Gomulka** was arrested and imprisoned in 1951. These purges continued on and off until 1953. In Czechoslovakia about half the old Communist leadership was removed.

Austria Resists Communism

After 1945 Austria proved an exception to the general Communist control in eastern Europe. Soviet forces entered Vienna in April, 1945, and the Russians agreed to the establishment of a coalition government of Communists, Socialists and Catholics under the Socialist leader **Dr. Karl Renner.** This was accepted by Britain, France and the United States, whose forces occupied their zones of Vienna. In the elections of 1946 only four Communists were returned to the Austrian parliament, and in 1947 the Communists also left the coalition government. After 1950 Austria received substantial American financial help under the Marshall Plan (see p. 194).

The Position in Greece, 1944–1949

Here the Communist-led resistance had taken over most of the country as the German army had retreated. An agreement was reached between the returning exiles and the Communists to form a coalition government. Trouble arose, however, when the government proposed to disarm the Communist forces. This was resisted, and the British troops who had entered Athens in October, 1944, were involved in fighting against Communist forces in Athens in December 1944. Eventually the Communist forces were disarmed, but were promised full civil rights. In March, 1946, the extreme Right-wing parties, fervent supporters of the returned Greek monarchy, won the elections. Unfortunately, this led to anti-Communist arrests on a wide scale, and the rights guaranteed by the disarming agreement were ignored. In reply the Communists began guerrilla activity against the government, and, under **General Markos,** were supplied with arms across the frontiers of Yugoslavia, Albania and Bulgaria. For three years they controlled the greater part of Macedonia. Tito, on bad terms with Russia, closed the frontier in 1949. The United States had also provided large financial aid to the Greek government. In 1949 the Communist military resistance was finally defeated.

Summary

By 1948 Communist control was consolidated in Poland, Rumania, Bulgaria, Yugoslavia, Albania and Czechoslovakia. By 1949 the Communist armed rising had been defeated in Greece, and in Austria Communist influence was very slight.

It should be noted that in all countries with a strong pre-war party representing the peasant interests, it was *a principal Communist aim to defeat and absorb these parties.* The programme of collective farms and attempts to abandon the old separate peasant holdings was then undertaken. In the case of the non-Soviet-occupied countries of Yugoslavia and Albania, the Communist governments were less under Russian influence and, adopting more independent lines of policy, were regarded with hostility by Moscow. This led to denunciations of 'Tito nationalists' in the other Communist states and purges on Stalinist lines between 1948 and 1953.

QUESTIONS

1. What were the general aims of Stalin's policy in eastern Europe in the immediate post-war period?

2. Describe the stages by which the Communists gained control in Czechoslovakia.

3. Why did Marshal Tito's dispute with the Soviet Union arise?

4. What was the effect of the Yugoslav-Russian dispute on the other Communist states?

5. Describe the situation in Greece in the years 1944–1949.

CHAPTER TWENTY-THREE

THE POST-WAR WORLD, 1945–1953 —WESTERN EUROPE

As after the First World War, there was a strong movement away from the older, traditional politics and parties towards Socialism and Communism. In western Europe, however, Communism, while powerful in France and Italy, did not gain the power it achieved in eastern Europe.

France

Communists had played a leading part in the French Resistance after Hitler's attack on Russia. They had also gained a strong hold over the French trade unions. The leader of the French Communist Party, **Maurice Thorez,** was a strong supporter of Stalin's policies—'France is my country,' he declared, 'but the Soviet Union is my fatherland.' However, despite rumours of a Communist attempt to seize power, Communist policy in France followed a constitutional or liberal parliamentary course. The Communists were represented in General de Gaulle's first government and helped to prepare the new constitution of the **Fourth Republic.** The Socialists under **Léon Blum** chose co-operation with the Christian Democrats (MRP) and refused all offers of alliance by the Communists. Unlike Czechoslovakia, the Communists in France failed either to absorb the Socialists or to break away any substantial part of the Socialist Party. In 1947 they left the government because they disagreed with its policies for industry and because they also demanded the complete independence of Indochina. There were other reasons, however, especially the Soviet Union's rejection of the Marshall Plan.

The French Communists now concentrated on trade-union industrial action, while *in the French parliament the political situation became unstable and chaotic.* Governments could only survive by pleasing Socialists, Radicals and Conservatives. This led to constant changes of government, political intrigue and manœuvre. Over such important questions as taxation, the state policy towards Catholic schools, and the French Empire (especially Algeria and Tunisia) there were constant crises. This prevented any clear lines of policy emerging, and eventually led to the re-emergence of General de Gaulle, who had retired from politics in 1947. (See also Chapter 27.)

Italy

In Italy the Communists had controlled the Italian Partisans during the latter part of the war, and in the elections of 1946 they gained 19 per cent of the votes, the Socialists 21 per cent and the Christian Democrats 35 per cent. A coalition government with Communist participation was the result. However, the Left wing of the Social Democratic Party under **Signor Nenni** formed a political pact with the Communists under **Togliatti.** This split the Socialists, whose anti-Communist elements broke away from the Social Democratic Party under **Signor Saragat.** The united Communist-Socialist group gained 32 per cent of votes in the election of 1948, and the Christian Democrats under **de Gasperi** gained 41 per cent: the latter formed a government, which was still in power in 1953. But, as in France, the government's position was never strong enough to carry through decisive measures. The position was nearly as unstable as in France.

The Communists, who had in Italy the largest Communist party in Europe, took a leading part in the trade-union movement and also attempted to expropriate the big landlords of southern Italy in favour of the impoverished peasantry. For this purpose they established *Committees of the Land* in imitation of the Russian Bolsheviks of 1917. This movement, however, was not successful.

Germany

After 1945, four zones were created for the occupation forces of Russia, the United States, Britain and France. Berlin itself also had four occupation zones, but, as we have noted, was entirely surrounded by the Soviet-held zone.

A central authority was created to control the zones—the **Allied Control Council** which met in Berlin. The ultimate aim was to form a German government with whom a peace treaty could be signed by the Allies. The division of Germany into two parts which arose later was never intended in 1945.

The Sudeten areas of Czechoslovakia were returned to Czechoslovakia and the union of Austria with Germany was annulled. Poland received back her territory lost in 1939, and the frontier extended further westward to the **Oder-Neisse line,** which gave Poland all the valuable industrial territory of Silesia. Russia also received the north-eastern part of East Prussia, and Königsberg.

Refugee Problem in Germany

The worst immediate problem was the vast swarm of ten million refugees from eastern Europe, of whom two million were the Sudeten Germans expelled by the Czechs. This imposed a tremendous strain on a Germany devasted by air raids and itself facing the problem of the survivors from the Nazi concentration camps. This situation was complicated by the Russian demand for £2,000 million in reparations, including industrial equipment from the Ruhr. (This area was in the British zone.) *Britain, France and the United States refused this demand,* for it would have added vast new economic difficulties to the situation in their own zones. *This was the first rift in the Allied Control Council.* In their own area the Soviet authorities dismantled much industrial equipment and transported it to Russia. They also brought about a fusion of the Social Democrats (Socialists) and the Communists into the **Social Unity Party (SED)** in 1946—a party effectively controlled by the Communists. The large landed estates in east Germany were divided among the peasantry while the whole area was divided into five provinces with local governments. The central administration was directed from the Soviet sector of Berlin. *Thus Communism dominated the Soviet zone from the beginning.*

Economic Union of British and American Zones

In the British, American and French zones free capitalist enterprise was adopted within the limits allowed by the occupying powers.

In 1947, with increasing difficulties arising in the Control Council, the British and American Zones were formed into one economic unit. In **1948** a **London Conference** of the Western powers agreed that a separate government for western Germany should be formed. The two main German parties allowed to function were the Christian Democrats under **Konrad Adenauer** and the Social Democratic Party under **Kurt Schumacher** (who had survived a Nazi concentration camp). In the Soviet Zone a People's Congress or parliament was set up.

The Berlin Blockade, June, 1948–May, 1949

The Western powers wished to bring about a currency reform in western Germany, including their zones of Berlin. The revaluation of the mark was declared necessary in order to assist the revival of trade and industry. A new German mark was issued to replace the old currency. The aim was to reduce inflation and weaken the illegal black market in various commodities. The Russian representative had already left the Allied Control Council in protest at the Western powers' London Conference on the future of western Germany, and the new measures were communicated to the Russian authorities in writing. They replied that the currency reform was contrary to the Potsdam agreements and that the existence of two currencies was a further division of Germany and would hamper trade between the zones. It also prohibited the circulation of the new notes in the Soviet zone and in Berlin, which it claimed was part of the Russian zone, economically speaking. *In June, 1948, the corridor enabling supplies to reach Berlin from the West was closed.* This constituted a blockade of the city by the Soviet authorities and was considered to be an attempt to force the Western powers out of Berlin altogether. The situation was tense and dangerous and armed conflict could have broken out. However, the British and United States air forces organized an *air-lift* of supplies into Berlin. This was maintained until May, 1949, at which point the Russians lifted the blockade. This was the first great trial of strength and determination between the Soviet Union and the Western powers. *It led on to the definite division of Germany*, and the **Federal Republic of Germany** was set up. In the elections which followed Dr. Adenauer gained a majority, with the Social Democrats under Schumacher in opposition. In the eastern zone the People's Council now became the government, and in October, 1949, the eastern zone was declared the **German Democratic Republic.** The first Prime Minister was the Socialist **Grotewohl,** with the Communist **Ulbricht** as Deputy Prime Minister (later to become Prime Minister).

Thus the so-called *iron curtain* was drawn through Germany, with fifty-two million people in the western Federal Republic of Germany and seventeen million in the German Democratic Republic.

The Truman Doctrine and the Marshall Plan

In his famous speech at Fulton, Missouri, in March, 1946, Mr. Churchill had warned against the development of what he called 'tyranny' and that '*from Stettin on the Baltic to Trieste on the Adriatic an iron curtain has descended across the Continent*'.

President Truman also made it clear that the U.S.A. must resist further Communist advance not only by military power (the U.S.A. had the monopoly of the atomic bomb in 1946), but by the *use of America's immense wealth to assist economic recovery in other countries*. The *Truman Doctrine* was followed by an important speech at Harvard by **George Marshall,** American Secretary of State, in which he urged the European states to consult together on the aid required and how it would be used. He later made it clear that his invitation to this co-operation included the Soviet Union. Russia's response was at first co-operative, and **Mr. Molotov,** Soviet Foreign Minister, met the Foreign Ministers of France and Britain for joint discussions on June 27, 1947, in Paris. However, difficulties arose, and Molotov *declined to support the Marshall Plan on the grounds that the conditions it laid down amounted to interference in the internal affairs of European states*. Poland, Hungary and Czechoslovakia had been inclined to accept Marshall Aid, but the Soviet decision to oppose the plan prevented their taking part in the full conference. Thus a further sharp division had occurred between Soviet and western policy, and Russia became even more interested in seeing that the governments of eastern Europe were Communist-dominated in order to maintain their loyalty to her. It meant increasing attempts to eliminate any parties in those states which looked towards the west.

The final stage by which the Marshall Plan began to operate for

Europe was the formation in April, 1948, of the **Organization for European Economic Co-operation (OEEC)**, consisting of sixteen European states. The U.S. Congress passed the Economic Co-operation Act, which enabled the United States to advance 12,000 million dollars' worth of aid to Europe between 1948 and 1951. Before this act, the United States had already given financial aid to Italy and Greece.

It was after the breakdown of Soviet co-operation in the Paris Conference of June 27 that the **Communist Information Bureau** (Cominform) was established to co-ordinate the policies of all Communist parties, including those of the eastern states and of France and Italy. This was a sign of the increasing control of Moscow over the Communist movement.

The Western Alliances

After the war a series of important European alliances grew up.

1. **The Anglo-French Pact of Dunkirk,** March, **1947.** This was a pact of mutual defence, and was directed against Germany rather than the Soviet Union.

2. March, **1948,** the **Brussels Treaty** between Britain, France, Belgium, Holland and Luxembourg. This guaranteed mutual assistance against aggression.

3. March, **1949,** the **North Atlantic Treaty.** The five Brussels powers were joined by U.S.A., Canada, Denmark, Norway, Iceland, Italy and Portugal. This provided for mutual support against aggression and covered not only the European territories but North America, Algeria, and islands in the Atlantic north of the tropic of Cancer and vessels at sea within this area. In 1951 Greece and Turkey joined the alliance. A permanent central organization was set up in Paris known as the North Atlantic Treaty Organization **(NATO).** A Supreme Headquarters Atlantic Powers Europe **(SHAPE)** was also set up at Versailles under General Eisenhower.

The NATO treaty was intended not only as a defence against possible Communist aggression, but also to secure the unity of Europe. An eventual aim was to assist in the ending of the old conflicts between France and Germany by bringing the German Federal Republic into NATO at a later date. This took place in 1954. The treaty was regarded as part of the general move towards European union.

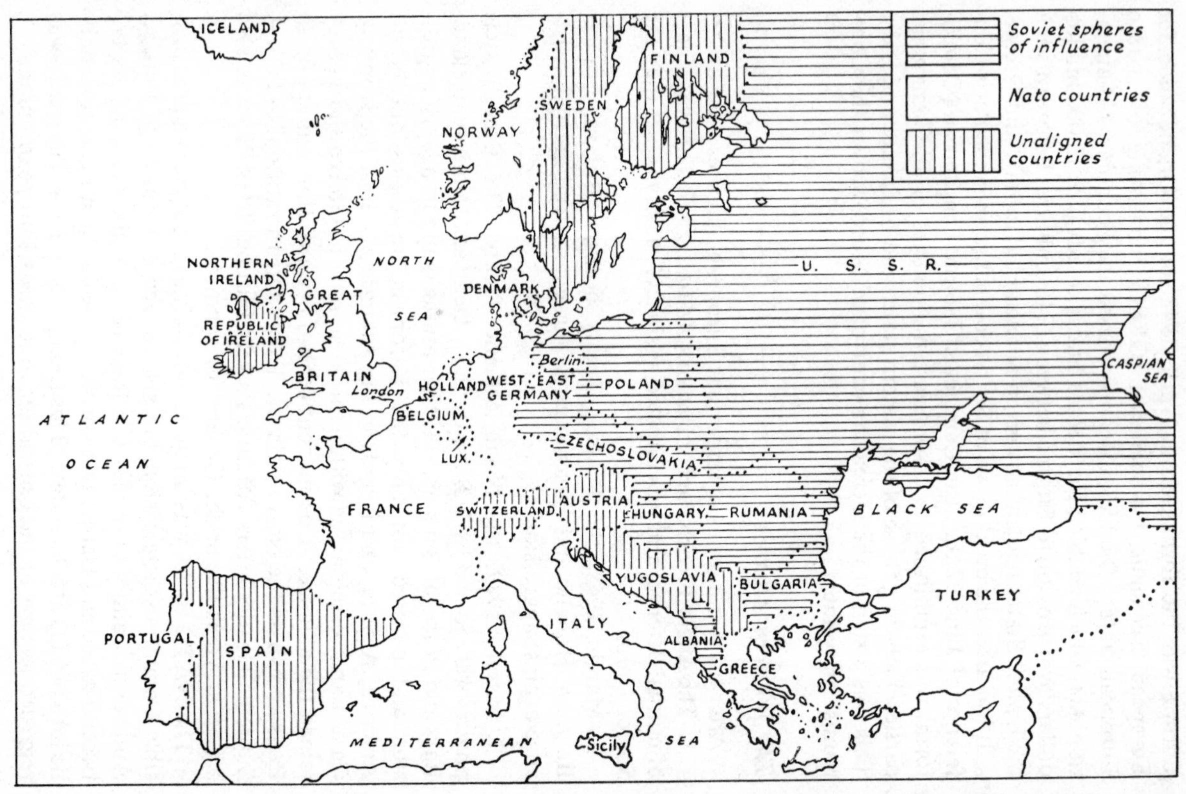
Soviet spheres of influence
Nato countries
Unaligned countries
ICELAND
FINLAND
SWEDEN
NORWAY
U. S. S. R.
NORTHERN IRELAND
REPUBLIC OF IRELAND
GREAT BRITAIN
London
NORTH SEA
DENMARK
Berlin
WEST GERMANY
EAST GERMANY
POLAND
HOLLAND
BELGIUM
LUX.
CASPIAN SEA
ATLANTIC OCEAN
CZECHOSLOVAKIA
FRANCE
SWITZERLAND
AUSTRIA
HUNGARY
RUMANIA
BLACK SEA
YUGOSLAVIA
BULGARIA
TURKEY
ITALY
ALBANIA
GREECE
PORTUGAL
SPAIN
MEDITERRANEAN SEA
Sicily

The Soviet attitude was hostile. In a communication to the member states Mr. Molotov declared that the treaty was contrary to the United Nations Charter which forbade members to form alliances directed against other members and that it was a breach of war-time Anglo-Russian and Anglo-French treaties. The Russian view was that the alliance was aggressive.

Other Movements of European Union

The **Schuman Plan,** put forward by the French Foreign Minister, **M. Schuman,** in 1950, proposed that a single authority should be set up to control the French and German coal and steel industries. This proposal cut right across the old frontiers and was an important advance in European economic co-operation. The **European Coal and Steel Community** was set up in July, **1952.** A governing body or High Authority was established to control the industries of France, the Federal German Republic, Belgium, Luxemburg, Holland and Italy.

Attempts were also made to establish a European army (the **Pleven Plan**), but France disliked the inclusion of Germany, and Britain also refused to join. However, in September, 1954, the Brussels Treaty Organization became known as the **Western European Union** and admitted the German Federal Republic and Italy. The Western Union was to form part of NATO, and this would bring German armed contingents under NATO control. At the same time the German Federal Republic was now recognized as a fully sovereign and independent state and British and American occupation troops only remained there with the agreement of the German government. The status of the occupation forces had gradually changed from that of forces occupying a conquered country to that of defensive forces against the east.

The Atomic Bomb

On September 22nd, 1949, the governments of the U.S.A., Canada and Britain reported that an atomic explosion had been detected in the Soviet Union. *The conclusion became clear that the U.S.A. no longer had a monopoly of the atomic bomb.* The governments stressed the growing importance of the international control of atomic energy.

Summary

1. During the period 1945–1953 the outlines of the so-called *Cold War* between the Communist and non-Communist world took clear shape.

2. The Western powers became increasingly consolidated through such organizations as NATO, Western Union, the Iron and Steel Community.

3. The east European states were consolidated under Communist control—a process hastened after the Russian refusal to entertain the Marshall Plan for eastern Europe.

4. The existence in France and Italy of strong Communist parties outside their governments after 1947 left the conduct of political affairs in those countries to weak coalitions, producing constant changes of government and the slowing down of progress through the resultant political chaos.

5. A competition in atomic power was proceeding between the U.S.A. and the U.S.S.R.

The Korean War and its effects, which come within this period, are dealt with in Chapter 24.

Dates

1946 **Churchill's Fulton speech ('Iron Curtain').**
Communists in coalition governments in France and Italy.
Socialist Unity Party formed in eastern zone of Germany.
The Truman Doctrine and the Marshall Plan.

1947 **Economic union of British and American zones in Germany.**
Anglo-French Pact of Dunkirk.
Communists leave French government.
Molotov rejects the Marshall Plan at Paris Conference (June).

1948 **London Conference decides on creation of separate government for western Germany.**
Western currency reform in Germany.
Berlin blockade begins.
OEEC set up.

1949 **End of Berlin blockade** (May).
German Democratic Republic established (East Germany)

NATO and SHAPE established.
Soviet Union explodes atomic bomb.
1952 European Coal and Steel Community.
1954 Brussels Treaty Organization becomes the Western European Union, including Federal German Republic and Italy.
German Federal Republic accorded full sovereignty.

QUESTIONS

1. What forms did Communist activity take in France and Italy between 1945 and 1953?

2. What problems arose between the Western powers and the Soviet Union over Germany in the years 1945–1953?

3. What were the aims and importance of the Marshall Plan?

4. In what ways was the unity of Europe developed between 1945 and 1953?

CHAPTER TWENTY-FOUR

THE POST-WAR WORLD, 1945–1953 —THE MIDDLE AND FAR EAST

Syria, Lebanon and Palestine

In 1946 both Syria and Lebanon became independent of France and soon after were admitted to the United Nations. But France once again assumed full control of Morocco and Tunisia, as well as Algeria.

There were special problems for Britain. Palestine had been assigned to Britain as a mandate of the League of Nations after 1919, and in 1945 British forces were again in the country. There was, however, increasing opposition to Britain from the extreme Jewish elements, especially the **Stern Gang,** who carried out a terror campaign against British soldiers and civilians. *The Arabs were opposed to the Jewish settlement of Palestine*, and their opposition had strong backing when the **Arab League** consisting of Egypt, Transjordan, Iraq, Syria, Lebanon, Saudi Arabia and Yemen was formed in 1945. The question of Palestine was brought before the United Nations, which proposed its *partition between Jews and Arabs*—a solution which pleased neither. In May, 1948, Britain withdrew her forces, and this was followed by a proclamation of the **State of Israel.** Immediately the Arab states began attacks on Israel, but these were repulsed, and an armistice was signed between Israel and the Arab states. This remained an armistice, and the Arab states have never recognized the existence of Israel. In 1953 there were over 900,000 Arab refugees from Israel in camps in the Arab states, and the humanitarian work of the United Nations was scarcely able to cope with the problem. Over 200,000 Jews were expelled from Iraq and entered Israel in poor health. An extremely bitter problem had thus arisen in the Middle East.

Egypt

There was now a strong revival of Egyptian nationalism, and demands for the removal of British forces. Britain concluded a treaty with Egypt to evacuate British forces by two stages, with the right to return if Egypt or neighbouring countries were threatened with aggression.

The national movement had been led for many years by the main nationalist party, the **'Wafd'** under **Nahas Pasha,** but they were now subject to pressure from the more fanatically anti-western **Moslem Brotherhood.** Britain was regarded as the real creator of the State of Israel and the latter's victories against the Arab states made anti-British feeling in Egypt more intense. The 'Wafd' now demanded the removal of British troops from the Canal Zone. In 1951, a treaty of 1936 which had made these arrangements, was declared null and void by the Egyptians and **King Farouk** was declared King of Egypt and the Sudan. Britain wished to see the Sudan independent. Increasing popular agitation against Britain led to serious riots in Cairo in January, 1952, when British civilians were killed and many buildings associated with the British occupation were destroyed by mobs. There had also been growing discontent with both the King and the 'Wafd' leaders, and on July 22, **1952,** a group of officers led by **General Neguib** and **Lt.-Colonel Nasser** seized control. At this point King Farouk abdicated. By 1953, Egypt was a republic and under new leadership pledged to improve the social conditions of the people and to remove the last vestiges of British power.

North Africa

1. **Tunisia.** The movement for national independence from France had grown during the war period. Its most determined exponent was **Habib Bourguiba,** who, on the resumption of French power in 1945, left Tunisia and carried on a nationalist agitation from abroad. An important development was the formation of a Tunisian trade union movement which advocated national independence. Although Bourguiba was allowed to return to Tunisia, the French continued to oppose national independence, and he was arrested in December, 1951. He was later released and long negotiations took place with the French

government, who were concerned to safeguard the position of the French residents in Tunisia. In January, 1952, Bourguiba and other leaders, including Communists, were deported to special detention in northern Tunisia. The situation became more tense, with attacks on French civilians, soldiers and police. Numerous popular demonstrations occurred throughout Tunisia. By 1953 no solution had yet been found, despite the fact that the Tunisian question had been brought before the United Nations.

2. **Morocco.** Here also the French resisted strongly all demands for independence. **General Juin** was appointed French Resident in 1949 and a policy of arrests and repression was carried out. In 1953 the Sultan, Sidi Mohammed, who sympathized with national demands, was deported to Madagascar and another Sultan installed who was prepared to co-operate with the French authorities.

3. **Algeria.** Algeria had always been an *integral part of France* and had her own representatives in the French National Assembly in Paris. However, the post-war nationalist agitation had some effect in modifying French policy, and in 1947 an *Algerian Assembly* was given some powers of legislation for the special conditions of Algeria, and also had the task of adapting French laws to local conditions. This Assembly, however, in the absence of a wide popular franchise, was under the control of the European minority and the French authorities. It did not satisfy nationalist demands.

Turkey

After the war Turkey, who had remained neutral until her declaration of war against Germany in February, 1945, three months before the end of the war in Europe, was *subjected to immediate pressure from the Soviet Union.* This was in line with Stalin's general policy of reinforcing as many of the frontiers of Russia as possible. It was a revival of Russian aims of the nineteenth century. Firstly, Russia demanded the cession of **Kars** and **Ardahan** which she had held before the Congress of Berlin, 1878. Secondly, she demanded bases inside both the **Dardanelles** and the Bosphorus. Thirdly, that the Montreux Convention of 1936 which put the Straits under international control should be repudiated and a joint **Soviet-Turkish control** established. The pressure for these concessions was maintained for a long period, but the Turkish government refused. Turkey maintained troops on her frontiers, and was supported by *financial aid from America* through the Truman Doctrine and the Marshall Plan. Here the *Cold War* had a very obvious battlefront.

Communist and Soviet propaganda was launched against the Turkish political system established by Mustapha Kemal. This was countered by **President Inonu,** the successor of Kemal as leader of the Republican People's Party. *The opposition Democratic Party was now allowed to take part in elections*, and in 1950 it won an overwhelming victory. This was a complete break from the dictatorship which had existed from 1922, and tended to strengthen Turkey internally.

Persia

During the war Persia had been divided between the Soviet Union and Great Britain, as a safeguard against German aims which had sympathizers in Persia. In the northern zone occupied by Russian forces and administrators there arose, with Soviet encouragement, the **Tudeh (Communist) Party.** In September, 1945, the Communists established the self-governing province of Persian **Azerbaijan** with its capital at Tabriz. A Kurdish self-governing area was also set up with its capital at Mahabad, and it served as a centre for Kurdish agitation against Persia, Iraq and Turkey. Soviet troops remained beyond their allotted time in Persia until the Persian government agreed to the formation of a joint Soviet-Persian company to exploit the oil resources of northern Persia and until Communists were brought into the Persian government.

In October, 1947, however, the Persian parliament refused to ratify these agreements and in 1949 the Tudeh party was banned. *The nationalists not only turned against the earlier agreements with the Soviet Union, but against Britain as well.* The Anglo-Iranian Oil Company was nationalized by the Persian parliament. The nationalist **Mossadeq** gained power in **1951** and the **Shah of Persia** was forced into exile, but he returned after a military coup overthrew Mossadeq in **1953.**

Although the Soviet Union had supported the policies of the Tudeh party, she made no effort to intervene in support of the anti-British and anti-American Mossadeq. She was not prepared for a head-on collision with Britain and the U.S.A. in the Middle East. As in the case of Turkey, Russian policy had halted at the point at which armed conflict with the Western powers could have occurred. Nevertheless the social and political influence of Communism in alliance with anti-western nationalism had increased greatly in Persia, as in other areas of the Middle East and North Africa.

French Policy in Indochina (Vietnam)

The French Vichy government under Pétain accepted the Japanese occupation of strategic points in the French colonial territory of Indochina. In April, 1945, the Japanese created the state of **Vietnam** under the **Emperor of Annam, Bao-Dai.** During the whole war period many French administrators as well as the **Communist Vietminh** under **Ho Chi-Minh** had resisted the Japanese. After the Japanese surrender in August, 1945, the Communist Vietminh gained control of Hanoi in the north and also had strong support in Saigon in the south. By agreement, British troops occupied south Vietnam (Cochin China) and the Chinese nationalist troops of Chiang-Kai-shek occupied the north and collaborated with the Communist Vietminh. The division of north and south was at the 18th parallel.

French trading and financial interests were very important in Saigon, and when French troops arrived in October, 1945, they *fought against the Vietminh* who were attempting to control the city. However, they were not strong enough to oppose both the Vietminh and the Chinese in the north. Saigon came once again under French control.

In the north Ho Chi-Minh, who distrusted the nationalist Chinese, got rid of them by temporarily achieving peace with the French who officially recognized the Republic of Vietnam established by the Communists. However, Ho Chi-Minh then *demanded the inclusion of south Vietnam in the Republic*. In reply to this the French established a government in Saigon which opposed the Vietminh and the north. This led to a general rising by the Vietminh against the French in December, 1946. To this the French replied by recognizing the former Japanese puppet Bao-Dai as ruler of the whole of Vietnam.

The situation was changed in favour of the Vietminh by the arrival of Chinese Communist forces on the northern border, who gave direct aid to Ho Chi-Minh. By this time the whole of China was under Communist control and **Chiang-Kai-shek** had been driven out into the island of **Formosa** with the remnants of his forces under American protection. The Communist victory in China under **Mao-Tse-tung** had radically changed the situation in the east in favour of anti-western Communism and nationalism. Both China and the Soviet Union now recognized the Vietminh as the rulers of all Vietnam. In reply to this the French continued their military operations against the Vietminh and attempted to strengthen the position of Bao-Dai. Reinforcements arrived from France and the over-all direction of the struggle was assigned to General Juin. Despite attempts at negotiation, the struggle was still continuing in 1953. Its outcome is dealt with in Chapter 26.

Communism Under Mao Tse-tung in China

During the war there had been collaboration between the Communists and Nationalists against the Japanese, but it was uneasy. As representatives of the big landlords and Capitalist elements, the Nationalists under Chiang-Kai-shek were distrusted by the Communists who, in the territories controlled by them, had expropriated the landlords in favour of the peasants. In 1945 the Communist armies occupied their own areas in the north. General Marshall was sent out to China, but his efforts to bring the two sides together failed. Fighting between Communists and Nationalists broke out in Manchuria.

The Communist armies swept everything before them, and their popularity with the peasantry was immense. *By 1949 the Communist Party under Mao Tse-Tung was in control of China*, and Chiang-Kai-shek was in Formosa. *The victory of Communism in China was a defeat for the U.S.A. and one of the most important events in world history*. It altered the whole balance of world forces, for there were now two vast powers, Russia and China, under Communist rule. Communist China tended to become the centre of inspiration for Asian Communism rather than Moscow. *In 1965 China exploded her first atomic bomb.*

In 1949 the British government gave full recognition to Communist China, but the U.S.A. would not do so. The U.S.A. also continued to *oppose the entry of Communist China to the United Nations* and this attitude has been maintained to 1966. Her support for Chiang-Kai-shek in Formosa ruled out her recognition of Peking.

The Korean War, 1950–1953

Korea had come under Japanese rule in 1910, but the Allies decided that Korea should be independent after 1945. Russian and American troops occupied temporarily the north and south respectively, divided approximately at the 38th parallel.

The Allied aim was to unify Korea under one government, and in March, 1946, negotiations between American and Russian representatives in Korea took place for this purpose. A conference in Moscow in 1946 had agreed that the unified Korea would be under the temporary trusteeship of the U.S.A., the U.S.S.R., China and Great Britain (i.e. they would be answerable to the United Nations for the general supervision of the country). The North Koreans now objected to the Representative Democratic Council, set up by Dr. **Syngman Rhee** in South Korea, being allowed to function in a united Korea because it had opposed the trusteeship idea. The Americans, however, declared that they could not agree to the exclusion of a body which comprised a union of over 100 political parties in South Korea (in Korea altogether there were about 400 'political parties').

Following this breakdown of the first efforts to unify Korea, a **United Nations Commission** under **Mr. Menon** (India) went to Korea in 1948 and suggested the election of leaders from north and south to meet together for consultations on unification. This, however, was rejected, and the American proposal for elections in South Korea was adopted. It should be noted that Mr Menon's proposals were rejected by the 'Little Assembly' of the United Nations, comprising only a part of its membership. Its powers to do this were questioned by some members who demanded a vote of the whole General Assembly.

On February 16th, 1948, the North Korean People's Committee, comprising a union of various political groups with strong Communist control, announced the creation of a separate **Democratic People's Republic** and a North Korean people's army. This consisted of 200,000 men mainly equipped with Russian weapons. The United

Nations Commission established to supervise elections was refused entry to North Korea. Elections were then held in both South and North Korea and new constitutions adopted, each side claiming that their system was intended for the whole of Korea. Dr. Syngman Rhee was elected President of South Korea and soon afterwards began discussions with Chiang-Kai-shek for the defence of the Pacific area against Communism.

Russian forces had left North Korea in 1948 and American forces left South Korea in 1949.

Great tension developed between North and South Korea, and there were constant armed clashes at the 38th. parallel and along the coasts. At the end of June, 1950, North Korean forces crossed the 38th parallel. President Truman decided that American forces should be sent to the assistance of South Korea, and the Security Council of the United Nations, condemning North Korea as the aggressor, declared that members of the United Nations should do all possible to support South Korea. Russia not being present at this meeting of the Security Council, the veto was not applied. Forces sent were mainly American, with British, Commonwealth and Turkish troops also being involved. The North Korean forces were driven back over the 38th parallel, and *the war was carried into North Korea.* At this point Chinese *Volunteers* entered North Korea, and in 1951 the United Nations forces were driven back. As Communist forces were being supplied from north of the Yalu River, the United Nations Commander, the American **General MacArthur,** wished to bomb Manchuria.

This was a critical point of the Korean war. China had signed a treaty of alliance with Russia in 1950, and if MacArthur's strategy had been carried out, it was possible that the Soviet Union would have entered the war, which could have become the third world war. The possession of stockpiles of atomic bombs by the Soviet Union was now a certainty. In these circumstances *President Truman dismissed MacArthur* and the possible extension of the war was avoided. Soon afterwards, in July, 1951, truce talks began between the two sides, and dragged on until 1953, when the 38th parallel, with slight adjustments to meet the defensive requirements of each side, became the frontier between North and South. The repatriation of prisoners of war and other negotiations for the eventual armistice had been long and tedious. The difficulties did not come only from the Communists, for President Rhee proved very difficult to the United Nations negotiators, and in a visit to the United States advocated an attack on Communist China.

Effects of the Korean War on World Affairs

1. It increased the fear of general war and speeded up the formation of *various defensive alliances* between the Great Powers on both sides of the 'Iron Curtain'.

2. It led to anti-Communist hysteria in the United States and the emergence of **Senator McCarthy** as 'Communist-baiter-in-chief' and the spreader of political smears against persons of even mildly liberal opinion. This damaged the United States in the eyes of her western allies.

3. The support given to Right-wing elements such as Chiang-Kai-shek in Formosa and Syngman Rhee in South Korea by the United States *tended to turn the Asian peoples against America.*

4. In Communist China the war led to a harsher and more totalitarian policy. This was allied to violent anti-American propaganda and to charges that the U.S.A. was waging germ warfare against China. There was increasing pressure to bring everyone more under the influence of Communist ideology and the toleration so far shown to non-Communists was replaced by *more direct indoctrination.*

5. On the credit side, the MacArthur incident had shown a nervous world the dangers of minor wars becoming atomic holocausts, and *it strengthened the growing demand for effective international control of atomic energy.*

Summary

The situation in Asia after the end of World War II was one of general ferment. The movement for independence was widespread—in French Indochina, in Korea, in the empires of Britain and the Netherlands (Malaya, Burma, India, Indonesia). World Communism was attempting to consolidate and extend the influence it had gained during the war against the Axis powers. Its influence was also seen in the Middle East and North Africa, and everywhere it was attempting

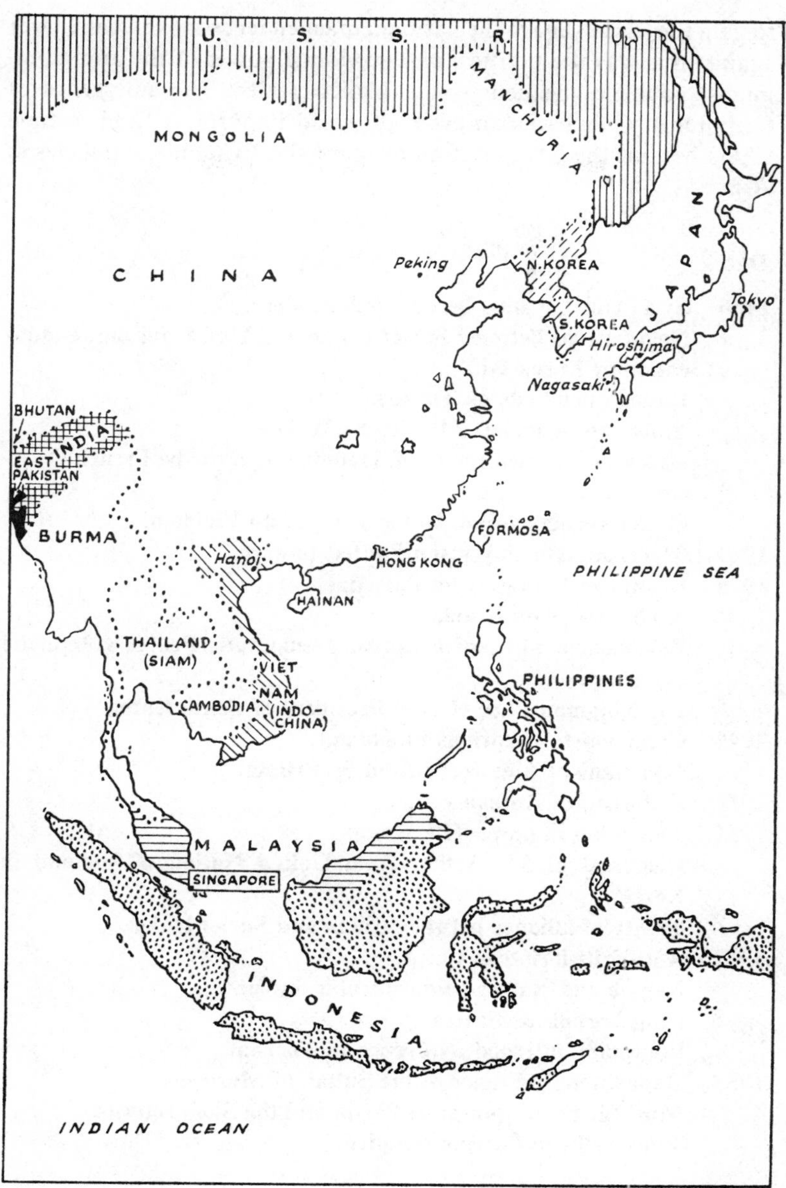
U. S. S. R.
MANCHURIA
MONGOLIA
CHINA
Peking
N.KOREA
S.KOREA
JAPAN
Tokyo
Hiroshima
Nagasaki
BHUTAN
INDIA
EAST PAKISTAN
BURMA
Hanoi
HONG KONG
FORMOSA
PHILIPPINE SEA
HAINAN
THAILAND (SIAM)
VIET NAM (INDO-CHINA)
CAMBODIA
PHILIPPINES
MALAYSIA
SINGAPORE
INDONESIA
INDIAN OCEAN

to gain the leadership of the national independence movements. Over against this was the political and economic power of the anti-Communist countries headed by the United States. The emergence of Communist China was an event of world importance, and in time China became the inspirer of more aggressive Communist policies in Asia.

Dates

1946 **Syria and Lebanon become independent.**
Negotiations between Soviet Union and U.S.A. for the re-unification of Korea fail.
Russian demands on Turkey.
American financial aid given to Turkey.
December, armed rising of Vietminh against the French (Vietnam).
French recognize Bao Dai as ruler of all Vietnam.

1947 **Algerian Assembly given limited powers.**

1948 **Britain withdraws from Palestine.**
Arab attacks on Israel.
Establishment of North Korean Democratic People's Republic and army.
Dr. Syngman Rhee elected President of South Korea.

1949 **Communists victorious in China.**
Communist China recognized by Britain.

1950 **Outbreak of Korean war.**

1951 **Mossadeq in power (Persia).**
Dismissal of MacArthur from United Nations Command in Korea.
Treaty of alliance between China and Soviet Union.

1952 **Anti-British riots in Cairo.**
Neguib and Nasser gain control in Egypt.
King Farouk abdicates.
Bourguiba interned by French in Tunisia.

1953 **Deposition by France of the Sultan of Morocco.**
Mossadeq loses power in Persia and the Shah returns.
Truce talks in Korea concluded.

QUESTIONS

1. *Outline the changes which occurred in this period in two of the following:* (a) *Palestine;* (b) *Egypt;* (c) *Algeria;* (d) *Persia.*

2. *What were Soviet aims in respect of Turkey after the war and how were they resisted?*

3. *Describe the course of events in Indochina in the years 1945 to 1953.*

4. *Outline the developments in Korea which led to the war of 1950–1953.*

5. *What were the effects of the Korean war on world affairs?*

CHAPTER TWENTY-FIVE

THE YEARS 1953–1977 IN EUROPE

The Post-Stalin Period

MARSHAL STALIN died on March 5, 1953, and in the next few years important changes took place in the states of eastern Europe. In view of the rigid and personal control which he had exercised over every aspect of Russian and Communist policy, his death was certain to produce changes. **Malenkov** became Russian Prime Minister, and **Nikita Khrushchev** First Secretary of the Soviet Communist Party.

To a certain extent there were signs of a weakening of Communist control in the eastern states. In Czechoslovakia, the President, Klement Gottwald, a complete follower of the 'Stalin line', died soon after attending Stalin's funeral. In the same year, 1953, *expressions of working-class discontent* showed themselves in Czechoslovakia. There were a number of strikes to protest against the lowering of the standard of living by a currency reform, and in the industrial town of Pilzen the workers in a number of industries came out on strike, and there were demands for a change of government. These were isolated movements, and were suppressed by the use of troops, but *they were a new phenomenon in the Communist world.*

In East Berlin a dispute between building workers and management led to strikes and demonstrations. Similar signs of discontent appeared in other parts of eastern Germany. Soviet armoured units moved into the areas concerned and the disturbances were suppressed.

The Russian Communist leaders had to take account of these events, and a certain disavowal of Stalinist policies began to make itself felt. The most obvious sign of this was the trial and execution of **L. P. Beria,** head of the Soviet security police under Stalin.

These disturbances also led to changes in other states. In Hungary

Imre Nagy replaced the Stalinist **Rakosi** as Prime Minister. This was followed by more freedom of expression in the press. It also brought a modification of the Stalinist policy of extreme concentration on heavy industry, and more attention was now given to the production of consumer goods. The Hungarian peasantry received more government financial assistance. They were also given freedom to opt out of the collective farms and by the end of 1954 about 10 per cent of the collective farms had been broken up. This produced a 'mixed economy' on the land—the Communist collectives on one hand and private peasant occupation on the other. Political prisoners were released on a wide scale and internment camps broken up.

In Czechoslovakia rather similar movements occurred, especially efforts to produce more consumer goods for the people. There was also a general increase in wage levels.

In Poland more freedom of expression was permitted on the radio and in the press, and the activities of the secret police were drastically reduced.

All these were immediate signs of important changes in the Communist world, and coincided with changes both inside Russia and in her foreign policy. There gradually emerged the avowed Russian policy of *peaceful coexistence* with the Capitalist world—the acceptance of the idea that the two systems could compete peacefully and that war was not inevitable. The Communist leaders still avowed that Communism would in time show its superiority over the Capitalist world and would gain the peaceful victory. In other words, *the aim of spreading world Communism was by no means abandoned,* but it now tended to take on less harsh and aggressive forms, as far as Moscow was concerned. (In the 1960's Communist China was to revive the more aggressive line, causing a considerable rift between herself and Moscow.)

Eastern Europe, 1955–1956

The changing situation in eastern Europe reached its climax in the years 1955–1956.

In 1955 Malenkov resigned as Soviet Prime Minister and Khrushchev assumed more power. Khrushchev had had a distinguished record in administration during the war, but he now reinforced the anti-Stalinist policies which had been developing in Russia and world Communism. The greater freedom of discussion in the Soviet Union since 1953, especially for writers and artists of all kinds, continued to develop. But the most significant event was the speech of Khrushchev at the twentieth congress of the Communist Party of the Soviet Union in Moscow on February 25th, 1956. This meeting was secret, but details of Mr. Khrushchev's speech were given by Communist leaders in other states. It was a wide-ranging attack on Stalin's methods and policies. The main charges against Stalin were that he had:

1. Abandoned collective leadership and made himself supreme.
2. Permitted the imprisonment or execution of loyal Communists who had opposed him.
3. Made bad mistakes in agricultural policy.
4. Failed to prepare for the German invasion.
5. Made grave mistakes of strategy during the war.
6. Been responsible for the quarrel with Yugoslavia in 1948.

Khrushchev denounced the *cult of personality* by which Stalin had achieved almost a personal dictatorship in Russia.

This speech had a profound effect not only in the Communist world but everywhere else. In Russia itself *it was followed by the release of persons imprisoned during the purges of 1937*, including a former Commissar for Education. The reputations of many who had been executed were now officially re-established. This rehabilitation now occurred in other states—for example, of **Rajk** in Hungary and **Kostov** in Bulgaria and others of their supporters who had been imprisoned or executed. In Poland about 30,000 political prisoners were released and the sentences of another 70,000 were drastically reduced. In Czechoslovakia the Prime Minister, **Mr. Siroky,** denounced the personal power achieved by the late president, Gottwald, and the methods of the security police; a number of political prisoners were also released. In all the eastern states the security police were subjected to criticism and to drastic changes.

Developments in Poland and Hungary were of great importance and require a more detailed reference.

Poland, 1955–1977

Besides the changes already mentioned in Poland Mr. Gomulka, who had been in prison since 1951, was now released. This was later followed by demands, especially from the industrial workers of Warsaw, for his re-instatement as First Secretary of the Communist Party, which was done. In public speeches he made it clear that Socialism could be achieved in different countries by differing means and that domination by the Soviet Union or anyone else in Polish internal affairs would not be tolerated. At the same time friendship and co-operation with the Soviet Union in international affairs would be maintained. (This was very similar to the line originally taken by Tito in Yugoslavia.) He declared that riots by the workers in Poznan were due to poor living conditions which must be improved.

At the same time, **Marshal Rokossovski,** who had been Stalin's nominee as Polish Commander-in-Chief in 1949, was removed from his post.

In some respects this was going further than Mr. Khrushchev liked, but Poland was prepared to resist any Russian pressure, even armed, and he accepted the situation.

These changes in Poland led to further breaks with the policies of the Stalinist period: (1) The dissolution of the collective farms was allowed, and a great exodus from them followed. (2) Taxation on the peasantry was reduced and better prices allowed for their produce. (3) Agreement with the Catholic Church was achieved and religious instruction was once again allowed in the schools. In general, the priesthood supported the new government and political leadership. (4) Greater freedom of political expression in the press was allowed and non-political art and literature were almost entirely free from official control. (5) The Polish parliament, the **Seym,** was given more powers of legislation and at the same time the government's powers to govern by decree were drastically reduced. (6) New economic policies increased the output of consumer goods and the standard of life greatly improved in the following years. (7) The workers in the factories were brought into closer consultation on all matters affecting production—an increase of *industrial democracy*.

The year 1970 produced important events in Poland, one of the key states of the eastern bloc. The economic condition of the country was bad—low production, high unemployment. A rigid state control of industry was leading to the production of many goods for which there was no public demand. The government's own income was low, while poor agricultural production led Poland to rely on grain imports from the Soviet Union, Canada, France and West Germany. The younger generation in Poland were especially critical of government censorship and the absence of real freedom of discussion. A few newspapers dared to raise these questions. When the government attempted a drastic increase in prices, rioting broke out and a general state of emergency was declared. There were many fatal clashes between the government militia and demonstrators, and for a time the government sealed off the whole Polish coastline and rail traffic was suspended.

These events in Poland led to the removal of Gomulka as Secretary-General of the Communist Party and his replacement by a less dogmatic communist, Edward Gierek. The price rises were cancelled, and gradually order was restored. Gierek's policy was to reduce government control of industry and give more freedom to industrial concerns to carry out their own planning. This change led to great improvements. In 1973 industrial production rose by 33 per cent and real wages also rose steeply. The years 1971–77 saw internal improvements in Poland under Gierek, but the disturbances were a serious challenge to the government of one of the most important communist states.

The Rising in Hungary

Here events took a more tragic turn. In October, 1956, *student demonstrations on a wide scale took place in Budapest.* The general demand was couched in liberal terms—demands for social and political freedom and for free elections. The Prime Minister, **Gero,** at first resisted, but eventually he was replaced by Imre Nagy who had been Prime Minister at an earlier period. He formed an all-party government which had wide support throughout Hungary and announced a programme which included: (1) withdrawal from the Warsaw Pact and the adoption of neutrality in international affairs; (2) negotiations with Russia for the withdrawal of her troops from Hungary; (3) the holding of free elections; (4) the release of **Cardinal Mindszenty** who had been in prison since 1948.

The Soviet Union suddenly moved large numbers of infantry, artillery and tanks into Hungary on November 4th and *began a concerted attack on the armed supporters of the new government.* These attacks were made in strength against Budapest and other centres where the insurgents were strong. At the same time a government was set up under **Janos Kadar,** First Secretary of the Communist Party, who had deserted Nagy's government. In a few days the uprising was crushed with considerable loss of life and the Kadar government was set up.

This action of the Soviet Union was widely condemned, but the United Nations could only protest. In any case, two of the most important Western powers, France and Britain, were already involved in the Suez affair (see pp. 232–3).

The reasons for Soviet armed action are a matter for debate, but certain points seem clear: (1) the demands for neutral status by Nagy were coupled with the proposal that the United Nations should guarantee this neutrality—a supervision which Russia was not prepared to tolerate on her frontiers; (2) the success of the Nagy government would have shaken the whole foundation of Soviet influence in eastern Europe and could have spread to other states.

The Common Market

This was one of the most important economic developments in post-war Europe. By the **Treaty of Rome, 1957,** the European Economic Community was formed **(EEC)**, its purpose being to establish a Common Market. The states entering the agreement were six in number—France, the German Federal Republic, Italy, Belgium, Holland and Luxembourg, comprising about 170,000,000 people. The area is separated from the other European states by a common tariff barrier, and the aim is progressively to reduce tariffs between the member countries so that eventually no tariffs will exist between members. The member countries have agreed to impose the same rates of tariffs against outside countries. The Secretariat of the Common Market was set up in Brussels. In general it has proved successful, there being a 29 per cent increase of trade between members in 1961 compared with 1960 and an 8 per cent increase with countries outside. The Common Market also aims to have common funds for investment and to enable labour to pass freely from one member state to another.

Earlier attempts by Britain to enter the Common Market were vetoed by the French under General de Gaulle, who considered that Britain, especially on account of her close attachment to the United States, would not be able or prepared to accept all the conditions laid down in the Rome Treaty of 1957. But in 1970 the Conservative government of Mr Heath re-opened negotiations, and the attitude of France was less rigid than had been the case in de Gaulle's presidency. The negotiations were long and tedious, and a considerable part of British opinion appeared to be doubtful of the value to Britain of entering the market. But parliamentary approval was obtained, and on January 1, 1973, Britain became a member of the Common Market. The Irish Republic and Denmark also entered at the same time. Britain secured agreements which were satisfactory to the Commonwealth producers of dairy products (mainly New Zealand) and of sugar (the West Indies). In Britain the Labour Government which came into power in 1974 organised a referendum on the question of Britain's membership of the EEC. The referendum showed national approval by a majority of about two to one.

Closely connected with the Common Market is the Strasbourg Assembly containing representatives of the political parties of the member states of the Market. This is a consultative body and can advise the Common Market Commission on matters raised and approved by the Assembly, but has no powers to enforce its opinions. In Britain the Labour Party, opposed to the terms of entry by Britain, decided not to send to Strasbourg the proportion of its M.P.s which it was entitled to send.

The European Free Trade Area, 1959

Known as **EFTA,** this is a free-trade area promoted especially by Great Britain and containing seven European states (Norway, Sweden, Denmark, Portugal, Austria, Switzerland and later Finland) which are not members of the Common Market.

After Britain's entry to the Common Market in 1973 she, together with Denmark, ceased to be a member of EFTA, but EFTA continued to have special trading arrangements with the Common Market countries.

Euratom

This is a further development of European co-operation for the development of atomic energy and its membership consists of the same six nations belonging to the European Coal and Steel Community (see p. 197).

German Re-unification Fails

The permanent division of Germany had never been a declared policy of any of the war-time Allies, and the problem of German re-unification was again raised in 1953. This led on to the important **Berlin Conference** of January–February, **1954.** The powers represented were the U.S.A., the Soviet Union, Britain and France.

The conference showed a fundamental difference between the Western powers and the Soviet Union in their approach to this problem. The Western powers' proposals were based on these principles: (1) the holding of a free election for the whole of Germany; (2) a new German government would then sign a peace treaty with the anti-Nazi powers; (3) the new German government would then be free to decide with which countries, if any, to make alliances. The Soviet Union's proposals were: (1) a provisional government composed of equal numbers of representatives of east and west Germany; (2) elections then to be held; (3) the new government then to sign a peace treaty which would include the stipulation that Germany would form no alliances at all, but maintain an international policy of neutrality.

Besides wishing to maintain Communist power in east Germany, Russia was determined to keep to her demand for the neutrality of Germany. In view of Germany's record this was regarded by many as a reasonable demand. On the other hand, the Western powers wished to bring Germany into the western system of alliances. The Soviet Union claimed that it was the Western powers' refusal to accept German neutrality which caused the breakdown of negotiations.

The failure of the Berlin Conference led on to the recognition by the Western powers of the German Federal Republic as a fully independent and sovereign state in October, 1954. An important undertaking was given by the new state—that it would not alter the frontiers of Germany or seek to re-unify Germany by the use of armed force.

Russia had at least agreed to discuss German re-unification, and this was followed by agreement with the Western powers to sign a *peace treaty with Austria*, now declared independent and neutral. All occupation forces were withdrawn from Austria in 1955.

In May, **1955,** Russia signed the **Warsaw Pact** with Poland, Czechoslovakia, Hungary, Rumania and Bulgaria. This was a defensive alliance which permitted Soviet troops to be stationed in these countries, and was a reply to the Western European Union and NATO which the Soviet Union had declared to be a breach of peace treaties between herself and Britain and France.

A sign of the further modification of the 'Stalin line' was a visit by Mr. Khrushchev to Belgrade in 1955, when *friendly relations were resumed with Yugoslavia.* Russia accepted the independence of Yugoslavia in foreign policy, and the Yugoslav Communist Party was also confirmed in its independence.

Summit Conference, 1960

In 1958 Mr. Khrushchev raised the question of a *Summit Conference* between the heads of state of the Great Powers to settle outstanding international problems. The problems were those of disarmament (especially nuclear disarmament and the testing of nuclear weapons), the problem of Berlin and of Germany and the whole question of relations between the NATO and the Warsaw Pact countries. It was hoped that all causes of dispute between the Communist and non-Communist world would be dealt with and that a meeting for this purpose of the Premiers of the Soviet Union and Britain and the Presidents of the United States and France would be the most effective way of dealing with these matters.

After two years of discussions and counter-proposals on the aims and methods of the conference, including preliminary meetings of the Foreign Secretaries of the Western powers, the date of May 16th, 1960, was finally agreed upon. On that date President Eisenhower, Mr. Khrushchev, General de Gaulle and Mr. Macmillan were to meet in Paris.

On May 1, 1960, an unarmed American reconnaissance plane was shot down near Sverdlovsk, over 1,200 miles inside the Soviet frontiers. The pilot was captured alive. This U-2 incident was sensational. The U.S.A. later admitted that this type of reconnaissance was taking place over the U.S.S.R. for information purposes which were aimed at preventing surprise attack on the U.S.A.—in other words, defensive purposes only. Mr. Khrushchev denounced the U.S.A. and cast doubts on the good faith of the U.S.A. in the desire for *peaceful co-existence.* On arriving at Paris on May 16th he demanded that the U.S.A. condemn the actions of its air force, punish those guilty and give an undertaking not to repeat these actions. On these conditions he agreed to continue with the Summit Conference. President Eisenhower replied that these flights had in fact not been resumed and that he was preparing proposals for the United Nations for a system of aerial reconnaissance which would prevent preparations for surprise attack. He declared that Mr. Khrushchev was using the incident to wreck the conference. After three days of intense diplomatic activity and attempts to secure a modification of Mr. Khrushchev's attitude, the latter left Paris on May 19th.

Thus a conference on which great hopes had been built never started. The few days served only to underline the tensions and dangers of the *Cold War*, although Mr. Khrushchev declared that he was still prepared for Russia to continue negotiations for an atomic test-ban treaty.

The Cuban Crisis

The **Cuban Crisis** of October, **1962,** when Russian rocket installations were detected on Cuba by American reconnaissance planes, brought the world once again to the brink of atomic war. **President Kennedy's** demands for the removal of these installations and his decision to intercept Russian ships carrying missiles to Cuba brought about a Russian-American confrontation. Mr. Khrushchev's decision to divert the Russian ships and to undertake the removal of the rockets from Cuba under Red Cross supervision was a statesmanlike decision in the face of American firmness. The later installation of the hot-line telephone communication between Washington and Moscow was a constructive outcome of this dangerous situation.

The Test-ban Treaty

During these years both the United States and Russia had continued an intensive programme of nuclear test explosions. The problem of the nuclear pollution of the atmosphere became serious. After long negotiations, a treaty banning all atmospheric tests (i.e. not those underground) was signed between the U.S.A., the U.S.S.R. and Britain in Moscow in the summer, **1963.** General de Gaulle had declared that France would participate in a general treaty among all the nuclear powers to prohibit all nuclear weapons and destroy stockpiles, but in the meantime would continue her efforts to develop her own nuclear weapons. Despite the attitude of France, the **Test-ban Treaty** was a first important step towards the possibility of banning all nuclear tests.

Czechoslovakia

During the 1960s several states of Eastern Europe were tending towards more independence of Moscow, although their allegiance to the military Warsaw Pact remained firm. At the same time bad relations developed between Russia and Communist China, where Mao-Tse tung regarded himself as the protector of the pure doctrine of communism as against the Russian tendency to compromise with western capitalism. Despite this, however, in 1972 President Nixon of the United States visited China, and a new phase of better relationships between Moscow and Peking began. Most important of all was the lifting of numerous trade restrictions between the United States and China which had been imposed by the United States many years before. This development coincided with the admission of Communist China to the United Nations in 1972 and the expulsion of Nationalist China (Taiwan).

In Eastern Europe important developments centred on Czechoslovakia, where, in 1967, a severe inflation led to fall in earnings, to unemployment and widespread discontent. Demands arose for less state control over economic affairs and the creation of a 'free market' for the sale of consumer goods. In Slovakia there was a strong movement to secure more independence from the government in Prague. At the same time writers denounced the government literary censorship and young people were showing little interest in joining the Communist Party.

In 1968, Dubcek, the new First Secretary of the Czech Communist Party, sought to meet these criticisms by liberal-type reforms. The Stalinist President Novotny was replaced by the more liberal General Svoboda. The reforms now introduced were a drastic change from the past—such as the right to hold public meetings, the abolition of press censorship, the curtailing of the powers of the Security Police, the right of minority parties to be represented in the government. Above all, the National Assembly was to be free to criticize any aspects of government policy. Moscow showed disapproval of these measures and was strongly supported by the East German government. In the summer of 1968 Warsaw Pact military manoeuvres were held near the Czech borders and suddenly in August, after an apparent withdrawal of Russian troops stationed in Czechoslovakia, Russian forces moved into Prague and, after meeting some resistance, overthrew the Dubcek government. A new government was formed of which Dubcek was a member, but he was gradually removed from positions of power and became Ambassador to Turkey. The complete repudiation of the liberal-type reforms was consolidated in 1970 when Dr Husak, a strong supporter of Russian policies, became prime minister.

The Berlin Wall

In 1961 the East German government completed the building of a dividing wall between East and West Berlin, in an attempt to prevent the movement of Germans from East to West Germany. By the early 1960s this movement had entailed a great loss of manpower to the East German economy and at one point reached the level of 20,000 a month. The Berlin Wall was constructed with armed towers, and those attempting to pass over it were liable to be shot. This led to a number of deaths of would-be escapees, and increased tension between West and East Germany. However drastic and unpleasant, the measures taken were effective in sealing the boundary, and by 1970 the East German economy was showing signs of increased production and greater strength. Important changes occurred as the result of the formation of the Social Democratic government in the German Federal Republic under Willi Brandt. He was a strong advocate of attempts to bring about agreement between West and East Germany, and his efforts resulted in a new agreement in 1972 by which easier access between East and West Germany was obtained. Closer trading relations were to be developed and ambassadors appointed. This change was ratified by the West German public in the elections at the end of 1972 when Brandt obtained a clear majority in the West German parliament at Bonn. These important developments led on to other countries making arrangements for ambassadors or other representatives in East Germany. Arrangements also began to be made in 1973 for the representation of East Germany in the United Nations. None of these arrangements precluded the future unification of the two Germanys, but this possibility had certainly receded. To all intents and purposes there existed even more clearly by 1973 two German states.

International Developments, 1974–1977

These years were politically some of the most important of the twentieth century. In Greece the nine-year ruthless dictatorship of the generals collapsed and a liberal democratic parliamentary system was restored. This was mainly a consequence of the failure of the generals' attempt to secure Greek control of Cyprus, which was followed by the Turkish invasion of the island and its division into Greek and Turkish zones.

In Italy, where poor industrial production, a low value of the currency, unemployment and a lethargic and corrupt administration led to increasing discontent throughout the country, the ruling Christian Democratic Party was under great pressure. The Communist Party of Italy, declaring its support for Euro-communism and its opposition to Russian domination of communist practice and theory, made considerable gains in the election of June, 1976, despite the Pope's efforts to influence the Catholic electorate against the communists. The Christian Democrats remained the largest party in parliament, but were dependent on communist support. At the beginning of 1978 this support was withdrawn, and a serious political crisis arose. In the meantime elements of the extreme right (neo-fascist) and the extreme left were constantly involved in riots, while terriorism, kidnapping or shooting of prominent politicians and industrialists and bomb-throwing were very frequent.

Another drastic change occurred in 1975 by the overthrow of the thirty-year-old fascist dictatorship of Dr. Salazar in Portugal. The main challenge to the old regime came from within the armed forces and the revolution was almost bloodless. In the autumn of 1975 an attempt by the newly-legalised Communist Party to seize control was defeated, and a moderate socialist government was formed.

In Spain the change from fascism to a democratic liberal system occurred after the death of the fascist leader General Franco in 1975. The monarchy was restored in the person of Don Juan Carlos, who had Franco's blessing. Despite the violent opposition of the old Francoist party, the Falange, the Spanish parliament adopted in 1976 a liberal constitutional monarchy, involving freedom of elections and of speech and publication. After much controversy, the Communist Party of Spain was itself legalised in 1977. The general election of 1977 led to the formation of a government of the moderate centre.

In Africa radical changes occurred in these years. Portugal lost control of Mozambique to the national guerrilla forces which had waged resistance to the Portuguese colonial forces for some years. In Angola also the MPLA (Popular Movement for the Liberation of Angola) gained control, defeating the non-communist rival movements with the aid of forces from Dr. Castro's Cuba.

From Mozambique guerrilla forces were now organised for operations against the Smith regime in Rhodesia, and in general these developments represented a considerable advance for communism in Africa.

In the Middle East conflict, the tendency developed for the Soviet Union to support the Arab cause and for the United States to redress the balance by support of Israel. However, at the end of 1977, President Sadat of Egypt made a dramatic gesture towards peace in the Middle East, when he made an historic visit to Jerusalem and addressed the Israeli parliament. But Syria, Libya and Jordan did not support the Sadat initiative, and organised their own separate conference, in which the PLO took a prominent part in denouncing Sadat's move as a betrayal of the Arab cause. At this point the United States began to play an even more positive role. When Sadat's effort's seemed to be on the brink of failure, he visited the United States in February, 1978, and at the same time military talks between Israel and Egypt, which had been broken off, were resumed. It seemed that a new dimension in the general problem was developing.

In 1975 a fierce struggle took place in the Lebanon between the Christian right-wing forces and the Moslem left. After widespread destruction, especially in the capital Beirut, a united Arab force was organised from outside to police a cease-fire. Reasonable calm was re-established in the latter part of 1977.

In July, 1976, Palestinian skyjackers seized an Air France plane carrying a considerable number of Israeli passengers and forced the pilot to fly to Entebbe in Uganda. A daring Israeli airborne raid succeeded in releasing and returning to Israeli all but a very few of the hostages. The skyjackers had demanded the release of a number of Palestinian guerrillas held prisoners in Israel and elsewhere.

The Helsinki International Agreement, 1 August, 1975

The Helsinki accord on human rights and other questions was signed by the representatives of thirty states, including the principal states of Western and Eastern Europe. All states pledged themselves to refrain from the use or threat of force in their relations with one another, and declared that disputes between them would be settled by peaceful means. However, more important even than these declarations was the declaration of their support and 'Respect for human rights and fundamental freedoms, including the freedom of thought, conscience, religion and belief.' It was agreed that a meeting of representatives of the participating states should be held in Belgrade in June, 1977, to exchange views on the working of the agreements and to make provision for future developments. The declaration clearly presented problems for the eastern communist states, and an unofficial committee was established in the Soviet Union to monitor the extent to which the declaration was adhered to. During 1977 Soviet authorities took measures against this committee, and some of its members were arrested.

Summary

The death of Stalin in 1953 was followed by new developments in Russia and the east European states. A number of popular disturbances occurred in all of them and were succeeded by changes of party line in the various Communist countries. The production of more consumer goods and the de-collectivization of agriculture were important features of these changes. The denunciation of much of Stalin's policy by Khrushchev in 1956 was followed by further changes, such as the release of the victims of former purges or their political rehabilitation if dead. Movements both in Poland and Hungary represented efforts to gain more independence of Soviet policies. The suppression of the Hungarian rising by Soviet forces showed, however, that the Soviet Union would not tolerate a complete change of front by her satellites.

The problem of the unification of Germany proved intractable, and the failure of the Summit Conference of 1960, after the U-2 incident, was a serious setback to efforts to improve east-west relations. The Cuban crisis of 1962 saw the absolute confrontation of the Soviet Union and the United States and the most dangerous situation since the end of World War II. On the credit side the Test-ban Treaty of 1963 was a most important forward step.

Important international developments occurred in the last years of this period. Greece returned to democracy, as also did Portugal and Spain. In Africa both Angola and Mozambique gained their independence, and communism made considerable gains. In the Middle East President Sadat of Egypt undertook an important peace initiative.

Dates

1953 **Death of Marshal Stalin.**
Disturbances in east European states.
Modifications of Communist policies.

1954 **Failure of Berlin Conference on German re-unification.**

1955 **Khrushchev assumes power.**
Release and rehabilitation of many political prisoners in Russia and other states.
Re-instatement of Gomulka in Poland and important changes in Polish policies.
Austrian peace treaty.
The Warsaw Pact.

1956 **Denunciation of Stalinism by Khrushchev.**
October, student riots in Budapest.
Imre Nagy becomes Hungarian premier.
November 4th, Soviet forces move against Hungarian rebels.

1957 **Creation of the European Common Market.**
1958 **Khrushchev raises question of a Summit Conference.**
1959 **Creation of EFTA and Euratom.**
1960 **Summit Conference prepared for May 16th, Paris.**
May 1, U-2 incident.
1961 **Building of Berlin Wall.**
1962 **October, Cuba crisis.**
Khrushchev agrees to dismantle Cuban missiles under international supervision.
1963 **Nuclear Test-ban Treaty.**
Assassination of President Kennedy.
1968 **Dubcek reforms, Czechoslovakia, Russian occupation of Prague.**
1970 **Serious disturbances in Poland.**
1972 **New agreement between West and East Germany.**
1973 **January 1, Britain enters the Common Market.**
1974 **Turkish invasion of Cyprus.**
1975 **Overthrow of Salazar in Portugal.**
Helsinki agreements.
1976 **Gains by Italian communists in elections.**
1977 **General election in Spain.**
1978 **President Sadat visits Jerusalem.**

QUESTIONS

1. In which countries of eastern Europe did signs of unrest appear in 1953–1954, and what changes of internal policy occurred?

2. What were the results of Khrushchev's denunciation of Stalin on (a) *international affairs;* (b) *internal affairs of the east European states?*

3. How did the policies of the Western powers differ from those of Russia on the re-unification of Germany?

4. Write notes on (a) *'Peaceful coexistence';* (b) *the Warsaw Pact;* (c) *the U-2 incident;* (d) *the Nuclear Test-ban Treaty;* (e) *the Cuba Crisis;* (f) *the Common Market.*

5. For what reasons was the Berlin Wall constructed?

6. Why was the new treaty between East and West Germany possible in 1972?

7. What was the case for and against Britain's entry to the Common Market?

8. Why did Russia use military force in Czechoslovakia in 1968?

9. What important changes took place in European politics in the years 1974–77?

10. What were the causes of discontent in Poland in 1970, and what measures were taken to meet it?

CHAPTER TWENTY-SIX

THE MIDDLE AND FAR EAST, 1953–1977

Tunisia

THE French disasters in Indochina *caused radical changes in French colonial policy*. The new Prime Minister, returned by a large majority in 1954, **Pierre Mendès-France,** decided to bring Bourguiba to France and open negotiations. It was agreed that Tunisia should have control of her own internal affairs, and Bourguiba returned to Tunisia in 1955. Although Mendès-France was defeated in 1955 and resigned his premiership, the progress of Tunisia towards independence continued. Bourguiba controlled the key nationalist party in Tunisia, the **Neo-Destour,** and pursued a policy of pressure on the French leading to further concessions. In 1956, an agreement with France recognized Tunisia's right to have its own army and to control its own foreign policy—a very big step towards independence. France was to have the right to keep her troops there for a time and also to control the naval base of Bizerta. From this point the achievement of national independence was almost complete, for France had made fundamental concessions by 1956. Further pressures led to agreement for the withdrawal of all French forces outside Bizerta by October, 1958.

Morocco

After 1954 the basis of Moroccan independence was also laid. The French policy of placing a puppet Sultan on the throne caused extreme national discontent in Morocco. Military and civil action against the French took on a terrorist form—sabotage, assassination, the strike weapon, were all used, and the French for their part took harsh measures against their opponents. For nearly two years a state of civil war existed between the Moroccans and the French civil and military authorities. In 1955, however, the French agreed to re-instate the deposed Sultan. This was followed by new negotiations which *gave the Moroccans full independence in home and foreign policy*. The Moroccans also gained control of the old northern Spanish zone by agreement with Spain, and Tangier lost its international status and came under Moroccan control. As in the case of Tunisia, these gains led on to complete independence. The accession to power of General de Gaulle in France, 1958, led to better relations between Morocco and France, and many outstanding causes of dispute were settled.

Algeria

As an integral part of France, the situation in Algeria took on a different character from that of Tunisia and Morocco and fundamentally affected the political situation in France itself, leading to the re-emergence of General de Gaulle as President in 1958. This is dealt with in more detail in Chapter 27 on France in the period 1940 to 1963.

Britain and Egypt

In Egypt the group of officers which had ended the rule of King Farouk were strong nationalists and also determined to improve the lot of the ordinary people after the corrupt rule of Farouk. In 1952 **General Neguib** became Prime Minister and in 1953 the old political parties, including the 'Wafd', were dissolved and replaced by the National Liberal Rally. The Egyptian Republic was proclaimed, and Neguib became President and Nasser Vice-Premier. Differences arose between them and in 1954 Nasser made himself Premier. Immediately two important questions came to the fore—(1) the **Sudan** and (2) the **Suez Canal.**

Britain favoured the creation of an independent Sudan, and in 1953 Egypt had agreed to the election of a Sudanese parliament and government for three years, after which the Sudan would be free to decide whether to unite with Egypt or not. *In 1956 she declared for independence*, and the Egyptian aim of union was defeated. This in itself created bad relations between Britain and Egypt. However, Nasser's policy on the Canal Zone was at first moderate and he agreed to the British demand that the post-war treaty arrangement by which she would be entitled to reoccupy the Canal Zone in war-time should be maintained.

The Suez Crisis

The Arab states had never recognized the state of Israel, and Egypt quickly took up the anti-Israel campaign. At the same time Nasser wanted western financial aid for the building of the **Aswan Dam.** But America, who was pro-Israel, refused his requests for financial aid. *The failure to obtain western financial aid turned Nasser strongly against the west*, and he declared his intention to nationalize the Suez Canal and expropriate Britain and France. He had strong Arab sympathy in the Middle East, which at this time was anti-western. The Soviet Union was also on friendly terms with Egypt.

French official policy was strongly anti-Nasser, not only over the Canal question, but because *Egypt was a centre for anti-French activities in Algeria.* The French wished to bring Nasser down. The decision by the governments of Britain, France and Israel to use force was governed also by the fact that the Soviet Union was already involved in difficulties with Hungary and was unlikely to give Nasser direct support. On October 29th, Israel attacked Egypt and advanced rapidly. Britain bombarded Egyptian airfields and landed troops at Port Said. *Immediately the actions of the three powers were denounced in the United Nations* and by Britain's closest ally, the United States. The Soviet Union threatened to intervene. All this led to the withdrawal of British and French forces and the halting of the Israeli campaign.

The Suez affair was one of the most sensational events of the decade and really constituted a serious error by the opponents of Nasser. Britain and France were denounced as aggressors and were forced by sheer isolation to retreat. This also enabled Nasser to claim that his forces had repelled the invaders and greatly strengthened his position in Egypt. *It was to a certain extent a victory of the Soviet Union over the west*, for the Arab states tended to become increasingly anti-western, and the *Afro-Asian countries saw the Soviet Union as their supporter against the Western powers.* It led to greater unity in the Arab world, and in 1958 Egypt and Syria combined to form the **United Arab Republic.** It led to the Yemen seeking the friendship of Egypt for its campaign against British rule in the **Aden Protectorate.** In almost every way the Suez affair militated against the interests of the west and strengthened the unity of the Arab world. Although the U.S.A. had condemned the actions of Britain and France, she also lost influence in the Middle East.

The Baghdad Pact

Even before Suez, the Western powers had been losing ground in the Middle East and had failed to get the Arab states to join the system of western alliances. This was the main reason for American financial assistance to Turkey—to bolster her against the Soviet Union. American rocket bases were also set up on the Turkish frontier with Russia. Iraq, where there were British air bases, also feared Soviet intentions and in 1955 formed a defensive pact with Turkey. British air bases were then transferred to Iraqi control and only British air force advisers remained. Pakistan joined the defensive alliance, and after the fall of Mossadeq, Persia also joined. With the addition of Great Britain, the **Baghdad Pact** was thus brought into being, consisting of Britain, Turkey, Iraq, Pakistan and Persia. India was especially annoyed, particularly with her fellow Commonwealth member, Britain, for forming an alliance with Pakistan in view of the serious *conflict between India and Pakistan over Kashmir* (to lead to the outbreak of war between the two states in 1965). Britain made it clear, however, that she would not intervene in the case of a war between two Commonwealth powers.

The Baghdad Pact was another facet of the *Cold War*, but it was not particularly strong, especially as the United States declined membership.

Arab–Israeli Conflict

In the 1960s the Palestine Liberation Front became increasingly active. This organization aimed at the complete restoration of former Arab rights in Palestine and voiced above all the interests of the numerous Arab Palestine refugees who, since 1948, had been living in encampments. The Front operated from countries bordering on Israel, especially in Jordan, where it brought pressure to bear on King Hussein to take a more aggressive line towards Israel. Numerous clashes also developed along the Israeli–Syrian border in particular. In April 1967, both Syria and Egypt declared their intention of destroying the state of Israel. President Nasser of Egypt ordered the withdrawal of the United Nations Emergency Force which had been posted in Sinai between Egyptian and Israeli forces. On May 22, 1967, Nasser closed the Gulf of Aqaba to Israeli shipping, thus denying Israel access to her only southern port, Eilat.

On June 5, 1967, the Israeli air force attacked airfields in Egypt, Jordan, Syria and Iraq with devastating effects. This resulted in lack of air cover for Arab ground forces and, after serious defeats on land, Hussein and Nasser accepted a ceasefire on June 8 and Syria on June 9. The Arab states, however, refused to negotiate a peace settlement and Israel maintained her hold on Sinai, the Suez Canal and the Golan Heights in Syria. Russia then began to restore Egypt's military losses, while the U.S.A. continued to supply Israel.

A United Nations resolution of 1967 required the Israelis to relinquish their captured territories as a preliminary to peace negotiations. Mutual raiding continued. In Russia increasing difficulties were now placed in the way of Jews wishing to emigrate to Israel. However, an official cease-fire was agreed in 1970 and things became quiet along the Suez Canal, the opposite banks of which were occupied by Israeli and Egyptian forces. However, guerrilla pressure against King Hussein continued, and guerrilla forces gained control of some towns in the northern areas of Jordan. In 1971, after serious fighting between guerrilla and loyalist troops in the capital itself, Amman, Hussein succeeded in re-asserting his authority. Further developments in the Arab struggle against Israel from 1971 to 1973 included the hijacking of aircraft, while in 1972 several members of the Israeli Olympic team at Munich were murdered. In the autumn of 1972 there occurred a series of letter-bomb attacks on Israeli diplomats and business firms in Europe. To all these activites Israel replied with counter-measures, especially reprisal raids on guerrilla strongholds in Syria and Lebanon.

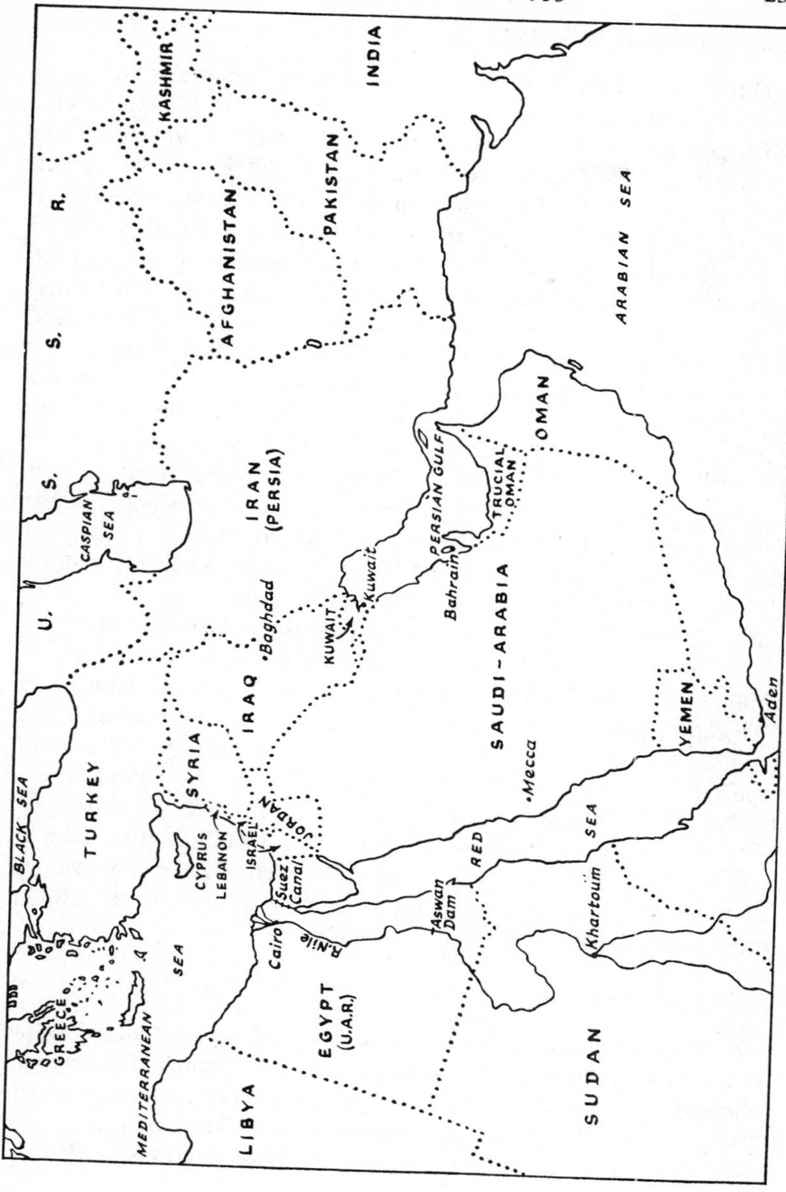
U. S. S. R.
KASHMIR
INDIA
PAKISTAN
AFGHANISTAN
CASPIAN SEA
IRAN (PERSIA)
ARABIAN SEA
OMAN
TRUCIAL OMAN
PERSIAN GULF
Bahrain
Kuwait
KUWAIT
Baghdad
IRAQ
SAUDI - ARABIA
YEMEN
Aden
BLACK SEA
TURKEY
SYRIA
JORDAN
ISRAEL
LEBANON
CYPRUS
Suez Canal
RED SEA
Mecca
Aswan Dam
Khartoum
SUDAN
R. Nile
Cairo
EGYPT (U.A.R.)
LIBYA
GREECE
MEDITERRANEAN SEA

The Yom-Kippur War, 1973

During the years 1970–73 relations between Israel and the Arab states had worsened. On October 6, 1973, the Day of Atonement, when general activity in Israel was at a standstill, Egypt and Syria launched massive attacks across the Suez Canal and on the Golan Heights respectively. The Egyptian drive was at first successful in getting large forces across the canal. However, Israel managed gradually, and after considerable losses of men and material, to redress the situation. After enormous tank battles east of the canal they succeeded in crossing to the west bank, where they destroyed many Soviet-installed SAM missile sites and also trapped the Egyptian Third Army east of the canal. At this point both the U.S.S.R. and the U.S.A. supported a United Nations resolution calling for a cease-fire, and this was achieved on November 11th. In 1975 mutual withdrawal of forces from some territory was arranged and a United Nations force was established between the former combatants. A further dramatic development took place at the end of 1977, when President Sadat of Egypt made his historic visit to Jerusalem to address the Israeli parliament. His peace initiative was strongly opposed by the Palestinian Liberation Organisation and by other Arab states, especially Syria and Libya. A conference called in Jerusalem in January, 1978, between Israeli and Egyptian representatives in the presence of a representative of the United States, Senator Vance, met with immediate difficulties, especially relating to the Israeli occupation of the West Bank of the Jordan and to President Sadat's demand that Israel should withdraw from all conquered Egyptian territory. When the initiative seemed to be faltering, President Sadat visited President Carter in Washington in an effort to gain clear support for his aims from the United States and to secure arms supplies from her.

Indochina (Vietnam)

In May, **1954,** the French key fortress of **Dien Bien Phu** fell to the forces of the Communist Vietminh, and this French disaster was followed by negotiations between north and south Vietnam which resulted in the division of the country at the 17th parallel. No new bases were to be set up by either side, and free elections were to be held by July, 1956, in both north and south to establish a government for the whole of Vietnam. Cambodia and Laos were declared independent, and Vietminh forces were to withdraw. This agreement, signed at Geneva between the Great Powers (with the exception of the United States), fixed the lines of demarcation which remained in force until 1965, when Vietcong (Communist) activity supported by the north spread into south Vietnam, leading to the military intervention of the United States. In 1954 the United States regarded Communist control of the north under Ho Chi-Minh as making free elections impossible. In south Vietnam the United States supported the Prime Minister Ngo Dinh Diem who had refused to recognize the 1954 agreement. The U.S.A. provided the government of south Vietnam with very great economic and financial aid.

The Manila Pact, September, 1954

This agreement led on to the formation of the **South East Asia Treaty Organization (SEATO).** This was intended as a counter to possible aggression in the South-west Pacific below 21° 30′ latitude. Its members comprised the United States, Britain, France, Australia, New Zealand, the Philippines, Thailand and Pakistan. The area covered included Cambodia, Laos and south Vietnam. The U.S.A. agreed only to take action *in the case of aggression from Communist states*, and would consult the other members in other cases. Indonesia, which had half the population of the area concerned, refused to join.

Vietnam, 1954–1975

Following the fall of Dien Bien Phu a peace conference at Geneva decided to partition Vietnam at the 17th parallel. But the North left many armed supporters in the South as the nucleus of future action. In Cambodia and Laos communist forces remained in control of considerable areas, especially those safeguarding the southward routes into South Vietnam.

The Diem government, supported by the U.S.A. refused to accept the Geneva settlement of 1954. President Diem established an inefficient and corrupt government in the South and soon social unrest flared up. In 1957 communist guerrillas began to take wider control of the countryside, and in 1961 the National Liberation Front was set up in Hanoi to control and direct the movement in the south. Although the U.S.A. continued to support Diem until his later removal, by 1963 communist influence in South Vietnam had greatly extended. In 1964 an American warship was attacked by a North Vietnamese torpedo boat in the Gulf of Tongking, and the U.S.A. adopted a policy of air bombardment of North Vietnam. By 1967 the U.S.A. had 400,000 troops in Vietnam, but even so the Vietcong were able in June, 1967, to launch serious attacks on South Vietnamese cities, including Saigon itself.

By 1967 the Vietnamese struggle had become the main centre of world communist and anti-communist conflict. Both Russia and China supplied war material to North Vietnam, and the Americans were aided by token forces from South Korea, Australia and New Zealand. In 1968 the out-going President of the United States called a halt to American bombardment of the North. Soon afterwards peace negotiations began in Paris between the warring parties. Under the new President, Richard Nixon, these negotiations were continued, with breaks at moments of deadlock—a situation which continued until January, 1973. In the meantime American bombing of the north was resumed, but at the same time Nixon effected a gradual withdrawal of American ground forces as the American policy of building up the native forces of President Thieu continued to develop. By the end of 1972 American ground forces were little more than 40,000. After the refusal of President Thieu to accept the peace conditions negotiated by Dr Kissinger, Mr Nixon's special representative, America resumed the bombing of the North in December, 1972, but now extended it to the area of Haiphong (whose harbour had already been mined by American warships some time previously) and Hanoi itself. B-52 bombers in great force carried out these raids and both military and civilian casualties in the North were heavy. The embassies of some friendly governments suffered in the raids on Hanoi. Losses of B-52 bombers were considerable—about 25, representing many millions of dollars. These raids were discontinued in January, 1973, and Kissinger conducted further negotiations with the North Vietnamese. These resulted in the signing of an agreement acceptable to both President Thieu and the North Vietnamese, and a cease fire, under international supervision, came into force on January 27, 1973. All American forces were to be withdrawn and all prisoners repatriated within sixty days. An appallingly destructive war was thus halted, but the future of Vietnam still involved political problems of ultimate control which had yet to be solved by North and South, by communists and anti-communists. The basic conflict was not yet resolved.

The cease-fire of 1973 appeared to be advantageous to the communists, for they were still in control of large areas of the South, where the communist Provisional Government ruled. More American troops were withdrawn, but fighting still continued widely in Vietnam. The American withdrawal continued in 1974 and at the same time the communist forces built up powerful new supply bases, while at the same time not undertaking any large offensive. However, in 1975 the North Vietnamese launched a tremendous offensive, using powerful forces of tanks, aircraft and big guns. Important coastal towns fell in rapid succession to the communists, and in May they entered Saigon. Thus the long war ended dramatically in communist victory. This was an enormous blow to American policies and a further decisive advance for communism in South-east Asia.

Summary

The movement of French colonial territories towards independence was carried to success by the colonial national movements, especially aided by de Gaulle's policy. In the same way Egypt, by nationalizing the Suez Canal, was now entire master of her own territory. During this period the Western powers lost ground in the eyes of the Middle and Far Eastern peoples—this applied especially to Britain and France after Suez. The Baghdad Pact was an attempt to bolster the Middle East against Communism and the Soviet Union, but the U.S.A. did not become a member. In the Far East, the Manila Pact leading to SEATO was a further move to strengthen the anti-Communist front, but Indonesia stood aside.

Dates

1953 Dissolution of the old political parties in Egypt.

1954 Fall of Dien Bien Phu, Indochina.
Geneva agreements for division of Vietnam and independence of Laos and Cambodia.
Pierre Mendès-France secures further concessions for Tunisia.
Nasser, Prime Minister in Egypt.
Manila Pact and SEATO.

1955 The Baghdad Pact.

1956 Tunisia gains right to control its own army and foreign policy.
Sudan declared independent.
Israel, Britain and France attack Egypt.
United Nations intervenes in Egypt.

1958 United Arab Republic of Egypt and Syria formed.

1961 National Liberation Front set up in Hanoi.

1963 Great extension of Communist control in South Vietnam.

1964 Incident in the Gulf of Tongking. American participation in the war greatly increased.

1967 The Communist Tet offensive makes considerable gains.
June, Arab–Israeli war.

1968 Peace negotiations begin over Vietnam.
American bombing of the North intensified.

1972 Strong South Vietnamese forces now existed, and American troops drastically reduced, but American bombing policy intensified.
December, American bombing extended to Hanoi and Haiphong.
Murder of members of Israeli Olympic team, Munich.

1973 January 27, cease fire came into effect in Vietnam.

1973 October–November, Yom-Kippur War.

1974 American troop withdrawals continue from Vietnam. Communists build up powerful supply bases.

1975 Powerful communist offensive succeeds, and Saigon captured in May. End of the war in Vietnam.

QUESTIONS

1. *Explain the origins of the Suez affair of 1956 and its results.*

2. *Write notes on:* (a) *the Baghdad Pact;* (b) *SEATO;* (c) *the Geneva agreements of 1954.*

3. *What advances had been made by Tunisian nationalism up to 1958?*

4. *What are the aims and methods of the Palestinian Liberation movement?*

5. *How do you account for the fact that peace negotiations over Vietnam lasted four years?*

6. *What were American reasons for intervention in Vietnam?*

CHAPTER TWENTY-SEVEN

FRANCE, 1940–1977

The War Period, 1939–1945

FROM September, 1939, to May, 1940, the 'phoney war' period saw France manning the Maginot Line and suffering increasingly from the inertia which waiting for attack had produced. During this period France, therefore, suffered *a loss of morale* due to the 'Maginot mentality', which was a complete reversal of the old French strategy of attack.

In March, 1940, Daladier, associated with the Munich agreement of 1938, which had led to the fall of Czechoslovakia, was replaced by **Paul Reynaud** as Premier. Soon afterwards, on May 10th, the Germans began their drive through the Netherlands, Belgium and Luxembourg. The defences of the Meuse River were penetrated and large French forces surrounded at Sedan. At this point Mussolini declared war on France. In general, the French had depended too much on the Maginot Line, which was by-passed. *They were also weak in tanks and aircraft.* Reynaud was replaced by Marshal Pétain and the Compiègne armistice was signed with Hitler in June.

The armistice conditions gave the French government nominal control of the whole country, but in fact *the Germans controlled northern France, and the Channel and Atlantic coasts.* The Vichy-controlled area was mainly the southern agricultural land and the Mediterranean coast. Pétain was Head of State with Pierre Laval as Vice-President.

General Charles de Gaulle was already in Britain at the head of the **Free French Movement,** to which in 1940 a number of colonial territories declared their allegiance. The most important of these were **Chad** and the **French Cameroons.** Also within France itself the underground **Resistance Movement** began to organize itself.

Vichy France became a semi-fascist state. The influence of nineteenth-century French royalism again became felt, and the motto of 'Liberty, Equality, Fraternity' derived from 1789 was replaced by 'Work, Family, Fatherland'. The press was strictly controlled, the trade unions abolished as independent bodies and special militia created as a police force to carry out government decrees. It was also used against the Resistance Movement.

Admiral Darlan replaced Laval for a short time as Head of Government, 1941–1942, but in 1942 Laval returned to office and stayed there until 1945. In general, *Laval wished for a more positive collaboration with the Germans*. This active co-operation was seen more strongly from 1942, the year in which British and American forces landed in North Africa and in which the whole of the Vichy area was occupied by the Germans. Any semblance of independence disappeared when the Germans dissolved the 100,000 strong army allowed to Vichy under the armistice. The Vichy régime was now completely under German control and outright French Fascists of the pre-war era, such as **Marcel Deat,** were included in the government. The Vichy militia co-operated with the Gestapo against the Resistance, and also aided the rounding up of younger Frenchmen for forced labour in Germany.

Committee of National Liberation

All resisting groups and parties eventually acknowledged de Gaulle as their leader, and from these movements developed in 1943 the **French Committee for National Liberation.** A provisional assembly was set up in Algiers and after D-Day, 1944, it moved to France and became the nucleus of a French provisional government under General de Gaulle.

In France itself the harsh German labour conscription forced the younger men into the hills, where the **maquis** resistance was organized. This was supplied with arms by aircraft from Britain, where the organization of such aid was under the control of Colonel Buckmaster. In the months immediately preceding D-Day the 'maquis' became increasingly active in its attacks on German troops, railway transport and road communications. In September, 1944, when the Allied campaign was making good progress, the Vichy state was declared abolished, and Laval and some of his supporters fled to

Sigmaringen in Germany. (He was later brought back to France, tried and shot as a traitor.)

In the elections of October, 1945, the Socialists, Communists and the Mouvement Republicain Populaire (MRP) parties were returned with nearly equal representation, and General de Gaulle was head of the first post-war government containing representatives of these parties. He resigned in January, 1946, and was succeeded by **Felix Gouin** (Socialist).

The Fourth Republic

A major task of the new parliament was to prepare a new constitution for France, which it was hoped by many would be an improvement on that of 1875. In fact, the first proposals were rejected by the people in a referendum. In the same year, 1946, amended proposals were put before the public. The result of the referendum *showed great uncertainty among the public*. In the first place, about one-third of all voters abstained, and the constitution was only accepted by the narrow margin of approximately nine million votes to eight. This was an inauspicious beginning.

Under the new constitution women had the vote for the first time. A system of proportional representation was introduced. The second chamber, the **Council of the Republic,** had very little say in law-making and in this respect was much weaker than the old Senate of the Third Republic. The **National Assembly** became the real ruling force. The President was chosen by both the National Assembly and the Council of the Republic. The system of local government remained almost the same as under the Third Republic. In practice, the Fourth Republic proved little different from the Third, and the considerable abstention over the referendum and the large vote against the constitution showed both the fears and apathy of the French people about the new government.

Decline of the Fourth Republic

The years 1946 to 1958 prove that the new system could scarcely cope with the vast problems facing France. The plan for the modernization of French industry did, in fact, under the inspiration of **Jean**

Monnet (the 'Monnet Plan') make good progress, but increasing labour discontent was a feature of the period. Production rose above pre-war levels, but wages fell behind prices, and a widespread 'black market' in foodstuffs developed in order to by-pass rationing. Industrial strife increased after 1947, in which year the Communists left the government and concentrated on direct industrial action. However, even the trade union movement was weakened by the split between the Socialists and Communists in the French General Confederation of Trade Unions (the **CGT**). Part of the Confederation seceded under **Léon Jouhaux** to form the **Force Ouvrière.**

Instability

The government of France consisted for many years of three-party coalitions. Against this system General de Gaulle, from his position outside parliament, continually waged political war. He formed in 1946 his own movement known as the **Rally of the French People (RPF)** to unite all those opposed to the new constitution and to Communism. In 1951 the RPF gained 120 seats in the National Assembly. This in itself introduced a further political complication in an Assembly which after the 1951 elections contained six parties of almost equal representation. Further criticisms arose in 1953 when thirteen ballots of the Assembly and the Council of State were required before the President (**Réné Coty**) was elected. As under the Third Republic, there had been constant changes of government since the war, and there was no necessity for elections to be held when a government was defeated.

One of the more successful Prime Ministers was **Pierre Mendès-France** (1954–1955). For the first time since the war a Prime Minister was elected by a large majority of the National Assembly, mainly because he had promised a 'new deal' for France and the ending of the war in Indochina. He succeeded in the latter task and remained in power for just over seven months, but was defeated in 1955 on his policies for Tunisia. He was succeeded by **Edgar Faure**, but the elections of January, 1956, produced more political confusion in the Assembly than ever. In this election the supporters of **Pierre Poujade** gained fifty-two seats and 2,500,000 votes. He waged a campaign of opposition to the constitution. denounced the weight of national

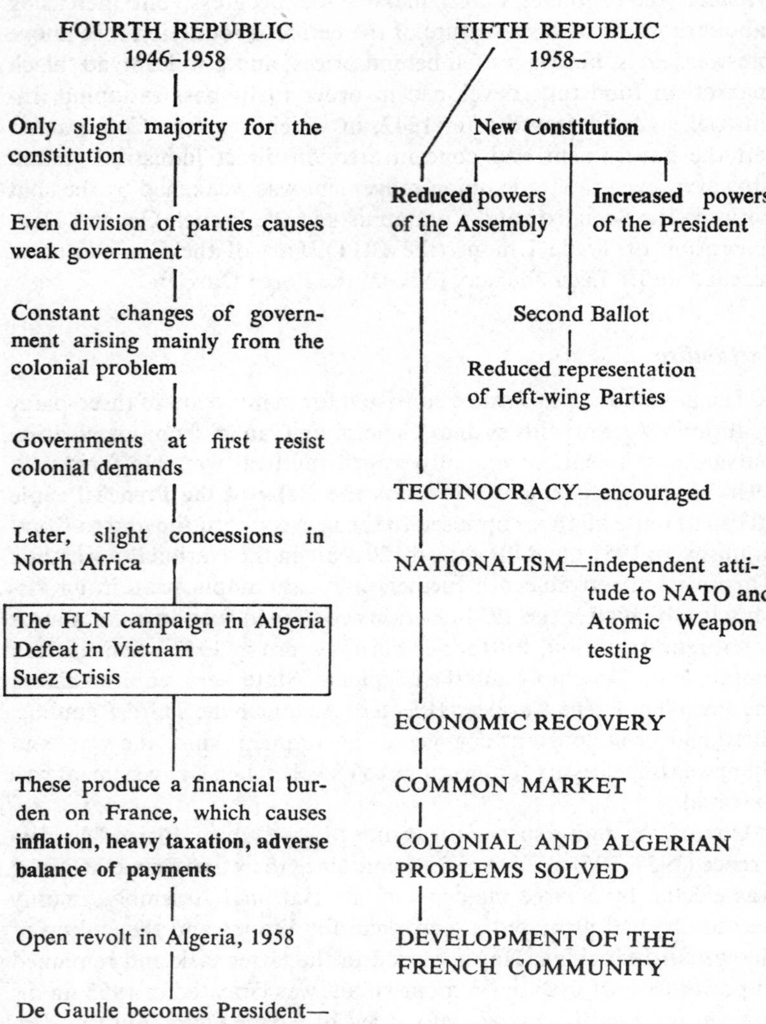
FOURTH REPUBLIC
1946–1958
Only slight majority for the constitution
Even division of parties causes weak government
Constant changes of government arising mainly from the colonial problem
Governments at first resist colonial demands
Later, slight concessions in North Africa
The FLN campaign in Algeria
Defeat in Vietnam
Suez Crisis
These produce a financial burden on France, which causes inflation, heavy taxation, adverse balance of payments
Open revolt in Algeria, 1958
De Gaulle becomes President—end of Fourth Republic, 1958
FIFTH REPUBLIC
1958–
New Constitution
Reduced powers of the Assembly
Increased powers of the President
Second Ballot
Reduced representation of Left-wing Parties
TECHNOCRACY—encouraged
NATIONALISM—independent attitude to NATO and Atomic Weapon testing
ECONOMIC RECOVERY
COMMON MARKET
COLONIAL AND ALGERIAN PROBLEMS SOLVED
DEVELOPMENT OF THE FRENCH COMMUNITY

taxation, and demanded an imperialist policy which would strengthen the French Empire and oppose the demands of the colonial nationalists in Algeria, Morocco, Tunisia, etc., for independence. General de Gaulle's RPF had fallen to twenty-one members. The new Prime Minister, **Guy Mollet** (Socialist), remained in office for eighteen months but suffered from the disastrous Suez policy of 1956 and from increasing troubles in Algeria.

The Algerian Problem

The position in Algeria had grown more and more critical and was a basic cause of the end of the Fourth Republic.

The French population in Algeria was one-tenth of the total (one million as against nine million non-French). Strong trading links with France had existed from the early nineteenth century, and in France itself over 400,000 Algerians were employed. In Algeria, the French were mainly townspeople and there was no French land-owning class holding down a feudal peasantry. The anxiety of the French settlers to maintain their position in Algeria was very great and they had strong and violent support from some leaders of the French army in Algeria. This army in 1954 numbered 500,000 and its maintenance and its operations against the Algerian nationalists were costing France something in the region of the *enormous sum of £700,000,000 annually*. This was an immense drain on France and was causing inflation and industrial discontent.

Serious trouble began on November 1, 1954, when bands of Algerian nationalists raided French installations. This movement was inspired and organized by **Ahmed ben Bella** from Cairo, who had formed the **Algerian National Liberation Front (FLN).** The FLN adopted the tactics not only of military rebellion but of terror and massacre against French residents and Moslems who supported them. Between 1954 and 1958 casualties on both sides were very great—over 200,000 Algerians and about 13,000 French officers and men. The war was savage on both sides, and there were serious cases of the use of torture by the French military. The French also regrouped 1,250,000 Algerians into special areas where they were isolated from FLN influence. On the other hand the FLN made sufficient military progress to be able to govern certain areas of the country independently.

Among the officer class of the French army there was already great discontent over the loss of national prestige involved in the defeat in Indochina and over the Suez affair. This discontent was very great in Algeria, where they feared that the French government intended to betray the interests of the army and of the French settlers ('colons'). In the National Assembly they were supported by a group of army leaders and Right-wing extremists known as the *Algiers lobby* who carried on activity against any government concessions to the Algerians. In May, 1958, **Pierre Pflimlin** became Prime Minister, and he was known to favour concessions to the Algerians. This was immediately followed by a seizure of control in Algiers itself by **Generals Salan** and **Massu.** Pflimlin resigned after fifteen days as Prime Minister, warning the country of the dangers of civil war.

At this point General de Gaulle came forward from his retirement and offered to 'assume the powers of the Republic'. President Coty declared his support for de Gaulle and on June 1, 1958, the Assembly accepted him by 329 votes to 224. He was granted full personal powers for six months and the task of producing a new constitution. Thus the Fourth Republic ended, because of internal confusion and discontent in France, the shifting and unsatisfactory politics of the Assembly, the instability of governments and the problems and divisions produced by the gradual break-up of the old French Empire. It had repeated too much of the pattern of 1875–1940.

The Fifth Republic

The position of President de Gaulle was difficult. He attempted to avoid being dependent on any one group. In the new government of **Michel Debré** (Prime Minister until April, 1962) only three members were open supporters of de Gaulle. The new government was composed of all groups except the Communists and the Poujadists. De Gaulle was regarded very differently by various interests—firstly, the Algerian rebels expected him to support the maintenance of French power in Algeria. Secondly, the Communists, Socialists, Radicals, etc., feared that he would establish a Bonapartist-type dictatorship. Thirdly, others expected him to achieve stability in government.

The New Constitution

In September, 1958, over *79 per cent of the voters supported the new constitution*, and 84 per cent of the electors voted (unlike 1946 when only about 66 per cent voted and nearly half of those against the constitution of 1946). The constitution as accepted by the majority had the following features:

1. Government by the National Assembly was greatly reduced and its general powers suffered considerable limitations. For example, the government now controls the parliamentary timetable and can give prior consideration to its own measures. In the vital matter of finance, the government *can legislate by decree*, if parliament delays a measure for more than seventy days. The government is still responsible to the Assembly, but a vote of censure on the government *requires a majority of the whole Assembly.*

2. The new powers of the President were considerable. He could dissolve the Assembly and order elections—and with a strong President *the knowledge that he would use these powers is effective in preventing irresponsible government defeats in the Assembly.* The President also has power to appoint the Prime Minister, and send special messages to parliament. He can assume emergency powers in case of internal revolt and disturbance.

3. The electoral system was changed. One member for one constituency was now introduced in place of the old system of proportional representation. The system of the *second ballot* was introduced. This meant that a clear majority by one candidate over others could be achieved by party agreements for the withdrawal of a candidate before a second ballot took place.

4. Members of the government cannot sit in the National Assembly, and this increases their independence of parliament.

5. The President was to be elected by the Electoral College, which is composed of all M.P.s, Councils of Departments and Representatives of municipal councils, and all overseas assemblies.

The general election of 1958 produced some interesting results from the change in the voting system. The Socialists were reduced to forty seats and the Communists to ten. The **Union pour la Nouvelle République (UNR)**, direct supporters of de Gaulle, gained 188 seats, and the **Poujadists** returned only one member and ceased to be of much account. De Gaulle depended on the support of the UNR, the MRP and the Independent Conservatives. Thus the elections showed a *strong swing to the Right.* The system of the second ballot had gone heavily against the Communists who, however, polled nearly four million votes. They later recovered much of their representation by second-ballot agreements with the Socialists.

De Gaulle's Foreign Policy

For the first time in French history the President came to direct and control the Prime Minister. He was no longer a figurehead, but an active political figure on which the future of the country greatly depended. Certain definite principles guided his actions. Above all, he distrusted those associated with the old parliamentary system. He removed many from government positions and *replaced them by technical experts.* In France **Technocracy** became the basic ruling force. Secondly, he was determined to get above the conflicts of parties and interests, and to govern in the interests of the nation as he saw them, and for this purpose the old parliamentarians seemed to him useless. In international affairs, while supporting the western alliances led by the United States, *he became increasingly nationalistic.* He has refused to accept any NATO schemes which would put French forces under complete NATO control. At the same time *he has continued to develop atomic weapons for France*, who now possesses her own atomic bombs. In default of a general agreement for the abolition of atomic weapons, he refused to accept the Nuclear Test-ban Treaty, and France has continued her own atomic testing in the Sahara. He has *adopted a line of independent criticism of any foreign government with whom he disagrees*—this particularly applies to his condemnation of the United States attitude to Communist China and to American intervention in Vietnam. The French were also in the main responsible for keeping Britain out of the Common Market in 1963.

De Gaulle's Domestic Policy

Between 1958 and 1963 more than three hundred decrees were issued which introduced essential reforms in French society. When he came to office in 1958, France was in a bad state financially. This was due to the drain of colonial wars. Her gold reserves were almost gone and government expenditure exceeded income by a disastrous amount (about 600,000,000,000 francs). Her balance of payments with foreign countries was adverse—that is, she was importing far more than she exported and was a debtor nation. By 1963 all France's colonial wars had ceased and this alone eased the economic situation. Some policies were drastic and led to discontent—for example, the franc was revalued and this caused some increase in prices and the cost of living but it helped French exports. However, dangerous price rises were prevented by direct control both of wages and prices and inflation was checked. By 1963 industrial production had greatly increased, the French balance of payments problem was solved and the gold reserves were high. This had been achieved by a certain amount of austerity imposed on all classes and by the reduction of the amount of money paid by the government in subsidies to industry. Industrial efficiency was intended to replace support by subsidy.

Discontent

De Gaulle's policies, however, gave rise to considerable social tension. Government control of Television and Radio and, to a certain extent, of the Press, gave rise to discontent. In 1968 Paris was the scene of both working-class discontent in general and violent protests by university students. The latter's demands ranged from outright opposition to the government of de Gaulle to demands for the radical reform of the university system, with student participation in decisions on matters both of university policy in regard to curricula, examinations, etc. The student unrest was heavily dealt with by the police and numerous arrests were made. De Gaulle himself was clearly shaken and produced a programme which included large wage increases for the workers and a programme of increased worker-participation at all levels. The election which followed gave the Gaullists an overwhelming victory. But confidence had been shaken and industrial production had slumped. An adverse balance of trade developed and de Gaulle's work in building up the gold reserve was endangered. Demands were made for the devaluation of the franc, which de Gaulle refused to sanction. Instead, new economies were imposed all round, leading to further unrest. In the national referendum of 1969 de Gaulle failed to obtain a clear national majority, and he resigned. He was succeeded by Pompidou. De Gaulle died towards the end of 1970. By 1973 a Socialist-Communist electoral alliance was threatening the existence of the Gaullist majority in the National Assembly.

Colonial Policy

The Algerian question was the most important of all. The Algerian 'colons' and army leaders *expected de Gaulle to take up their cause.* In this they became increasingly disillusioned. The President pursued his own course. In September, 1959, he declared that once fighting stopped the Algerians would have the right of self-determination after a period of four years. The FLN disliked the four-year wait and the 'colons' opposed the whole idea of self-determination. He then undertook negotiations with the FLN leaders in France, but these discussions broke down. However, in January, 1960, he *removed the extremist General Massu from his command in Algeria.* The situation became very tense when a number of rebel civilian and army units rose in revolt. The army, however, in general remained loyal and the rebel movement failed. The National Assembly in Paris then gave President de Gaulle special emergency powers for one year to deal with the Algerian crisis. In November, 1960, he made the important declaration that *an Algerian republic was inevitable*, and he followed this by a referendum in Algeria which showed overwhelming support for his policy. But the diehards were not yet finished. In April, 1961, *an outright military revolt took place in Algiers led by General Salan* and three others. For a time civil war in the city looked inevitable, but de Gaulle remained firm and in an important television broadcast appealed for the support of the French army and people. (There had been rumours of intended parachute drops in France itself by the rebels.) In four days the movement in Algiers collapsed. The rebels now organized the **OAS (Secret Army Organization)** for terroristic activities against de Gaulle and his supporters. An attempt to assassinate him was made in September, 1961, while he was being driven to his country estate. However, negotiations with the Algerian nationalists continued, and on *July 4th, 1962, Algeria became a sovereign state.*

Further attempts to assassinate General de Gaulle caused him to consider the future of the Presidency. He wished to change the method of electing the President by introducing the popular vote. Parliament was opposed to this and his government was defeated in the Assembly. He now put this question to a referendum, which supported his proposed change. In order further to test his standing in the country he ordered a general election for November, 1962. The result was a complete vindication of his popularity, for on the second ballot his supporters gained an absolute majority over all other groups in the National Assembly. No previous instances of this were known in the history of the French Republic.

His motive in securing an alteration of the method of presidential election was to ensure that the Presidency would not result from the manœuvres and intrigues of parliamentary groups, but would reflect the will of the people.

The French Community

De Gaulle's policies for the colonies recognized the inevitability of independence. Just as the British Empire was changing rapidly into the Commonwealth, so the old French Empire was changed into the French Community, with the colonies becoming independent and at the same time *free to make special arrangements for association with France*. The majority of the newly independent states took this course and made arrangements with France for trade, for technical assistance and for financial help. In 1960 Madagascar, Senegal and Mali became independent states within the French Community. Soon afterwards other territories became independent—Mauritania, the Republic of Gabon, Dahomey, the Ivory Coast, Niger and Upper Volta.

In essentials de Gaulle followed a liberal colonial policy, which alarmed and exasperated the French Algerians, but was welcomed by all who were not conservative imperialists of the old type.

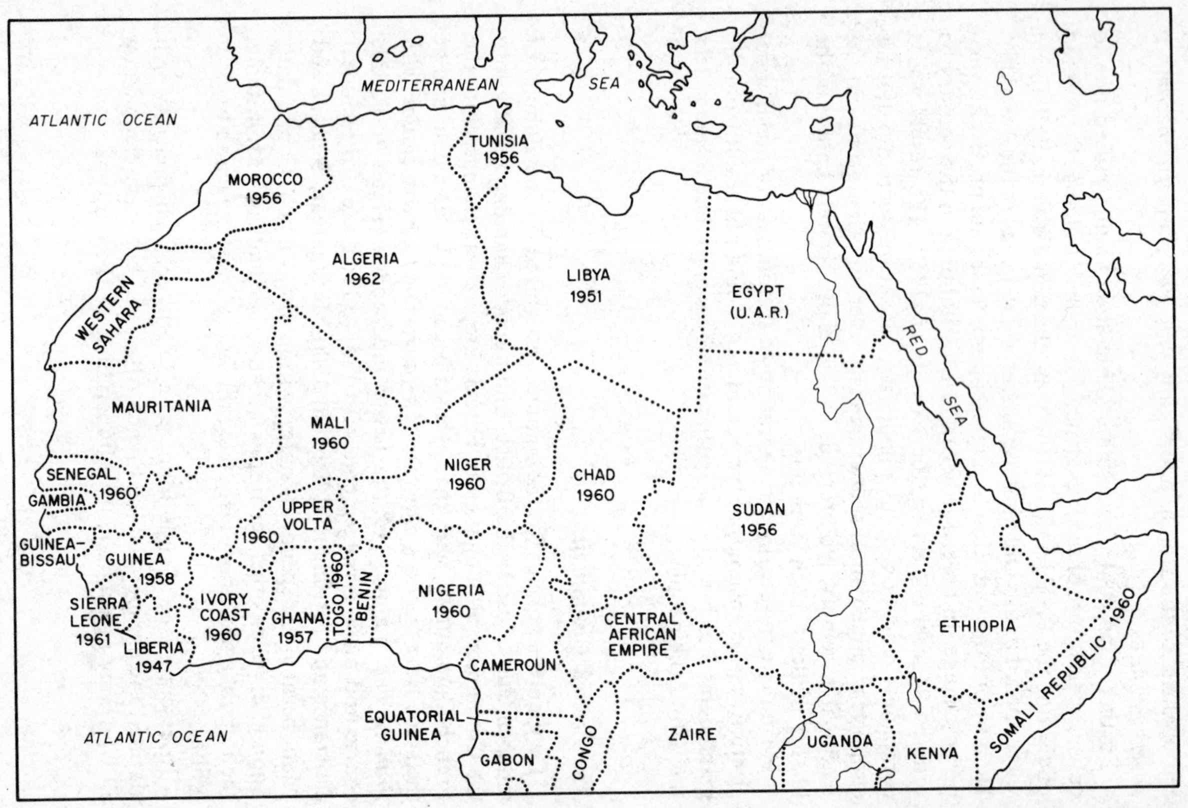
ATLANTIC OCEAN
MEDITERRANEAN
SEA
MOROCCO 1956
TUNISIA 1956
ALGERIA 1962
LIBYA 1951
EGYPT (U.A.R.)
RED SEA
WESTERN SAHARA
MAURITANIA
MALI 1960
NIGER 1960
CHAD 1960
SUDAN 1956
SENEGAL 1960
GAMBIA
UPPER VOLTA 1960
GUINEA-BISSAU
GUINEA 1958
SIERRA LEONE 1961
LIBERIA 1947
IVORY COAST 1960
GHANA 1957
TOGO 1960
BENIN
NIGERIA 1960
CENTRAL AFRICAN EMPIRE
ETHIOPIA
SOMALI REPUBLIC 1960
CAMEROUN
EQUATORIAL GUINEA
ATLANTIC OCEAN
GABON
CONGO
ZAIRE
UGANDA
KENYA

France, 1970–1977

These years saw critical developments in French politics, the most notable being the considerable growth in strength of the French Communist Party. In the elections of 1973 a united front of Socialists and Communists strengthened the position of both at the expense of the Gaullists. The communists now declared themselves in favour of the democratic process and joined the Euro-communist trend which implied criticism of some aspects of Soviet policy and a desire to pursue policies which were not the result of Soviet pressures. In the elections the Gaullist UDF (Union Democratique pour la République) managed to retain power with the aid of some smaller groupings in the Assembly. The leftist pressures, however, undoubtedly influenced President Pompidou to introduce such radical measures as a monthly minimum wage, more worker-participation in industry and more facilities for retirement at sixty. However, in April, 1974, President Pompidou died and in the ensuing presidential election M. Giscard d'Estaing gained the victory by the slender margin of 1.8 per cent over his Socialist–Communist opponent M. Mitterand. D'Estaing's policies now went further in a liberal direction—press censorship was abolished and also political censorship of films. Illegal telephone-tapping by the state security service was ended. All these practices had arisen during the Gaullist period. However, France had serious problems of unemployment, inflation and terrorism. In foreign affairs she continued on the Gaullist course of building up her own nuclear armament. By 1977 she was the world's third nuclear power after the U.S.A. and the U.S.S.R.

Summary

France was unprepared for war in 1939, and defeatism and the 'Maginot mentality' made matters worse. The fascist-type Vichy régime resulted from her defeat, but the strongest elements of the nation rallied to the Resistance and the Free French Movement. The post-war constitution of France showed little advance on that of the Third Republic, and the Algerian crisis was the final strain that brought de Gaulle back to power on his own terms in 1958 and saw the creation of the Fifth Republic. The years of de Gaulle's Presidency showed considerable national economic recovery, the solution of the

Algerian and colonial problems, and the development of the French Community. De Gaulle pursued a strongly national line in foreign policy, especially in relation to NATO, to the United States and to the question of atomic testing and weapon creation. The constitution of the Fifth Republic stabilized internal politics and in 1962 for the first time in French history the supporters of the government had an absolute majority in the Assembly. De Gaulle promoted the power of the technocrats in the state and tended to push out of key posts the old parliamentarians.

But the authoritarian elements in de Gaulle's policy gave rise to discontent, leading to student and industrial unrest of alarming proportions in 1968. De Gaulle gradually lost the overwhelming national support which he had so far enjoyed, and by 1973 there was a decided shift to the Left in French politics. De Gaulle's successor, Pompidou, came to support Britain's entry into the Common Market, one of the most important changes which took effect on January 1, 1973. This represented a marked change in France's foreign policy as compared with de Gaulle's rigid opposition to Great Britain's entry.

During the years 1973 to 1977 there was an attempt to unify the forces of the left under the Socialists and Communists. This greatly strengthened the opposition to d'Estaing and created the possibility of government by the left.

Dates

1940 **Paul Reynaud Prime Minister, March.**
Compiègne Armistice with Hitler, June.
Pétain heads the Vichy régime.
Free French Movement established by de Gaulle.

1942 **Pierre Laval Head of Government at Vichy.**
Policy of fuller co-operation with the Nazis.
British and Americans land in North Africa.
Germans take over Vichy territory.
French pre-war Fascists now in Vichy government.

1943 **French Committee for National Liberation established by de Gaulle.**
Development of the 'maquis' in France.
Provisional French Assembly set up in Algiers.

1944 D-Day, June 6th.
Liberation of France.
1945 Elections return mainly Socialists, Communists and MRP.
Coalition under de Gaulle.
1946 De Gaulle resigns (January).
New constitution of the Fourth Republic accepted in referendum by narrow majority only.
De Gaulle forms his Rally of the French People (RPF).
1947 Communists retire from government.
1951 RPF gain 120 seats in the Assembly.
1953 Thirteen ballots required to elect President Coty.
1954 Pierre Mendès-France, Prime Minister.
Rebellion in Algeria begins under the FLN.
1956 January elections produce more political confusion.
Poujadists win 52 seats.
1958 Pierre Pflimlin, Prime Minister.
Rising in Algiers under Salan and Massu.
De Gaulle comes forward and is elected President by National Assembly.
Michel Debré, Prime Minister (till 1962).
Large majority for the constitution of the Fifth Republic.
Drastic losses by Socialists and Communists under second-ballot procedure, and swing to the Right.
1959 September: de Gaulle promises Algerians right of self-determination.
1960 De Gaulle removes Massu from command in Algiers.
November: de Gaulle declares Algerian republic to be inevitable.
1961 Revolt in Algeria by group of officers and section of army under General Salan.
Failure of revolt.
OAS formed.
September: attempted assassination of President de Gaulle.
1962 Algeria becomes sovereign independent state. General de Gaulle gains absolute majority in general elections.
1968 Student and general unrest.
De Gaulle victorious in elections.
1969 Further unrest. De Gaulle fails in referendum and resigns.

1970 Death of General de Gaulle.
1973 United Front of Socialists and Communists.
1974 Giscard d'Estaing elected President.
1977 France the world's third nuclear power.

QUESTIONS

1. What were the main characteristics of the Vichy régime, 1940–1944?

2. What were the causes of the fall of the Fourth Republic in 1958?

3. What colonial problems faced France in the years 1945 to 1962, and how were they solved?

4. Give an account of the Algerian problem in the years 1945 to 1962.

5. What were the achievements of de Gaulle in the years 1958 to 1963?

6. Why was there increasing opposition to de Gaulle in 1968 and 1969?

CHAPTER TWENTY-EIGHT

THE UNITED NATIONS

THE Charter of the United Nations was drafted at San Francisco on April 25th, 1945. It was signed at that time by fifty-one nations.

The general purpose of the United Nations Organization is indicated in Article 1 of the Charter, which is to *preserve international peace and security*. It declares the right of self-determination for all peoples and the equality of all peoples. It aims to secure international co-operation to solve problems of an economic and cultural nature. Article 2 stresses the equality of all members in the Organization and emphasizes the point that it will not intervene in any internal affairs of states, except to enforce measures already decided upon.

New members can only be admitted by *a unanimous decision of the Security Council* and a two-thirds vote of the Assembly. Many of the new member states are those arising from changes in the former British, French and Dutch empires.

Organization

The principle of one member one vote in the General Assembly was adopted at the outset. The Assembly supervises the whole work of the organization. Voting in the Assembly is by a majority or by two-thirds according to the agreed importance of the questions before it. The Assembly receives annual reports from the Secretary-General and various commissions and committees appointed by the Assembly. It also has control of the finances. The Assembly meets annually, but during the year works by means of committees.

The Security Council

The Security Council has the main responsibility for the maintenance of peace, and all members of the UN agree to carry out its decisions. It is composed of eleven members, of whom six are elected for two-year terms and five are permanent members. The original five permanent members were the U.S.A., the U.S.S.R., the United Kingdom, France and the Republic of China (Nationalist China). Its decisions are taken on agreement by seven members, but on very serious matters involving such things as economic or military sanctions against a state, the seven must include all the permanent members. *Thus any one of the permanent members can exercise a veto.*

Economic and Social Council

The Council consists of eighteen members elected by the Assembly for a three-year term, and its work is to direct the economic and financial aid given to states and also to supervise work of a humanitarian nature—for example, the care of refugees or victims of natural calamities such as epidemics, floods, earthquakes, etc. The work of the Council is assisted by special committees for definite geographical areas—for Europe, Asia and the Far East and Latin America. These committees make special studies on the spot and pass their recommendations to the Economic and Social Council, which then puts them before the Assembly. As will be seen, the Economic and Social Council is one of the most important bodies of the United Nations.

The Trusteeship Council

This Council supervises the work of those states who took over the administration of various trust territories, some of which were the old mandates of the League of Nations. It was composed of those members administering trust territories and those permanent members of the Security Council who did not administer trust territories. An annual report is required by the General Assembly.

The International Court of Justice

This is established at The Hague, and is composed of fifteen judges elected by the General Assembly and the Security Council. The judges must be nationals of fifteen different states. The aim is to ensure that the Court *represents the main legal systems of the world.* The judges serve for nine years and may be re-elected. The Court deals with all cases of international disputes put before it where these involve international law and, if the disputing states agree, its decisions can be compulsory.

The Secretariat

This comprises the Secretary-General and his staff. The Secretary-General is appointed by the Assembly on the recommendation of the Security Council. Secretary-Generals past and present have been Mr. Trygve Lie (Norway), Mr. Dag Hammarskjöld (Sweden) and now Mr. U Thant (Burma). The Secretary-General has the duty of bringing before the Organization any matters threatening peace and he gives a yearly report to the Assembly. He has the right to advise on the measures he deems necessary.

Important Problems before the United Nations, 1945–1963

The early work of the United Nations was made difficult through the development of the *Cold War* and its effect on the working of the Security Council. *Within the Council the tendency arose for the Soviet Union to confront the other powers.* This led on numerous occasions to the use of the veto by the Soviet Union. In the case of the Korean war, 1950, the Security Council was able to act in the absence of the Soviet Union. Later a resolution adopted by the Assembly enabled it to act for peace where the Security Council was unable to act, and this to a certain extent got round the veto problem. The Assembly also requested member states to earmark armed contingents for use by the United Nations when needed. It also established the *Peace Observation Commission* to report on parts of the world where the danger of war existed.

One of the first matters before the Security Council was the Persian complaint in 1946 that Soviet troops were still in northern Persia beyond the agreed time. The Security Council requested Persia and the Soviet Union to report progress made in withdrawal by May 6th. By that date Soviet troops had been withdrawn.

Greece. The outbreak of the civil war in Greece in 1946 presented the United Nations with a number of difficult problems. The Greek government complained in December, 1946, that Albania, Bulgaria and Yugoslavia were aiding the Communist guerrilla forces across their frontiers. A Commission of Investigation was sent out and reported (not unanimously) that intervention was taking place. Owing to the opposition of the Soviet Union the Security Council was unable to agree on action to be taken, but the Assembly appointed a *United Nations Special Committee on the Balkans* to try to achieve a peaceful settlement. The Soviet Union and the Communist states did not take part in the work of this committee. The war only ended after the defeat of the guerrilla forces, due in part to American aid to Greece and to Tito's dispute with the Soviet Union. In this case the United Nations had found the east-west conflict cutting across its efforts to stop the fighting.

Indonesia. The position in Indonesia at the end of the war was difficult. British and Indian forces occupied Indonesia after the Japanese capitulation and remained there until the end of 1946 in order to supervise the evacuation of prisoners and the re-establishment of normal conditions. However, the more extreme Indonesian nationalists resisted the presence of British and Indian troops and fighting broke out. In 1946 a truce was achieved and British and Indian troops evacuated. The Dutch then sent in troops of their own. In the meantime the Indonesian Republic had been established, and the Dutch aim was to incorporate the Republic in the Dutch Commonwealth on similar lines to the British. But hostilities broke out between the Indonesian nationalists and the Dutch forces. This situation was brought before the Assembly, but the Dutch claimed that Indonesia was still under her control and that it was an internal matter. A truce between the Dutch and their opponents was signed in 1948, but hostilities broke out again soon afterwards. In January, 1949, the Security Council requested a cessation of hostilities and also recommended the creation of a completely independent Indonesia.

For this purpose a United Nations special commission was appointed to assist and the Republic of Indonesia became independent on December 27th, 1949.

Palestine. The British government brought the question of Palestine before the United Nations, and requested its assistance in dealing with the conflict between the Jews and Arabs. A United Nations Special Committee on Palestine was set up, and it proposed the division of Palestine between Jews and Arabs and the establishment of an international government for Jerusalem. This resulted in further strife between Jews and Arabs, and **Count Bernadotte** of Sweden was sent out to attempt mediation between the two sides. In 1948 Britain withdrew her forces and the State of Israel was proclaimed. The Arab states then attacked Israel, and the Security Council threatened action by the United Nations unless fighting ceased, and Count Bernadotte brought about a truce. He was soon afterwards assassinated by Jewish terrorists. The next United Nations mediator, **Dr. Ralph Bunche,** secured an armistice between Israel and the Arab states in 1949. However, the relations between Jews and Arabs did not improve, and after the accession of Nasser in Egypt great antagonism developed between Egypt and Israel. On October 29th, 1956, Israeli forces invaded **Sinai** and the **Gaza strip.** Israel had complained of Nasser's refusal to allow the passage of Israeli vessels through the Suez Canal and that Arabs had infiltrated over her borders. There also followed the French and British action against Egypt, and on November 2nd the General Assembly demanded the withdrawal of Israeli, French and British troops. It proposed to send a *United Nations Emergency Force* under **General Burn** to supervise the cessation of hostilities. Israel, Britain and France agreed to a cease-fire and Nasser accepted the United Nations force. The United Nations gave technical assistance to Egypt to clear the Canal, which had been blocked by Egypt at the time of the attack.

Hungary. A resolution was moved in the Security Council calling on the Soviet Union to cease military action in Hungary in 1956, but this was vetoed by the Soviet representative. The General Assembly also passed resolutions requesting the Soviet Union to respect the right of the Hungarian people to independence, but the resolutions were ignored by Russia and the Kadar government on the grounds that events referred to were internal.

India and Pakistan. Serious conflict arose immediately after the war over Kashmir. The government of Kashmir decided on union with India in 1947, but there was immediate opposition from the Moslem tribes, and at the same time Indian forces entered Kashmir. India accused Pakistan of encouraging Moslem opposition, but this was denied. United Nations observers assisted in securing a cease-fire in 1949, and a truce-line was established. But despite numerous efforts by the United Nations no agreement on the future of Kashmir was achieved, and increasingly bad relations led to the outbreak of war between India and Pakistan in September, 1965.

Korea. The failure of the Soviet Union and the United States to agree on the re-unification of Korea under one government led the U.S.A. to bring this matter before the Assembly. *The Assembly passed a resolution which suggested the supervision by the United Nations of elections throughout Korea.* As we have seen the North Koreans had objections to certain parties of the South being recognized at all, and the United Nations proposal was not accepted. Separate elections were held in the South and the Republic of Korea established. Soviet and American troops were withdrawn in 1948–1949. After North Korean forces crossed the 38th parallel on June 25th, 1950, the Security Council called for their withdrawal. When this was ignored the *Security Council called on members of the United Nations to give military aid to the Republic of Korea.* General MacArthur was appointed supreme commander of the United Nations force and American troops landed at **Inchon** in September, **1950**. When the North Korean forces were driven back over the 38th parallel the Assembly approved the decision to carry the war into the north. The Chinese Communist forces then entered the war and Communist China was declared the aggressor and trading and arms sanctions were imposed against her. The truce signed on July 27th, 1953, left Korea divided almost exactly as before, and United Nations efforts to secure the unification of Korea had not succeeded by 1965.

Other Moves by the United Nations

Other matters showed the apparently limited powers of the United Nations when purely political questions were involved. For instance, in January, 1947, some British warships were damaged by mines laid by Albania in the Corfu Channel. The Soviet Union vetoed a resolution of the Security Council which placed the blame on Albania, and, despite a ruling by the International Court, Albania refused to pay compensation. Similarly, in the case of the Berlin blockade of 1948–1949 the Soviet Union argued that the Security Council had no authority, and the question was finally settled by negotiations independently of the United Nations. In the matter of the former Italian colonies, the United Nations played a successful part. This involved Libya, Somaliland and Eritrea and the question of their future came before the Assembly in 1949. It was finally agreed that Libya should become independent by 1951, that Eritrea should be federated with Ethiopia and that Somaliland should also become independent at a time to be decided.

The United Nations also took up the question of the *racial policies of South Africa*, which the latter declared to be a domestic matter outside the scope of the United Nations. The question of **Cyprus** also came before the Assembly. At first Britain declared this to be a domestic matter, but after the agreement between Britain and Cyprus on independence and after the outbreak of further strife in 1963–1964 between Greek Cypriots and Turkish Cypriots, a United Nations force went to Cyprus to attempt to prevent further outbreaks of fighting between the two communities. After the independence of the **Congo,** Civil War broke out between opposing factions and a United Nations force was sent to the Congo to attempt to restore order. The Soviet Union was opposed to this action on the grounds that it was another form of imperialist intervention in the Congo and has refused to meet any of the costs involved in the Congo operation.

Disarmament

In January, 1946, the **Atomic Energy Commission** was set up to consider the control of the production of atomic energy. Considerable disagreement arose between Russia and the U.S.A. The

Commission aimed at the international control of atomic production and the ending of the veto in the Security Council so that its decisions could be enforced. The Soviet Union opposed international ownership, wished the veto to continue and for an arrangement by which atomic stockpiles of weapons should be destroyed and a control system developed later. The U.S.A. wanted the establishment of a full control system first. A Conventional Armaments Commission was also established, and attempts were made to reach an agreement that each state would give full details of its non-atomic armaments so that general reduction could begin. These attempts failed.

In 1952 the **Disarmament Commission** replaced the Atomic Energy and Conventional Armaments Commission, and was to prepare proposals for general disarmament. When immediate general disarmament seemed unlikely, attempts were made to get disarmament by stages. In 1957, the General Assembly gave the Disarmament Commission the task of *securing the cessation of nuclear tests, of working out methods of inspection to guard against surprise attack and of ending the production of nuclear weapons altogether*. The first important breakthrough was the Nuclear Test-ban Treaty of 1963.

In 1957 the United Nations established the International Atomic Energy Agency to study the peaceful uses of atomic energy and ways in which the nations can co-operate in this important work. This agency was set up by a unanimous vote of the Assembly—a rare occurrence.

General Work

The United Nations has established important agencies dealing with cultural, educational and economic and financial matters. The International Labour Organization (**ILO**) is concerned with labour conditions throughout the world. The Food and Agricultural Organization (**FAO**) is concerned with technical assistance to underdeveloped countries as well as the problem of food and population. The United Nations Educational, Scientific and Cultural Organization (**UNESCO**) is concerned with the co-operation of nations for educational research and development and for the general promotion of science and culture. Immediately after the war UNESCO, from its permanent headquarters in Paris, helped devastated countries to reestablish schools, libraries and other educational institutions. It assisted educational work among refugees both in Europe and the Middle East. It has established offices in many parts of the world and arranges international conferences of teachers, scientists and technical experts in order to promote the interchange of important knowledge.

The United Nations has provided funds and technical assistance to numerous countries since World War II. Special Economic Commissions for Asia and the Far East and for Europe were established, and after the Korean war a United Nations Korea Reconstruction Agency was set up to give direct help to the Republic of Korea (South Korea).

The International Refugee Organization, which existed till 1952, repatriated and re-established over five million refugees, and this was replaced in 1952 by a special High Commission for Refugees. The United Nations International Children's Fund (**UNICEF**) was set up in 1946 and has dealt with the problem of child-care in countries devastated by war, flood and famine. Other important organizations are the World Health Organization (**WHO**), the International Monetary Fund (to assist states to overcome crises in trade and balance of payments problems), the International Bank for Reconstruction and Development (to provide loans to countries undertaking economic developments beyond their own financial powers).

The Trusteeship System

This was a most important aspect of the United Nations work. Eleven territories taken from Germany, Italy and Japan came under the **Trusteeship Council.** This system replaced the old mandates system of the League of Nations and was in a number of ways an improvement on it. As under the mandates system, the country administering the territories was responsible to the Trusteeship Council and the Assembly. But, in addition, individual inhabitants of the territories could submit complaints directly to the United Nations, and many hundreds of such petitions were heard either in writing or by personal appearance before the Trusteeship Council and the Assembly. Secondly, the territories were visited by inspectors every three years. Gradually these territories were absorbed into other states or became independent, and in 1963 only Nauru (a small island of nine square miles), the Pacific Islands and New Guinea remained as trusteeship territories administered by Britain, Australia, New Zealand and the United States.

The Trusteeship Council system enabled the countries concerned to develop to such a point that they were absorbed easily by others (for example, the Northern Cameroons, administered by Britain, eventually became part of Nigeria) or became independent.

In the case of **South-west Africa** complications occurred. The South African government, which governed South-west Africa under the old mandates, refused to give it up to the United Nations. After 1950 they accepted inspection by the United Nations committee but refused to give it further information. *The principle of 'apartheid' was extended to the territory* (i.e. the separation of black and white communities) and in 1960 the South African government refused admission to the territory by an investigating committee.

Admission of Communist China

The main opponent of the admission of Communist China to the United Nations had been the United States who continued to give consistent support to Nationalist China (Formosa or Taiwan) until 1971. In April, 1971, numerous American trade restrictions on Communist China were removed, and President Nixon visited Peking in 1972. The United States now supported the admission of Communist China, but wished to retain the right of Nationalist China also to membership. But this policy was repudiated by the General Assembly, which voted for the exclusion of Nationalist China. In 1972 the Communist delegates took their seats and the delegates of Nationalist China withdrew, under strong protest. The admission of Communist China was a move of great historic importance in the relationship of East and West, and particularly between Communist China and the United States.

Summary

The United Nations is the most important international organization ever created. Its success in major political questions affecting the Great Powers depends deliberately on the unanimity of these powers, and the *Cold War* has therefore limited the success of its efforts or entirely frustrated them on a number of major questions, such, for example, as atomic disarmament. However, it has acted with considerable effect even in a number of major questions—for example, the Suez affair, in the Congo and in Cyprus. On the economic and humanitarian side, its work has been magnificent and has received great support on both sides of the *Iron Curtain.* Its success must be judged by its total work and not only by its failures or successes in political questions.

Dates

1945	**United Nations Charter at San Francisco.**
1946	**Security Council intervenes between the U.S.S.R. and Persia.**
	Civil War in Greece.
1948	**U.N. proposes division of Palestine between Israelis and Arabs.**
1950–53	**U.N. forces in Korea.**
1963	**Nuclear Test-ban Treaty.**
1967	**United Nations Resolution on Arab–Israeli conflict.**
1971	**U.S.A. removes trade restrictions on China.**
1972	**Communist China admitted to United Nations.**

QUESTIONS

1. Outline the general organization of the United Nations.

2. Describe the work of at least three of its component organizations.

3. What part was played by the United Nations in: (a) *Korea;* (b) *the Civil War in Greece, 1946–1949;* (c) *the question of the Italian colonies;* (d) *Indonesia?*

4. Give examples from the political activities of the United Nations which show: (a) *partial success;* (b) *failure;* (c) *complete success.*

GLOSSARY OF POLITICAL TERMS

Absolutism: Rule by one person, who does not have to answer to any individual or to any institution, such as parliament.
Annexation: The taking over of territory by another country.
Anti-clericalism: Opposition to the political claims of the Church in the government of a country.
Anti-semitism: Anti-Jewish movements and propaganda.
Arbitration: Settlement of a dispute through the acceptance of a decision by a neutral power.
Ausgleich: The compromise or agreement between Austria and Hungary, 1866.
Autocracy: Absolute government by an individual.
Bourgeois: Referring to the middle class. As used by Marxists it has a more specific reference to the ownership of property from which rent or interest is derived. The 'petite bourgeoisie' are the lower middle classes, such as shopkeepers, who are less powerful than the big capitalists.
Clericalism: During the nineteenth century this movement was the attempt by the Roman Catholic Church to increase its influence within states and governments.
Collectivization of agriculture: A system by which the land of peasants and private holdings are absorbed into larger units owned and run by the state.
Communism: The doctrine put forward by Marx and Engels. It anticipates the overthrow of Capitalism by the working class or proletariat and the establishment of the 'dictatorship of the proletariat' as the preliminary to the creation of a new society, in which all the means of production and exchange of goods are in the hands of the state. Each member of this society will work according to his capacity and receive according to his wants.

Constitution: A form of government involving fundamental principles by which a state is governed and by which the monarch or other head of state is controlled.
Coup d'état: The overthrow of a previous government by conspiracy or military uprising.
Covenant: An agreement or compact.
Despotism: Arbitrary rule by a despot or tyrant.
Diet: An assembly of delegates: the name used for assemblies of the German, Austrian or Hungarian parliaments.
Fascism (see chapter on Italy after 1919).
Federalism: A system by which several states form one large country but each state retains the right to control its internal affairs.
Franchise: The right to vote in elections.
Free trade: A system of trade without customs duties.
Indemnity: Compensation for loss.
Left-wing: A term given to Radical, Socialist, Communist movements, etc., as opposed to Conservatism or Right-wing movements. Derived from the positions of parties in the semi-circular French Chamber of Deputies.
Liberalism: A general term to include those movements advocating freedom from dictatorship of any kind, and upholding the rights of freedom of speech, of the press and of assembly and other general individual rights.
Minority: People of a different nation, race or culture living within another state.
Nationalism: The movement for freedom from the domination of another country and the desire to create one united people with similar historic background and culture.
Nihilism: A movement of denial which aims to destroy everything derived from the past.
Plebiscite: A vote by all enfranchised persons on some important issue concerning the state.
Pogrom: Systematic persecution of Jews, or other minorities, leading to murder and massacre.
Proletariat: The labouring or 'working' class section of a country.
Protocol: A written record of a conference agreement signed by the participants.
Purge: A wiping-out of political opponents.

Racialism: Discrimination by one race against another. The preaching of the superiority of one race over another.

Radicalism: A movement for a basic or 'root' change in society.

Reactionary: Opposed to reform or wishing to return to past forms of society or government.

Referendum: A vote by all enfranchised citizens on an important state issue (see also 'plebiscite').

Sabotage: Malicious wrecking or damage to machines, military installations, etc., often to achieve a political aim.

Sanctions: Penalties against a country—such as the withholding of vital raw materials—by other countries who object to the policies of the condemned country.

Syndicalism: Control of factories, workshops, etc., by the organized workers.

Tariff: A duty on imported goods.

Technocracy: An organization of society in which technologists control the basic industries, and in this way influence the politics of that society.

Terrorism: The use of violent methods, involving murder or assassination, usually to achieve a political aim.

Ultra-reactionaries: Extreme Conservatives.

Ultra-royalists (Ultras): Extreme supporters of absolute monarchy allied to clericalism in France.

Unilateral action: Action by one state alone without consultation of others.

ANSWERING EXAMINATION QUESTIONS

At First

The answering of questions in a history examination is a test of both knowledge and method. The way a candidate approaches a paper may make a great difference to his chances of success. Here are some points which may prove useful:

(1) It is a good idea to spend a few minutes at the beginning of the examination studying the paper as a whole. Read the instructions at the head of the paper to see how many questions must be attempted. If the paper is divided into sections, be sure that you know from which sections you must answer questions.

(2) Success in a history examination depends a great deal upon a correct use of time. Make sure you know how much time you will have to answer each question in the paper. If, for instance, you have to attempt five questions in three hours, then you must reckon on about 35 minutes a question.

(3) Read through the questions carefully and decide which you think you can and cannot answer. At this stage you need not make up your mind definitely about this. You should, however, answer first the questions you think you can do best. This will make a good impression on the examiner at the start; and also you will probably be able to answer these questions more rapidly and leave more time for those about which you know less.

(4) Do not waste time copying out the questions, but be sure to number them carefully.

Planning the Answer

As you come to each question, it is advisable to think about your answer before you write anything. However simple the question may appear, read it through carefully until you are sure that you understand its full meaning. Jot down in rough the headings of your paragraphs in order, so that you can see that you have included all the relevant points and put them in proper sequence. In planning your answer in this way, remember that there are three types of examination questions in history, each of which must be approached in the correct way:

(1) *Narrative Question.* This asks you to tell a straightforward story. Examples of this type of question are, 'Describe the steps by which Bismarck united Germany' and 'Give an account of the work of either Garibaldi or Mazzini in the unification of Italy.' Very similar is the descriptive type of question, such as 'Give an account of the reforms introduced into Russia by Alexander II.' To answer questions like these, you must consider what facts are required and put them down in the right order; and do not fail to explain their importance where necessary.

(2) *The Discussion Question.* In this type of question you are asked to discuss some definite point or problem and make a judgement on it. This sort of question appears in many forms, but none of them must be answered as if it were a narrative question. For instance, the question, 'Why were the revolutions in the Austrian Empire in 1848–1849 unsuccessful?' does not require a mere account of the revolutions; it wants you to say exactly what the question asks, namely, why did the revolutions fail? Again, 'Account for the early successes of Napoleon and his later defeat' is not asking you to give a long *account of* the Napoleonic Wars. The distinction between '*account for*' and an '*account of*' must always be borne in mind.

A form of the discussion question is the comparative question, such as, 'Compare the character and achievements of Bismarck and Cavour.' This does not require first an account of the life of one and then of the other. Rather you should consider the problems facing them and compare them, side by side, in their methods and achievements.

Another sort of discussion question gives a quotation which you are asked to consider, such as, '*The sick man of Europe.* To what extent was this description of Turkey in this period justified?' Explain the meaning of the quotation and discuss why this description was used, and to what extent it was justified from your knowledge of the Eastern Question in the period.

In attempting any sort of discussion question, make sure first that you understand what you are being asked to consider and keep it in mind all the time you are writing your answer. Resist the temptation just to tell a story or describe events.

(3) *The Question on Several Topics.* This type of question begins, 'Write shortly on . . .' or 'Write notes on . . .'. It never means write in note form. It means writing a paragraph or two on each of the required number of subjects, giving the important points about each. If it is a special piece of law-making or reform, give its date, the circumstances in which it was passed, its main clauses and its significance; if it is a battle, when it was fought, who between, its outcome and importance; if it is a person, do not write a biography, but give the aims and achievements which make that person important; if it is a treaty, give its date, who it was between, its main clauses and results.

Writing the Answer

(1) Whatever type of question you answer, you must know something about it. In answering a discussion question, for instance, you must be able to support your arguments or judgements by reference to facts, and there is no substitute for them. A frequent criticism in the reports of examiners is that candidates attempt to disguise ignorance of a subject by 'waffling'.

(2) Another common criticism made by examiners is that candidates do not keep to the point in answering questions. Many marks are lost in examinations for irrelevancy. When you answer a question, make sure that you understand what it is about. Be certain that you realize what information the examiner wants and what he does not want. A question about the domestic policy of an English king, for instance, does not require information about his foreign policy as well. If you do not know much about the subject of a question, it is no use including information about some other subject which is related to it.

From time to time, therefore, while you are writing, glance again at the question to see if you are keeping to the point. In your final paragraph refer directly to the question and make sure that you have really answered it. A test of relevancy is to see if you could guess the question simply by reading the answer.

(3) A history examination is also a test in English composition. Handwriting, neatness and spelling are important. In particular, if you spell proper names and historical terms wrongly, the examiner may assume a lack of reading on your part. Be sure also to arrange your answers properly in sentences and paragraphs.

(4) Use dates when you can, but if you are unsure of a date it is better to leave it out rather than put a wrong date. It is important, however, to show the examiner that you know in what period events occurred and in what sequence.

(5) Occasionally a question says that you may illustrate your answer with a map or diagram, and you may always do this when it is suitable; but only attempt this if time allows. It is best to finish writing all your answers first and very unwise to leave a question unanswered in order to complete a map or diagram.

(6) Indeed, remember always the importance of time in an examination. Unless otherwise stated, each answer is allotted the same number of marks. It is, therefore, very important to answer properly the required number of questions. You should never misuse your time so badly that you have to answer your last question in note form. It is, of course, even worse not to have time to answer your last question at all. If you are required to attempt five questions, you are throwing marks away by only doing four questions, however well you answer them. Always keep to the correct amount of time you should allow for each question.

In Conclusion

When you have finished all your questions, you should have allowed yourself time to read carefully through all that you have written. Check your statements, punctuation and spelling. When you write in a hurry, you are very likely to make careless mistakes. It is very valuable, therefore, to have an opportunity to put these right and have a well-presented paper for the examiner to see.

BIBLIOGRAPHY

Grant, A. J. and Temperley, H., *Europe in the Nineteenth and Twentieth Centuries* (Longman)
Thomson, D., *Europe since Napoleon* (Longman)
Taylor, A. J. P., *The Struggle for Mastery in Europe, 1848–1918* (O.U.P.)
Thompson, J. M., *The French Revolution* (Blackwell)
Fisher, H. A. L., *Napoleon* (Home University Library, O.U.P.)
Brogan, D. W., *The Development of Modern France* (Hamish Hamilton)
Bury, J. P. T., *France, 1815–1941* (Methuen)
Taylor, A. J. P., *Bismarck* (Hamish Hamilton)
Trevelyan, G. M., *Garibaldi and the Making of Italy* (Longman)
Trevelyan, G. M., *Garibaldi and the Thousand* (Longman)
Trevelyan, J., *A Short History of the Italian People* (Allen & Unwin)
Taylor, A. J. P., *The Habsburg Monarchy* (Hamish Hamilton)
Sumner, B. H., *A Survey of Russian History* (Duckworth)
Marriott, J. A. R., *The Eastern Question* (O.U.P.)
Mansergh, N., *The Coming of the First World War* (Longman)
Bullock, Alan, *Hitler* (Odhams and Penguin)
Churchill, W. S., *The Gathering Storm* (Cassell and Penguin)
Hill, C., *Lenin and the Russian Revolution* (English University Press)
Fleming, Prof. D. F., *The Cold War and its Origins, 1917–1960* (Allen & Unwin)

INDEX

Abdul Hamid II, Sultan, 103–4, 126
Aberdeen, Lord, 101
Abyssinia (Ethiopia), 123, 165, 265
Addington, Lord, 25
Adenauer, Konrad, 193
Aden Protectorate, 233
Adowa, Battle of (1896), 123
Adrianople, Treaty of (1829), 99
Afghanistan, 125
Afro-Asian bloc, 232–3
Agadir crisis (1911), 126
Air warfare, 133, 172, 174, 176, 178
Aix-la-Chapelle, Congress of (1818), 43
Albania, 98, 164, 184, 262
Alembert, Jean d', 7
Alexander I, Czar of Russia, 28, 29, 32–3, 36, 38, 40, 43–4, 97–8, 113–14, 120
Alexander II, Czar, 92, 101, 115–17, 120
Alexander III, Czar, 94, 117, 120
Alexander I, King of Rumania, 102
Algeciras, Conference of (1906), 125
Algeria, 191, 200, 202, 231, 232, 246–7, 252–3, 255; National Liberation Front (FLN), 247, 252; Secret Army Organization (OAS), 252
Allenby, General, 136
Allied Control Council, 192
Alsace-Lorraine, 60, 107, 128–9, 140, 143
Amiens, Peace of (1802), 25
Anglo-Japanese Alliance (1902), 124
Anti-Semitism, 110, 156, 158, 162
'Appeasement', 165
Arab–Israeli War (1967), 233–4
Arab League, 200, 225
Arab Revolt (1917), 135–6, 141, 144
Armenian Massacres (1896), 104
Artois, Comte d', *see* Charles X
'Aryan Myth', Nazi, 156, 159

Aspromonte, Battle of (1862), 76
Asquith, H. H. (Lord), 133
Aswan Dam, 232
Atlantic Charter, 181
Atomic bombs, 177, 178, 197, 205, 244
Atomic Energy Commission, 265–6
Attlee, Clement (Lord), 183
Ausgleich (1867), 67–8
Austerlitz, Battle of (1805), 28–9
Austria, Republic of, 142, 184, 188, 218
Austria-Hungary (Dual Monarchy, Hapsburg Empire), 67–8, 137, 140, 141–3
Austrian Empire, 13–14, 17, 21, 22, 23, 25, 28, 32–3, 38–9; Revolution of 1848, 66–7, 71
Austro-German Union (*Anschluss*), 81, 166, 192
Austro-Prussian War (1866), *see* Seven Weeks' War

Babeuf, François, 21
Badoglio, Marshall, 175
Baghdad Pact (1955), 233, 239
Bakunin, Michael, 116
Palance of Power, 38–40, 52
Balkan Wars (1912–13), 126–7
Bao-Dai, Emperor of Annam, 204–5
Belgium, 38, 40, 51, 86, 143
Ben Bella, Ahmed, 247
Benesh, President, 167, 186
Beria, L. P., 212
Berlin, 182, 191, 192, 193, 212
Berlin-Baghdad Railway, 124, 125, 129
Berlin Colonial Conference (1884), 122–3
Berlin Conference (1954), 218–19
Berlin, Congress of (1878), 93, 104, 123
Berlin Wall, 222–3
Bernadotte, King of Sweden, 30, 39
Bernadotte, Count, 263
Berri, Duc de, 49
Bessarabia, 97, 113, 141
Bismarck, Prince Otto von, 59–60, 80, 83–6, 89–95, 104, 116, 124
Blanc, Louis, 52, 54
Blanqui, Louis, 52
Blücher, General, 34
Blum, Léon, 190
Boer War, 123, 124
Bolsheviks, 118, 148, 151
'Bomba', *see* Francis II
Bonaparte, Jerome, 29, 30
Bonaparte, Joseph, 30–31
Bonaparte, Lucien, 24
Bosnia and Herzegovina, 94, 102–4, 126–7, 141
Boulanger, General, 95; Boulangist crisis, 109
Bourguiba, Habib, 201–2, 230
Brazil, 44
Brest-Litovsk, Treaty of (1918), 148
Briand, Aristide, 163, 168
Britain: (pre-1914), 16, 17, 22–9, 33–4, 38–40, 43–5, 51–2, 57, 84, 92–5, 98–105, 122–5, 128; (1914–39) 131–7, 140, 142, 144–5, 148, 165, 167–8; (Seond World War) 170–8, 181–3; (post-war) 184, 192–8, 200–3, 218, 222, 231–3, 232, 239, 263
Broglie, Marshal de, 10
Brunswick, Duke of, 14–15
Brussels Treaty (1948), 195
Bucharest, Treaty of (1812), 97
Bukowina, 141
Bulgaria: 'Big Bulgaria', 93–5, 103–4, 132, 140; Communist, 184, 185
Bulgarian atrocities (1875), 103
Burma, 184
Byron, Lord, 98

Cambodia, 237
Cameroons, 122, 242, 268
Camperdown, Battle of (1797), 23, 36
Campo Formio, Treaty of (1797), 22
Canning, George, 44–5, 98
Cape Colony, 39
Cape St. Vincent, Battle of (1797), 22–3, 36
Carbonari, 57, 70
Carlos, King Don Juan, 225
Carlsbad Decrees (1819), 79
Carnot, General L.N.M., 16–17, 21–2, 23, 48
Caroline Islands, 123
Carter, President, 236
Castlereagh, Viscount, 38–40, 43–4
Catherine II (the Great), Czarina of Russia, 21, 113
Cavour, Count Camillo, 58, 72–4, 76
Ceylon, 25, 39
Chad, 242
Chamberlain, Joseph, 124
Chamberlain, Neville, 167, 171
Chambord, Comte de, 108
Chanak crisis (1922), 145
Charles, Archduke of Austria, 32
Charles X, King of France, 48, 49–50
Charles, King of Rumania, 102
Charles IV, King of Spain, 30

Charles Albert, King of Sardinia, 70, 71
Chaumont, Treaties of (1814–15), 40
Cheka, 148
Chiang Kai-shek, 182, 204–6, 207–8
China, 123, 184; Communist, 205, 210, 213
Christian Democrats: France (MRP), 190, 238, 244; Germany, 193; Italy, 191
Churchill, Sir Winston, 133, 171, 173, 177, 181, 183, 194
Cintra, Convention of (1808), 31
Cisalpine Republic, 22, 39–40
Clemenceau, Georges, 140
Coalitions against France: First (1793), 16, 21, 22; Second (1799), 23–5; Third (1805), 28–9
Code Napoleon, 27
'Cold War', 184, 198, 203, 221, 233, 261, 268
Collingwood, Admiral Lord, 28
Colombia, 45
Cominform, 187, 195
Common Market, 217–18, 250
Communism: European, 184–9, 190–95, 198; France, 54–5, 108, 190–91, 244, 248–9, 255–6; Germany, 154–9, 192, 194; Greece, 262; Indochina, 204–5; Italy, 159, 160–2, 191, 225; Middle East, 203–4, 239; world, 185, 208–9, 213; Spain, 225
Communist League, 82, 90
Communist Manifesto, 90
Concentration camps, Nazi, 158, 162
Concert of Europe, 45
Congo (formerly Belgian), 123, 265
Congo (formerly French), 126
Continental System, 29–30, 32–3, 34
Copenhagen, Battle of (1801), 25
Corfu incident (1923), 164, 165
Corporate State (in Italy), 161
Coty, President, 245, 248
Crete, 52, 100
Crimean War, 57, 72, 100–2, 115
Croats, 65, 141
Cuban crisis (1962), 221
Custozza, Battle of (1848), 71
Cyprus, 104, 224
Czechoslovakia, 64, 66, 141, 142, 166–7; Communist, 184, 185–6, 188, 192, 194, 212, 213, 220

Dahomey (Benin), 253
Daladier, Edouard, 167, 242
Dalmatia, 39
Danton, Georges-Jacques, 13, 14–15, 17, 20
Danzig, 141, 168
Dardanelles, 99, 143, 202; Straits Convention (1841), 100, 114; Campaign (1915), 133
Dawes Plan, 156
Déak, Francis, 65
Debré, Michel, 248
Delcassé, Théophile, 125
Denmark, 25, 39, 83–4, 218
Desmoulins, Camille, 10, 14
d'Estaing, Giscard, 255–6
Diderot, Denis, 6
Dien Bien Phu, Battle of (1954), 236–7
Disarmament, 128, 142, 258–9; Disarmament Commission (1952), 266
Disraeli, Benjamin (Lord Beaconsfield), 93, 103
Dollfuss, Engelbert, 166
'Dreadnought', 128
DreiKaiserbund, 92, 94, 95
Dreyfus case, 110
Dual Alliance: Austro-German (1879), 94; Franco-Russian (1893), 124
Dual Monarchy, *see* Austria-Hungary
Dupont, Marshal, 30

Eastern Question, 97–105
Ebert, Chancellor, 154–5
Edward VII, King, 124
Egypt, 23, 27, 51–2, 122, 124, 172, 184, 200, 201, 225, 227, 231–3, 234, 236, 239, 263
Einstein, Albert, 178
Eisenhower, General, 174–5, 195, 220
Ems telegram, 60, 86
Encyclopedists, 6
Engels, Friedrich, 90
Enghien, Duc d', 28
Entente Cordiale, 124–5
Eritrea, 123, 265
Estonia, 113, 141
Ethiopia, *see* Abyssinia
Eugènie, Empress, 59
Euratom, 219
European Coal and Steel Community, 197
European Economic Community (EEC), *see* Common Market
European Free Trade Area (EFTA), 218–19

Farouk, King of Egypt, 201
Fascism, 159–61
Fashoda incident (1898), 122

Ferdinand, Archduke of Austria, 127
Ferdinand I, Emperor of Austria, 66
Ferdinand IV, King of Naples (and Ferdinand I of the Two Sicilies), 39, 44, 69
Ferdinand II, King of the Two Sicilies, 71
Ferdinand VII, King of Spain, 30, 39, 44
Ferdinand, Prince of Bulgaria, 95
Ferry, Jules, 109
Fiji, 123
Finland, 39–40, 113, 148, 170
Foch, Marshal, 136
Food and Agricultural Organization (FAO), 266
Formosa, 205, 206
Fourteen Points, President Wilson's, 136, 140, 142–3
France (pre-Revolution), 1–4, 9
France (Revolution, 1789–95), 1–18: causes, 1–8; States-General, 9; National Assembly, 10, 11–12; Tennis Court Oath, 10; Bastille captured, 10; Constituent Assembly, 10–11; émigrés, 11, 13, 14; Declaration of the Rights of Man, 11; Jacobins, 11, 12, 13, 14–15, 18; March on Versailles, 11; Feuillants, 11, 12, 14; Flight to Varennes, 12; Civil Constitution of the Clergy, 12–14; Girondins, 13–17; Declaration of Pillnitz, 13–14; La Vendée insurrection, 14, 16; war with Austria, 14–15; Brunswick Manifesto, 15; Paris Commune, 15, 17–18; September Massacres, 15; the Convention, 15–18; Battle of Valmy, 15; Republic declared, 16; war with Britain, 16; Committee of Public Safety, 16–17; Revolutionary Tribunal, 16; the Terror, 17–18; Worship of Reason, 17
France (The Directory, 1795–99), 21–4
France (The Consulate, 1799–1804), 24–27; Concordat, 27
France (The Empire, 1804–14), 27–36
France (The Restoration, 1814–48): Louis XVIII, 33–4; the Hundred Days, 34; Prussians withdraw, 43, 49; ulta-Royalists, 44, 48–50, 61; Charter of 1814, 48, 49; white terror, 48–9; Grenoble revolt, 49; Republicans, 49–54; Legitimists, 49, 51–3; Ordinances of St. Cloud, 50; 1830 Revolution, 50, 79; Orleanist monarchy, 50–4; Charter of 1830, 50–1; Bonapartists, 51–4; workers' revolts, 53; Reform Banquets, 53
France (Second Republic, 1848–52), 54–6
France (Second Empire, 1852–70), 56–61; Napoleon III, 56; Compact of Plombières, 58, 73; Italian campaign (1859), 58, 67; 'Liberal' Empire, 59; Napoleon III's downfall, 60–61
France (Third Republic, 1870–1940), Thiers government, 107; attempted restoration, 108; Constitution of 1875, 108
France (Vichy régime, 1940–44), 242–3; Committee for National Liberation, 243
France (Fourth Republic, 1945–58), 190–1, 244–7, 248; Rally of the French People (RPF), 245–7
France (Fifth Republic, 1958–), 231, 248–56; Constitution, 249; Union pour la Nouvelle République (UNR), 249–50; (1970–77), 255–6
Francis I, Emperor of Austria, 32, 38, 43, 64
Francis II ('King Bomba'), King of the Two Sicilies, 74
Francis Joseph, Emperor of Austria-Hungary, 66
Franco, General, 166, 225
Franco-Prussian War (1870), 60, 86, 107–8
Frankfort, Treaty of (1871), 60
Frankfort Parliament (1848–49), 81–2
Frederick William III, King of Prussia, 32, 38, 43
Frederick William IV, King of Prussia, 80–3
Free French movement, 171, 242
French, Sir John, 131, 132
French Community, 253, 255

Gabon, 253
Galicia, 66, 133, 141
Gallipoli campaign, 133
Gambetta, Léon, 60, 107–8
Garibaldi, Giuseppe, 56, 71, 74, 76
Gasperi, Alcide de, 191
Gastein, Convention of (1865), 84
Gaulle, General de, 171, 190–1, 220, 222, 231, 239, 242–6, 248, 250–3, 256
Geneva Protocol (1924), 165

Germany (pre-1871): states of, 16, 22; German Confederation, 39, 79; North German Confederation, 85
Germany (Empire, 1871–1918): declaration of, 86; 1871 Constitution, 89; May Laws, 90; national insurance (1881), 91; colonial policy, 92; anti-French policy, 92, 94–5; naval programme, 124, 128; collapse, 141
Germany (1919 on): Weimar Republic, 154–8; Nazi régime, 1566, 158–9, 162; post-1945, 184, 191–3; German Federal Republic (West Germany), 193–4, 195, 197, 219–20; German Democratic Republic (East Germany), 194
Gestapo, 158
Gierek, Edward, 216
Gioberti, Vincenzo, 70
Gneisenau, Count von, 32
Goebbels, Josef, 158
Goering, Hermann, 158
Gomulka, Wladyslaw, 188, 215–16
Gottwald, Klement, 186, 212, 214
Great War (1914–18): origins, 122–130; Austrian ultimatum, 127; invasion of Belgium, 128, 131, 137; Mons, 131; First Marne, 131; Tannenberg, 132; Falkland Islands, 132; Ypres, 132; Verdun, 133; Somme, 133–4; Jutland, 134; Vimy Ridge, 134–5; Passchendaele and Caporetto, 135; Salonica, 136; summary, 136–7
Greece, 98, 141, 144, 172–3, 184, 188–9, 224, 227, 262
Greek War of Independence (1821), 44–5, 97–9
Grégoire, Abbé, 49
Grotewohl, Otto, 194
Guizot, François, 52, 53

Hague International Court, 144, 261, 265
Hague Peace Conferences, 128
Haig, Field-Marshal Earl, 132, 135
Hapsburgs, 39, 64–8
Haussmann, Baron, 57
Haynau, General, 66
Hébert, Jacques, 17, 20
Heligoland, 39
Helsinki Agreement, 1975, 226
Henlein, Konrad, 166
Himmler, Heinrich, 185
Hindenburg, Field-Marshal von, 133, 158, 159
Hiroshima, 177
Hitler, 142, 154–9, 162, 164, 165, 170–9
Hoare-Laval plan, 165
Ho Chi-Minh, 204–5, 237
Hohenlinden, Battle of (1800), 25
Hohenzollerns, 60
Holland, 16, 21, 23, 38
Holy Alliance (1815), 40
Hong Kong, 123, 173
Hungary, 64–8, 140–2, 184; Communist, 184, 185, 188, 194, 213–14, 216–17, 220, 227, 263–4

Ibrahim Pasha (son of Mehemet Ali), 98–9
India, 233, 264
Indochina, *see also* Vietnam, 109, 184, 204–5, 236–8
Indonesia, 184, 238–9, 262–3
Industrial development: Germany, 156; Russia, 117; Soviet Russia, 150–1
Inonu, President, 203
International Atomic Energy Authority, 266
International Developments, 1974–77, 224–6
International Labour Organization (ILO), 144, 266
Iran, 203–4, 233, 261–2
Iraq, 144, 164, 184, 184, 200, 233
Irish Republic joins EEC, 218
Iron Curtain, 194, 208, 269
Israel, 200, 225–6, 232, 233–4, 236, *see also* Yom-Kippur War
Italy: states of, 16; Cisalpine Republic, 22, 39–40; Napoleonic kindgom, 29; 1830 revolt, 51; 1848 revolt, 71–2; kingdom of, 76, 132, 137, 143; Fascist regime, 159–62, 175; post-war, 191, 224
Ivory Coast, 253
Izvolsky, Alexander, 125

Japan, 123, 165–6, 168, 173–4, 177, 184
Jellacic, Count, 65
Jellicoe, Admiral, 134
Jervis, Admiral (Lord St. Vincent), 22–3
Joffre, General, 131
Josephine, Empress, 32
Juin, General, 202, 205
Junkers, 80, 154

Kadar, Janos, 217, 264
Kara George of Serbia, 97

Kashmir, 233, 264
Kellogg Pact (1928), 165
Kemal Atatürk (Mustapha Kemal) 145, 203
Kennedy, President J. F., 221
Kenya, 122, 172
Kerensky, Alexander, 147–8, 152
Khrushchev, Nikita, 212, 213–15, 220–1
Kirov, 151
Kitchener, Lord, 122
Kléber, Jean-Baptiste, 23
Kolchak, Admiral, 148
Korea, 118–19, 184
Korean War (1950–53), 206–8, 261, 264
Kornilov, General, 147
Kossuth, Louis, 65–6, 68, 114
Kotzebue, August von, 43, 79, 114
Kulaks, 120, 149
Kulturkampf, 90

Lafayette, Marquis de, 4, 11, 14, 50
Laibach, Congress of (1821), 44
Lamartine, Alphonse de, 54
Laos, 237–8
Lateran Treaty (1929), 160
Latvia, 113, 141
Lausanne Treaty (1923), 140, 145
Laval, Pierre, 242–4
Lawrence, Colonel T. E., 135–6, 144
League Covenant, 144
League of Nations, 141, 143–4, 163–5, 168
Lebanon, 184, 200, 226, 234
Lend-Lease Act, 172
Lenin, V. I., 118, 120, 147–50
Leo XIII, Pope, 90
Leopold II, Emperor of Austria, 13, 14
Leopold of Saxe-Coburg (Leopold I of Belgium), 51
Lesseps, Ferdinand de, 110
Lettres de cachet, 4, 12
Liberalism: European, 43–4, 45; France, 51–3; Germany, 79–80, 92; Italy, 69; Russia, 113–16, 118
Libya, 236, 265
Liebknecht, Karl, 154
Lithuania, 133, 141, 164
Little Entente, 163
Lloyd George, David, 133, 135, 140, 142
Locarno Treaty (1925), 155–6, 165
Lombardy, 58
London, Conferences of (1840), 100
London, Treaties of: (1827), 45, 98; (1839), 51; (1912), 126
Louis XVI of France, 3, 9, 10, 11, 14, 15, 16, 18–19
Louis XVIII of France, 33–4, 49–9
Louis Napoleon Bonaparte, *see* Napoleon III
Louis Philippe, King of the French, 50–4
Louvel, Louis, 49
Lunéville, Treaty of (1801), 25
'Lusitania', 135
Luxembourg, 85–6, 195
Luxemburg, Rosa, 154

MacArthur, General, 207, 208, 264
MacMahon, Marshal, 107–8
Macmillan, Harold, 220
Madagascar, 109, 253
Magenta, Battle of (1859), 58, 73
Maginot Line, 170, 242
Malaya, 173, 184
Malenkoy, G. M., 212, 213
Mali, 248
Malta, 23, 27, 28, 39
Mamelukes, 23
Manchukuo, 165
Manchuria, 118–19, 123, 184
Mandates, 143, 144
Manila Pact (1954), 237, 239
Manin, Daniele, 71
Mao Tse-tung, 205
Marat, Jean Paul, 13–16
Marengo, Battle of (1800), 25
Marie Antoinette, Queen, 3, 11, 17
Marie Louise, Empress, 32
Marshall Plan, 188, 190, 194, 198, 203
Marx, Karl, 82, 90, 118
Masséna, General, 31
Massu, General, 248, 252
Matteotti murder, 160
Mauritania, 253
Mauritius, 39
Maximilian, Emperor of Mexico, 59
Mazzini, Giuseppe, 56, 70, 71, 74, 76
McCarthy, Senator, 208
Mehemet Ali, 51–2, 98–100
Memel, 164
Mendès-France, Pierre, 230, 245
Mensheviks, 118, 119, 148
Mentana, Battle of (1867), 76
Metternich, Prince, 38–40, 43–5, 64, 66–7, 70, 71, 79, 114
Mexico, 45, 58–9
Milan, 71
Mindszenty, Cardinal, 216
Mirabeau, Count, 10, 13

Modena, 69, 70, 73
Mollet, Guy, 247
Molotov, V. M., 194, 197
Moltke, Count von, 83
Monnet Plan, 244–5
Monroe Doctrine, 45, 59
Montenegro, 93, 102–3, 143
Montesquieu, 6, 7
Montgomery, Field-Marshal Lord, 174–6
Montpensier, Duc de, 52
Montreux Convention (1936), 202
Moore, Sir John, 31
Morocco, 125–6, 129, 184, 200, 202, 230–1
Mossadeq (Persian prime minister), 203–4
Mosul, 164
Munich Agreement (1938), 167
Munich *putsch* (1923), 155, 156
Mussolini, Benito, 160–2, 167, 171–3, 175–6

Nagy, Imre, 213, 216
Naples, Kingdom of, 27, 39, 44, 70, 114
Napoleon I (Bonaparte), 22, 23; appointed First Consul, 24, 27, 36; Emperor, 27, 36; marriages, 32; exiled to Elba, 33, 37, and to St. Helena, 34; career summarized, 34–6; body returned to France, 53
Napoleon III, Emperor of France, 53, 55–63, 73, 74, 76, 84, 85, 100–1
Napoleonic Wars: Italian campaign, 22; Egyptian campaign, 23; Marengo and Hohenlinden, 25; Copenhagen, 25; seizure of Hanover, 28; plans to invade Britain, 28; Trafalgar, Ulm, Austerlitz and Jena, 28, 29; Corunna, Fuentes d'Onoro and Toulouse, 31; Wagram, 32; Borodino and Moscow, 33; Dresden and Leipzig, 33; Waterloo, 34, 36
Nasser, President, 201, 231–2, 263
Nationalism, 32, 34, 37, 40, 64–6
Navarino, Battle of (1827), 45, 99
Necker, Jacques, 3–4, 9, 10
Nelson, Admiral Lord, 22–3, 28
Nemours, Duc de, 51
Netherlands, 38–40, 51
Neuilly, Treaty of (1919), 140
New Guinea, 123, 174, 267–8
Ney, Marshal, 48
Nice and Savoy, 58, 70, 74
Nicholas I, Czar of Russia, 45, 66, 67, 98–101, 114–15, 120
Nicholas II, Czar of Russia, 117, 120, 146, 148
Niger, 253
Nigeria, 122
Nightingale, Florence, 101
Nihilism, 116
Nile, Battle of the (1798), 23, 36
North Atlantic Treaty Organization (NATO), 195, 198, 220, 250, 256
Norway, 39–40
Novara, Battle of (1849), 71
Nuclear Test-ban Treaty (1963), 222, 250, 266

Obrenovich, Michael, 102
Oder-Neisse line, 181, 192
Olmütz, Treaty of (1850), 82, 83
Organization for European Economic Co-operation (OEEC), 195
Orsini, 58, 73
Orthodox Church, Eastern: Balkans, 97, 102; Russia, 114, 117
Oudinot, General, 55–6, 62, 71

Pakistan, 233, 264
Palestine, 101, 136, 144, 184, 200, 233, 263
Palmerston, Lord, 51–2, 74, 84, 99–100, 123
Panama scandal, 110
Papal Infallibility, Dogma of, 90
Papal States and the Pope, 27, 30, 36, 70, 71, 74, 76, 224
Paris, Comte de, 108
Paris, Siege of (1870–71), 60, 107
Paris, Treaty of (1856), 57, 102
Paris Commune (1871), 107–8
Parlement of Paris, 4
Parma, 69, 70, 73
Paul, Czar of Russia, 25
Peaceful coexistence, 213
Pearl Harbor, 173
Peninsular War, 30–31, 37
Persia, *see* Iran
Pétain, Marshal, 133, 135, 171, 242
Peter the Great, 113
Pflimlin, Pierre, 248
Philippe 'Egalité', 50
Philippines, 174
Physiocrats, 4, 6
Piedmont, 22, 38, 44, 69–70, 73
Pilsudski, Marshal, 149
Pitt, William (the Younger), 16, 28, 29
Pius IX, Pope, 70, 71, 90
Pleven Plan, 197
Poincaré, Raymond, 163

Poland, 21, 38, 114, 141–3; revolts of 1830, 51, 115; 1848, 66, and 1863, 116–17; Polish National Government, 149; Russo-German occupation, 168, 170; Communist, 184, 185, 192, 194, 213, 215–16, 220, 227
Polish Corridor, 167–8
Pompidou, President, 252, 255, 256
Port Arthur, 118–19, 123
Portsmouth, Treaty of (1905), 119
Portugal, 30–31, 33, 225, 227
Potsdam Conference (1945), 182
Poujadists, 245–7, 248–50
Prague, Treaty of (1866), 85
Pressburg, Treaty of (1805), 28–9
Protocol Powers, 44
Prussia, 13–15, 17, 21, 25, 28, 29, 31, 32–4, 38–40, 80–6
Prussian League, 82
Pyramids, Battle of the (1798), 23, 36

Quadrilateral fortresses, 71, 72
Quadruple and Quintuple Alliances (1814–18), 40, 43
Quesnay, François, 6

Radetsky, Josef, 71, 72
Rakosi, Matyas, 213
Rasputin, 146
Refugee problem: Arab, 200; Balkan, 164; German, 192; world, 267
Reichstag fire, 158
Reparations, 155–6, 163, 182, 192
Revolutions of 1848: Austria-Hungary, 65–7, 71; France, 53–4, 67, 80; Germany, 80–2; Italy, 71
Reynaud, Paul, 242
Rhee, President Syngman, 206–8
Rhine, Confederation of the, 33, 38–9
Rhineland, 141, 159, 165
Rhodes, Cecil, 122
Rhodesia, 122, 225
Richelieu, Duc de, 43, 48–9
Riga, Treaty of (1921), 149
'Risorgimento, Il', 72
Robespierre, Maximilien, 12–15, 17–18, 20
Rocket bases, U.S., 233
Roehm, Captain, 156, 158
Rokossovski, Marshal, 215
Romagna, 58, 73
Roman Catholic Church: Austria-Hungary, 64; France, 2–3, 12–13, 17, 27, 49, 109, 111, 191; Germany, 89–90, 95; Italy, 160; Poland, 215
Roman Republic, 55–6, 71, 74
Rome, Treaty of (1957), 217
Rome-Berlin-Tokyo Axis, 166, 168
Rommel, Field-Marshal, 173
Roosevelt, President F. D., 172, 174, 181
Rousseau, Jean-Jacques, 6–7, 17
Ruhr, occupation of, 155, 163
Rumania (Moldavia and Wallachia), 57, 99, 102, 141, 143; Communist, 184, 185, 220
Russia, Imperial, 21, 23–4, 25, 28–9, 31–33, 36, 38–9, 43–5, 113–120; Decembrist revolt (1825), 114; zemstvos, 115–17; Red Sunday (1905), 119; October Manifesto, 119; the Dumas, 119–20, 146; collapse, 141
Russia, Soviet: Kronstadt mutiny, 149; New Economic Policy, 149; collectivization, 150; 5-year plans, 150–1, 152; 1936 Constitution, 151; purges, 151, 152; in Second World War, 173–4, 176–9, 183, 184; post-war, 212–14, 225
Russian Revolution (1917), 135, 141, 143; Lvov Government, 146–7, 152; Kerensky Government, 147, 152; October Revolution, 147; civil war and intervention, 148–9; Communist Party rule, 149
Russo-Japanese agreement (1907), 125
Russo-Japanese War (1904–5), 118–19

Saar, 140
Sadat, President, 225, 227, 236
Sadowa, Battle of (1866), 67, 84
St. Germain, Treaty of (1919), 140
Salan, General, 248, 252
Salazar, Dr., 225
Samoa, 123
Sanctions, 144, 165
San Francisco Conference (1945), 181–2, 259
San Stefano, Treaty of (1878), 93, 103
Sarajevo assassination (1914), 127
Sardinia, Kingdom of, 58, 69–73
Saudi Arabia, 200
Savoy, *see* Nice and Savoy
Schleswig-Holstein, 81–5, 141
Schlieffen Plan, 128, 129, 131
Schuman Plan, 197
Schwarzenberg, Chancellor Prince, 66
Second World War (1939–45): Polish campaign, 168, 170; Denmark and Norway, 170–1; Belgium and Holland, 171; Dunkirk and the fall of France, 171, 230; Battle of Britain, 172, 178; African campaigns, 172–174; Russian campaign, 173–4;

Pearl Harbor, 173; Italian campaign, 174–5; Second Front, 175; V 1s and V 2s, 176; German defeat, 176; Hiroshima, 177; Resistance movements, 178, 184, 186–8, 190–1, 242–3
Secret Reinsurance Treaty (1887), 95
Security Council (UN), 181–2, 259; veto, 183, 207, 260, 261–2, 266
Sédan, Battle of (1870), 60
Senegal, 253
Serbia, 93, 97, 102–3, 126–7, 143
Serfs, emancipation of: Austria-Hungary, 65, 66; Balkans, 102; France, 1; Italy, 71; Prussia, 32; Russia, 113–14, 116
Seven Weeks' War (1866), 59–60, 67, 76, 84–6
Sèvres, Treaty of (1920), 140, 144–5
Siberian exiles, 113–14, 116
Sieyès, Abbé, 24, 25
Silesia, 141, 163–4, 192
Sinope, Battle of (1853), 101
Slovakia, 142
Smyrna (Izmir), 144–5
Social Democrats: Czechoslovakia, 186; Germany, 90–1, 154, 193; Italy, 191; Russia, 118, 119, 147
Socialism: France, 52–5, 110–11, 190–191, 238, 242–4; Germany, 154, 156; Italy, 160–2, 191; Russia, 116–17
Socialist International, 116, 128
Solferino, Battle of (1859), 58, 73
Somaliland, 123, 172, 265
Soult, Marshal, 31
South Africa, Union (later, Republic) of, 265, 268
South American republics, 44–5
South East Asia Treaty Organization (SEATO), 237, 239
South-West Africa, 122, 268
Soviet-German Non-aggression Pact (1939), 168
Soviets, 119, 146
Spain, 16, 21, 23, 30–2, 34, 36, 39, 44, 114, 225, 227
Spanish Civil War (1936–39), 166, 168
Spanish Marriages question, 52
Spanish Succession question (1869), 60, 86
Spartacist rising, 154
S.S. (Nazi protection squads), 158
Stalin, 147, 150–2, 170, 173–5, 181, 184, 212; de-Stalinization, 214, 227
Stolypin, Peter, 119–20
Storm Troopers (Nazi S.A., Brownshirts), 156–7, 158
Stratford de Redcliffe, Lord, 101
Stresa Front (1935), 166
Stresemann, Gustav, 155–6, 163, 165, 168
Submarine warfare, 135, 137, 172, 174
Sudan (formerly Anglo-Egyptian), 172, 201
Sudetenland, 142, 166–7, 192
Suez Canal, 110, 122, 236
Suez crisis (1956), 232–3, 247
Summit Conference (1960), 220–1
Supreme Headquarters Atlantic Powers Europe (SHAPE), 195
Suvoroff, Prince, 24
Sweden, 25, 39–40
Switzerland, 52
Syria, 51–2, 99–100, 144, 184, 200, 233, 236

Talleyrand, 38–9
Tanganyika, 122
Tangier, 231
Tangier crisis (1905), 125
Tanks, 133
Tariffs, 142
Thiers, Adolphe, 51–2, 59, 100, 107–8
Thorez, Maurice, 190
Tilsit, Treaty of (1807), 29, 113
Tirpitz, Admiral von, 128
Tito, Marshal, 173, 186–9
Todleben, Franz, 101
Togliatti, Palmiro, 191
Togoland, 122
Trafalgar, Battle of, 28
Transjordan (Jordan), 184, 200
Trans-Siberian Railway, 117, 123
Transylvania, 141
Treaty Ports of China, 123
Trianon, Treaty of (1920), 140, 142
Trinidad, 27, 39
Triple Alliance (1882), 94
Triple Entente (1907), 105, 125
Tripoli, 126
Troppau, Congress and Protocol of (1820), 43–4
Trotsky, 118, 147–50, 152
Truman, President, 182, 207
Truman Doctine, 194, 203
Tunisia, 94, 122, 184, 191, 200–2, 230
Turgot, Baron de, 3, 6
Turkey, Empire, 39, 51–2, 93, 97–105, 114–15, 126, 132–6, 140–1, 144–5; Republic, 202–3, 224, 233
Tuscany, 73
Two Sicilies, Kingdom of the, 69, 71
Tyrol, 39, 132, 141, 143

Uganda, 122
Ukraine, 148, 149
Ulbricht, Walter, 194
Unemployment, 156–7
UNESCO, 266–7
UNICEF, 267
United Arab Republic, 233
United Nations Organization (UNO), 181–2, 236, 252–69; Economic and Social Council, 260; Trusteeship Council, 260, 267–8
U.S.A., 3, 4, 59, 135, 136, 145, 172–8, 210, 225, *see also* United Nations
Unkiar-Skelessi, Treaty of (1833), 99, 100, 114
Upper Volta, 253
U–2 incident (1960), 220–1

Venetian Republic, 71, 76, 84–5
Verona, Congress of (1822), 44–5
Versailles Treaty (1919), 140 ff., 156–9, 165
Victor Emmanuel I, King of Sardinia, 69
Victor Emmanuel II, King of Sardinia, later of Italy, 71–2, 74, 76
Victor Emmanuel III, King of Italy, 160, 161
Victoria, Queen, 51, 92, 124
Vienna, Congress of (1814–15), 34, 38–40; Congress system, 43–5
Vienna, Peace of (1809), 32
Vietnam, *see also* Indochina, 204–5, 237–9
Villafranca, Truce of (1859), 58, 73–4
Villèle, 49–50
Villeneuve, Admiral, 28
Voltaire, 4, 6, 7

Wall Street crash (1929), 156, 161
Warsaw, Grand Duchy of, 32, 38, 40
Warsaw Pact (1955), 220
Wellington, Duke of, 31, 34, 36, 44
Western European Union, 197
Westphalia, Kingdom of, 29
William I, King of Prussia, 83, 86
William II, Emperor of Germany, 95, 124–9, 136
Wilson, President, 135, 140, 145
Windischgratz, General, 66
Witte, Sergei, 117, 124
World Health Organization (WHO), 267

Yalta Conference (1945), 181
Yemen, 200, 233
Yom-Kippur War, 1973, 236
Young Italy, Society of, 70, 74
Young Turk movement, 126
Yugoslavia, 141, 143, 173, 184, 186–8, 220

Zola, Emile, 110
Zollverein, 80